World of Relations

Publication of this volume was made possible in part by a grant
from the National Endowment for the Humanities.

Copyright © 1998 by The University Press of Kentucky

Scholarly publisher for the Commonwealth,
serving Bellarmine College, Berea College, Centre
College of Kentucky, Eastern Kentucky University,
The Filson Club Historical Society, Georgetown College,
Kentucky Historical Society, Kentucky State University,
Morehead State University, Murray State University,
Northern Kentucky University, Transylvania University,
University of Kentucky, University of Louisville,
and Western Kentucky University.

Editorial and Sales Offices: The University Press of Kentucky
663 South Limestone Street, Lexington, Kentucky 40508-4008

98 99 00 01 02 5 4 3 2 1

Library of Congress Cataloging-in-Publication Data
Robinson, David M. (David Miller), 1947-
    World of relations : the achievement of Peter Taylor / David M.
Robinson.
        p.   cm.
    Includes bibliographical references (p.   ) and index.
    ISBN 0-8131-2063-2 (cloth : alk. paper)
    1. Taylor, Peter Hillsman, 1917-   —Criticism and interpretation.
2. Domestic fiction, American—Southern States—History and
criticism.   3. Interpersonal relations in literature.   4. Southern
States—In literature.   5. Family in literature.   I. Title.
PS3539.A9633Z85   1998
813'.54—dc21   97-32640

This book is printed on acid-free recycled paper meeting
the requirements of the American National Standard
for Permanence of Paper for Printed Library Materials.

Manufactured in the United States of America

To Gwendolyn

Contents

Preface

I came to Peter Taylor's stories in the middle 1980s, when his literary reputation was beginning to accelerate. The first story I read, "The Old Forest," happens to be his best, and I fell under his charm immediately. Soon afterward I began teaching Taylor's stories to university students, and this opportunity to discuss them in greater detail deepened my sense of their accomplishment. Thus the writing began: first, essays in which I tried to delineate the workings of two of his strongest stories, "Venus, Cupid, Folly, and Time" and "The Old Forest"; and finally this volume, which attempts to offer one unifying perspective on the development of his principal ideas and fictional techniques. In each stage of the process, my appreciation for Taylor's craft and for his passionate curiosity about human relationships has grown.

My first debt of thanks is to my friend and colleague Kerry Ahearn, who shared with me his enthusiasm for Taylor and encouraged me to look into his work. I will always be grateful for those conversations. Another friend and colleague, Dieter Schulz, helped to arrange the conditions, during my year as a Fulbright Guest Professor at the University of Heidelberg, in which I could read Taylor in depth and teach his stories to a sympathetic seminar group on Southern writers. I still remember the response of one student to my attempts to explain the nuances of regional detail in Taylor's work. These stories, she said, happen every day in all the small towns around Heidelberg. The local is indeed the universal, I thought, and the question of the possible limitations of Taylor's "regionalism" was forever settled in my mind.

My sense of Taylor's impact and of the importance of a growing critical commentary on his works was greatly advanced by the 1991 Peter Taylor Symposium in Baltimore, organized by C. Ralph Stephens and Lynda B. Salamon. As both a tribute to Peter Taylor and a stimulus to the reading, teaching, and criticism of his works, this was a landmark event. I owe Ralph

Stephens many thanks for his continuing interest and support, and also for bringing me into contact, at the symposium, with Hubert H. McAlexander and Albert J. Griffith. Their contributions to Taylor studies are signal— their publications constitute the starting point for all studies of Peter Taylor's life and work—and their generosity has been notable.

I also thank Nancy Grayson Holmes, editor-in-chief of the University Press of Kentucky, for her faith in this project and her encouragement at important moments as I was bringing the work to completion. Early versions of some of these chapters appeared in the *Southern Review*, nos. 2-3 (1987) and the *Southern Literary Journal* 22, (1990); I am grateful to those journals for their support and their permission to include revised versions of those essays here.

This is a book about family, and I want to express my love and thanks to my wife, Gwendolyn, and my children, Elena and Paul, for their loving support. One "hears" Peter Taylor's prose, and I am sure that my ability to hear it is due in part to the good talks and fondly remembered family stories told by my mother, Beverly Chamlee Robinson—especially those of my Post family ancestors, all of whom seemed to have loved to tell and hear good tales.

Abbreviations

I have used the following abbreviations parenthetically in the text after the first quotation from each story, to indicate the volume cited by page number.

CS   *The Collected Stories of Peter Taylor.* New York: Farrar, Straus & Giroux, 1969.

MD   *In the Miro District.* New York: Carroll & Graf, 1983.

OF   *The Old Forest and Other Stories.* Garden City, N.Y.: Dial Press, 1985.

OSC   *The Oracle at Stoneleigh Court.* New York: Knopf, 1993.

Stand   *A Stand in the Mountains.* New York: Frederic C. Beil, 1985.

Summons   *A Summons to Memphis.* New York: Knopf, 1986.

TC   *In the Tennessee Country.* New York: Knopf, 1994.

TD   *Tennessee Day in Saint Louis: A Comedy.* New York: Random House, 1957.

WM   *A Woman of Means.* New York: Avon, 1986.

Introduction

In 1959 Peter Taylor published his third collection of stories under the title *Happy Families Are All Alike*. Both the historical moment of its publication and the nuances of the title's implications reveal Taylor's overall purposes as a writer of fiction and drama. Launching his career in the late 1940s and 1950s, Taylor wrote during the Cold War era, in which the cultural pressure for a national consensus centered on the construction of the "family," usually defined as the nuclear unit of father, mother, and children.[1] The normative quality of this concept was perhaps most memorably reinforced through the 1950s television sitcoms, in which the cohesiveness of family relationships came to represent an ideal of cultural unity as well; external threats and internal tensions were invariably overcome and, whatever the challenges, the stability of the family restored.

Taylor's work engaged that consensus, for his great subject was the family and its interrelations. But he responded to the consensus not by reinforcing it but by complicating and resisting it, as the full meaning of the title of his story collection suggests. It is drawn from a quotation from Tolstoy's *Anna Karenina*, which Taylor uses as an epigraph to the volume: "Happy families are all alike; every unhappy family is unhappy in its own way." It was the second half of Tolstoy's proposition that Taylor took as his fictional territory, and his stories and novels are in fact chronicles of the myriad ways that families devise to make themselves unhappy.

In this book I offer a reading of Peter Taylor that emphasizes his persistent concern with family relations and their impact on the emergence and wholeness of the personality. Beginning with his treatment of the relationship between fathers and sons, I trace the ways that such familial and generational conflict alters and in some cases thwarts the transition to maturity, creating lasting damage to adult relationships and ultimately replicating itself in continuing generational conflict. This portrayal of familial strife is reinforced by Taylor's consideration of the tensions generated by rapid social change in the South of the early and middle twentieth century, tensions that further complicate and intensify the internal and familial conflicts of his characters.

Robert Penn Warren's introduction to Peter Taylor's first collection of short fiction, *A Long Fourth and Other Stories* (1948)—the first and still the most influential critical appraisal of Taylor's work—specified the mastery of locale that constituted his initial literary identity: "Peter Taylor's stories are officially about the contemporary, urban, middle-class world of the upper South, and he is the only writer who has taken this as his province." Warren noted Taylor's sense of the disquiet caused by rapid social change, which he took to be Taylor's essential theme: "the attrition of old loyalties, the breakdown of old patterns, and the collapse of old values" (viii). Taylor's "contemporary" South seemed both alien and familiar in the late 1940s. It was still a region with a haunting past, and Taylor's Southerners were still exorcising their ghosts. But these were no longer the ghostly cavalry of Faulkner's Hightower; they were family ghosts of a more ordinary but no less paralyzing quality—fathers, mothers, brothers, and sisters holding one another in a bondage both destructive and sustaining. Taylor represented family relationships as the clearest indices of the social unease in the modernizing South, and his stories record the psychic costs of that cultural transformation.

Taylor's identification as a "Southern" author, which began with Warren's influential statement, has been a mixed blessing for his reputation. Clearly, Warren perceived Taylor's depiction of region as a major element of his accomplishment and promise. Southern settings helped him to secure a loyal core readership, whether from a sense of familiarity with the South or a sense of curiosity about it. For those who like a firm sense of "place" in their fiction, Taylor's finely crafted depictions of the urban upper South in the period between the world wars was persuasive and illuminating. Taylor found a fascinating geographical and historical niche and had the insight and the artistic capability to bring it to life. "It may be that a writer's most important possession, after his talent, is his sense of belonging to a time and place, whatever the disadvantages or injustices or cruelties of that time and place may be," Taylor said in a 1973 interview.[2] But he wrote admittedly of a world that was already essentially lost, and his very concentration on it became to some extent a limiting factor in the growth of his reputation and readership. Even in the midst of late public acclaim in the middle 1980s, when *The Old Forest and Other Stories* and *A Summons to Memphis* made a significant impact on a national readership, John Updike dismissed

Taylor in a *New Yorker* review of *A Summons to Memphis* as an inconsequential minor regionalist: "After a lifetime of tracing teacup tempests among genteel Tennesseans, Mr. Taylor retains an unslaked appetite for local nuance. The rather subtle (to Yankees, at least) differences between the styles of Memphis and Nashville are thoroughly and repeatedly gone into, with instructive side-glances at Knoxville and Chattanooga" (158). Even discounting both professional rivalry and differing regional loyalties here, it is obvious that Taylor's Tennessee focus, a foundation of his accomplishment and recognition, was not of universal appeal.

But even a sympathetic discussion of Taylor's considerable success in depicting his region does not take us far enough into the basis of his work, and it is for this reason that I point to Taylor's persistent concern with family relationships as a productive critical starting point. The attrition and collapse of a social structure in the midcentury South that Warren identified as Taylor's milieu was a social transformation experienced not by a "region" but by its people, and the change exerted particular pressure on the family structure. Taylor's sensitivity to the experiential burden of these changes makes his characters the subjects for a study of the human personality under pressure. At his best, Taylor not only describes regional qualities but explores the ways that personality and self-comprehension are molded by particular social norms and expectations, usually communicated most directly through the family.

What gives these explorations particular resonance, however, is Taylor's tacit assumption, the burden of many of his better stories, that the psyche is formed in large part *against* such forces. It is clear that his characters usually do not fit neatly or happily in the molds in which their family life and their culture attempts to pour them. Taylor's stories thus have less to do with affirming or rejecting Southern culture than with exploring the difficulties that particular characters have in formulating an identity amid the assumptions and implied demands of a highly structured society. These struggles for identity and self-understanding are almost always given dramatic form within the context of familial relationships.

Taylor's use of narrative perspective has been of particular importance to the success of this project, particularly his growing mastery of a retrospective first-person narration, which at its best evolves into a compelling struggle between the desire for self-understanding and the impulse toward self-delusion.[3] The paradigm of this confluence of regional observation and psychological exploration mediated through retrospective first-person nar-

ration is "The Old Forest" (1979), in which the narrator, Nat Ramsey, recounts the crisis of coming to maturity within the world of upper-class
Memphis in the 1930s as that world was itself changing dramatically. Nat's
detailed recollection yields the strikingly realized detail of ordinary life that
is the mark of Taylor's craft.[4] But the story attains its resonance through
Nat's conflicting desires both to comprehend what he is remembering in a
way that he was unable to do while he was experiencing it and also to shield
himself from a self-recognition that would be too painful to bear. He feels
he has been a dutiful son and a faithful husband but fears that he may have
lost his chance to understand himself completely.

The gradually increasing recognition of Taylor's craft among readers
and critics, spurred by his particular achievement in the 1970s and 1980s,
brought Taylor to wider public notice in the 1980s. His *In the Miro District
and Other Stories* (1977), the title story of which is one of his strongest
works, was followed in 1985 by *The Old Forest and Other Stories*, a volume
that further extended his reputation as a master of the craft of the short
story.[5] "The Old Forest" seems to have taken a central place in Taylor's fiction, and its effective adaptation into film by Stephen John Ross (with
Taylor's help and cooperation) will certainly augment its importance. Taylor
was honored in 1987 with the Pulitzer Prize and the Ritz-Hemingway Prize
for *A Summons to Memphis*, a novel that plays out this theme of the haunting
past and the attempt to comprehend it at length.[6] "In the Miro District,"
"The Old Forest" and *A Summons to Memphis* each illustrate a crucial point
about Taylor's technique: it is not merely the recollection and presentation
of the past but the act of remembering and explaining it that gives his stories their dynamism. The narration of memory as it is juxtaposed with the
present reminds us that Nat Ramsey's or Phillip Carver's work of self-cre-
ation is still in progress. The events of the past continue to have resonance
in the present because they are still being assimilated.

Taylor's use of memory as a device for distancing his characters from
their earlier selves yields psychological portraits of depth and complexity,
with a full recognition of the nuances and ambiguities of human motivation. The juxtaposition of past with present in the texture of the narratives
is central to this accomplishment. In "The Old Forest," *A Summons to
Memphis*, and *In the Tennessee Country,* for instance, as the narrator moves
toward self-analysis through retrospection, the distance of the past becomes
illusory. The past ceases to be merely a subject and comes to dictate the

terms by which the narrator attempts to recreate it, and to understand himself. Taylor is committed to the utilization of the short story as a form of psychological revelation, always seeking the act or moment at which a deeper profile of a character's psyche can be understood.

This modern sensibility, part of what Warren meant in describing his "disenchanted mind" (ix), is blended with a commitment to the oral tradition of Southern culture in which the often repeated story or incident takes on a defining quality for both the individual and the family, whose identities are tightly intertwined.[7] In "Venus, Cupid, Folly and Time," for example, the narration is more than self-analysis; it is based in a much larger texture of rumor, gossip, and repeated and embellished tale that has sustained the Dorsets in their social position for years. Ross's decision to have Taylor himself do the voice-over narration for the film version of "The Old Forest" confirmed the importance of the nuanced pacing and intimate tone that most readers relish in Taylor's stories. So Taylor is, like his characters, caught between two worlds, the tender sense of commitment and relation evoked by his mastery of intimate voice, and the harder-edged modernism and implicit tragedy of his psychological orientation. His skill lies in his refusal to allow either of these to yield too completely and reductively to the other.

Taylor's portrayals of his characters' attempts at self-understanding inevitably evolve into reflections on family relations, and on the forms of identity that such relations generate. Warren understood this element of Taylor's work from the beginning, noting that in his first stories "the old-fashioned structure of family life still persists, disintegrating slowly under the pressures of modernity" (viii). As Taylor's work developed over the next four decades, his attention to the depth of complication in family relationships increased, and his relentless analysis of the cracks in the veneer of the Southern, and the American, family should be seen as an important cultural statement.

I have divided my readings of stories representative of Taylor's concerns with family and culture into two broad sections. The first four chapters focus on the relationships that constitute the family; the last three consider Taylor's treatments of the changing social hierarchies and cultural practices of the upper South. Chapters 1 and 2 take up a central aspect of interfamily dynamics, father-son and mother-son relationships, which Taylor portrays in a variety of stories from the beginning to the end of his career. In these stories the problems of psychological dominance and emotional bondage are important, but Taylor's analysis of each parent-child relationship is unique. These, like all his stories, resist any easy reduction to thematic simplicity, although his concern with domineering fathers and their injured sons is clear enough. Chapters 3 and 4 consider the emotional and erotic bonds between men and women that are the basis of conventional family life, bonds that Taylor shows to be complex and highly problematized. These chapters also emphasize Taylor's important portrayals of the struggle of the individual for maturity and independence within the family setting, best exemplified in "Venus, Cupid, Folly and Time" and "The Old Forest," two of Taylor's strongest works.

In Chapter 5 I consider stories in which Southerners of various classes undergo a significant loss of social place, and therefore of secure identity, in the modern South. These are complemented by Taylor's depictions of African American domestic servants and their employers in the modern South, which I discuss in Chapter 6. Taylor is most explicit in his analysis of the problem of a "Southern" identity in two of his plays, *Tennessee Day in St. Louis* and *A Stand in the Mountains*, which are the subject of the final chapter. The plays evince his understanding of the dangers of tying one's identity too closely to the South, and reveal his ironic distance from the region with which he has been so closely identified.

This assessment of Taylor's fundamental concerns with family and region provides the framework within which I believe fruitful readings of Taylor's major stories and plays can be presented. His critical reception is still relatively young, and his strongest work—much of it concentrated in his later career in the 1970s, 1980s, and early 1990s—has yet to be fully assimilated. His fiction depends on nuance of tone and mood, concealments of motivation, ironic reversals of intention, and depictions of complex characters whose personalities are marked by tension and inner contradiction; it demands close and detailed reading.

Fortunately for all his readers, Taylor has been generous in discussing his works and their backgrounds in a number of interviews, which Hubert H. McAlexander has collected and edited in *Conversations with Peter Taylor*. Readers of that illuminating volume will find Taylor an astute commentator on his own writing, an author who understood his own purposes and could articulate them persuasively. The beginnings of a body of critical commentary on Taylor's work are also beginning to appear now, best represented in Albert J. Griffith's *Peter Taylor* (1970, revised in 1990) and in two recent collections of essays which have been very helpful to me in preparing this study: Hubert H. McAlexander's *Critical Essays on Peter Taylor* (1993) and C. Ralph Stephens and Lynda B. Salamon's *The Craft of Peter Taylor* (1995). I hope that the readings I offer here will extend the work begun in these volumes and open new discussion, both in the discourse of academic criticism and in the university classroom, where Taylor's work has a solid future.

PART 1
❖❖❖
Family Relations

❖ 1 ❖
Fathers and Sons

Peter Taylor has made his own early conflicts with his strong-willed father, Matthew Hillsman Taylor, a matter of biographical record. After his high school graduation, Taylor had earned a scholarship to Columbia, where he hoped to prepare for a literary career. His father, an attorney who wanted him to become an attorney also, insisted that he go to Vanderbilt instead. "And we had a knockdown, dragout quarrel and stopped speaking," Taylor told J. William Broadway. "The trunk was packed and I was going. My mother supported me—you know how mothers always support you. But he wouldn't give in, and I didn't give in" (*Conversations*, 96). Taylor instead began to work for a newspaper in Memphis, eventually enrolled at Southwestern University, and there came under the influence of Allen Tate. A charismatic teacher, Tate offered a powerfully inspirational example of literary dedication and persuaded Taylor to go to Vanderbilt in order to study with John Crowe Ransom. When Ransom left Vanderbilt for Kenyon, Taylor followed him there. His course of life as a writer and teacher of writing was set.

Taylor's resistance to his father's controlling demands seems to have been one of the defining narratives of his life. It represented both an act of independent self-determination and a deliberate choice of the less conventional career of writing and teaching over that of the law, which had been something of a family tradition. And this conflict between son and strong-willed father is a central version of the generational conflict to which Taylor returns repeatedly in his work.

An early and representative formulation of this theme is "Porte Cochere" (1949), the narrative of a thwarted man's destructive use of his paternal authority. Although "Porte Cochere" is a somewhat greener version of what would eventually ripen into more finely nuanced and psychologically adept works such as "Dean of Men," "In the Miro District," and *A Summons to*

Memphis, it effectively demonstrates how men act out of their past identities as sons in forming their relations as fathers. One of Taylor's darkest stories, it depicts a seemingly inescapable psychic isolation that eventuates in frustrated and soul-withering anger. Its protagonist, Ben Brantley, known to his children as Old Ben, is an irascible man whose domination of his children finally leads to their emotional rejection of him. Their final rejection is ironically played out while ceremonial family proprieties are being observed on Ben's birthday. "Clifford and Ben Jr. [his sons] always came for Old Ben's birthday" (*OF,* 256), the story begins, but as Taylor shows, the observance works not to bring the generations together but to emphasize their separation and reinforce the fundamental isolation that Ben feels. The emblem of that psychological isolation is the location of Ben's study "directly above the porte cochere [or drive-under]" (257), a room in which Ben can separate himself from his children yet simultaneously spy on them. The story takes place while Ben is doing exactly that—overhearing their conversation from the vantage of his study, and fuming all the while—even though they are long since grown with families of their own.

The significance of Ben's perch above the porte cochere is of course apparent to his family, and delineated clearly in a tense exchange with Clifford. In what begins as a trivial squabble over the decision to go out for dinner, Ben picks testily at Clifford, asking if he considers him "childish," until he provokes an angry outburst: "What the hell do you want of us, Papa? I've thought about it a lot. Why haven't you ever asked for what it is you want" (261)? Ben's needs have smothered his children, as Clifford, wrestling out from under them in his own maturity, has come to see. He is thus capable of pronouncing the meaning and purpose of the location of his father's study, from which Taylor draws the story's title. "Free to come and go," he says mockingly to his father, "with you perched here on the landing registering every footstep on the stairs and every car that passed underneath" (261). The design of the house is thus an important expression of Ben's personality, which allows his children no escape except through confrontation and struggle with him.[1]

In angrily asking his father what he wants of his children, Clifford has asked the fundamental question of the story. Ben wants something that his children cannot give him, even though he seems to demand it of them in bullying ways, because his needs could have been answered only by his own father. The confrontation with Clifford sends him into a reverie of the past that constitutes the psychic core of the story. Ben remembers as a boy climbing down a ladder into his father's empty cistern and accidentally dropping the lantern as he swung it out to illuminate the cistern's sides. "Crashing on the floor, it sent up yellow flames that momentarily lit the old cistern to its very top, and when Ben looked upward, he saw the furious face of his father with the flames casting jagged shadows on the long, black beard and high, white forehead" (263). The image is one of hellish entrapment, and his father is the devilish tormentor. Taylor reverses the image of the father as a figure of refuge or protection, making Ben's fear of him greater even than his fear of the flames or the cistern: "He had climbed upward toward his father, wishing the flames might engulf him before he came within reach of those arms." Ben's fear is justified, as his father, in a military-style procedure that seems to be a regular occurrence, deals him "three sharp blows across the upper part of his back," using an "oak stick that had his own bearded face carved upon the head" (263).

The oak stick became the only means by which a significant bond of identity was formed between Ben and his father—a violent bond, and one against which Ben had spent his life in a painful rebellion. Ben despises his father, wishing to be in a place "where there would be no children and no fathers" (264). When he himself does become a father, he makes the conscious commitment never to abuse his children physically, refusing to repeat his father's violent example. "Never once in his life had he punished or restrained them in any way! He had given them a freedom unknown to children in the land of his childhood, yet from the time they could utter a word they had despised him and denied his right to any affection or gratitude" (264). But his superficial rejection of his father's physical violence has been displaced by a destructive psychic coercion of his own children. Ben's conscious denial of his father's example is thus paralleled by a subconscious desire to refigure himself as his father. The entrapment that he felt in the cistern as he faced his father's anger has deeply imprinted itself on his personality, and he reenacts this scenario as a father from his vantage above the porte cochere. Just as his father entrapped him in the cistern, he blocks the unimpeded development of his children, unable to grant them in reality the freedom he claims to have given them.

Ben's angry exchange with Clifford eventuates in a moment of painful self-realization in which he is humbled by a sudden recognition of what he has done to them, how he has "tortured and plagued them in all the ways that his resentment of their very good fortune had taught him to do" (265). The tragic irony of Ben's life is that the steps he takes to avoid assuming his father's identity had in fact become the means by which he assumes it. When, in the story's final scene, he takes the oak stick with his father's face on it and begins, in a fit of quiet rage, "beating the upholstered chairs . . . and calling the names of the children under his breath" (265), we are made vividly aware of his inability to escape the psychological entrapment that his father's violence created for him. Although he is imprisoned by a resentment generated in his own childhood, it is also clear that Ben aches for his children; his desire to control them and the anger that results are in large part the thwarted expressions of his deep emotional need. Deprived of a nurturing and constructive relationship with his father, he is starved emotionally as an adult, and his pattern of reenactment of the source of his isolation only serves to deepen it.

That children can come to represent the potential compensation for a life of disappointment is the recognition of Taylor's "The Gift of The Prodigal" (1981), a later story with certain thematic connections to "Porte Cochere." The narrator is an aging widower who has developed a crippling dependence on hearing of the wild and self-destructive exploits of his youngest son, Ricky. As the old man watches Ricky approach his house one morning, suspecting that he has gotten into some form of trouble and will need to be bailed out again, he remembers the past history of his son's troubles, a stark contrast to the ordered and constructive lives of his other children.

The old man's initial tone is that of contempt for his son's generally debauched behavior, episodes of which he recounts in detail—an almost loving detail, we begin to realize, as the story continues. Despite the conventional forms of reverence shown him by his other children, he lives vicariously through Ricky's exploits and actually relishes Ricky's knowing confidence that his father will ultimately use his money and influence to clean up the messes he makes. He is one version of a Jamesian character who frequents Taylor's fiction, a man who lacks the courage or force of will to realize life for himself and must live it at one remove through observation of others. Ricky understands intuitively that he lives the sort of life his father has wanted but has never had the courage to attempt, and exploits this understanding in manipulating him.

When Ricky arrives to tell his latest tale and make his plea for help, he observes his father's obvious physical discomfort and the array of medication that he must take as his age progresses and his health deteriorates. "Man, you've got problems enough of your own," Ricky tells him as he apparently decides to leave. "Even the world's greatest snotface can see that. One thing sure, you don't need to hear *my* crap" (*OF*, 28). This at first seems like a surprisingly mature recognition on Ricky's part that the entire world does not revolve around his problems, and that his father is a man with his own life and his own needs. But the words cut his father like a knife; he at first commands and then pleads with his son to continue with his story. Ricky's apparent gesture of understanding has in fact been a form of threat, a warning that he may not share with his father his latest escapade or allow him the pleasure of cleaning up the mess.

After his father's pleas, Ricky relents and begins to tell his story. His father clings to the opportunity with a pathetic desperation: "What will it be this time, I think. I am wild with anticipation." And as he recognizes that anticipation, he also recognizes the inner poverty that it suggests. "Whatever it will be, I know it is all anyone in the world can give me now—perhaps the most anyone has ever been able to give a man like me" (29). Although an edge of self-recognition is revealed here, the confessional tone hides the more important issue: as Ricky continues with his tale, his father listens with eager relish, ready to pay appreciatively for the privilege of his inclusion. He has made his own lack of courage, his inability to establish a genuine and constructive relationship with life, into an emotional need that also ties his son into a pattern of crippling and self-destructive behavior.

Although "Porte Cochere" and "The Gift of the Prodigal" both present the paternal bond as destructive, they outline quite different ways in which such damage can occur—one through an abuse of paternal authority, and the other through an abuse of paternal generosity. Each story is based on a man's debilitating desire to define or redefine himself through the molding and manipulation of his son. In "Porte Cochere" it leads to the son's tense emotional rejection of his father's demands; in "The Gift of the Prodigal" it leads to a parallel dependency of the son on the father, one that is ultimately injurious to both. Taylor's "Dean of Men" (1969), a more complex and accomplished story, offers a different and perhaps more typically modern version of paternal failure, a failure based in neglect rather than dependency or abuse. Framed as a letter from a father to his nearly grown son Jack, from whom he has been long separated by a divorce, it is the utterance of a man who has lost his tie to the succeeding generation and, in a larger sense, has lost himself in the process. The narrator's tone is poignantly wistful and alarmingly aggressive by turns, and his shifts in tone signal important, unresolved conflicts that now center on his son and on his memories of his own father and grandfather.

Permeating the story is the narrator's anxiety about masculinity and his desire to reestablish a male generational continuity that his divorce seems to have broken. The narrator, a university president who began his rise through the administrative ranks as a dean of men—a position that he chose at the expense of his marriage—begins his letter with an aggressive attack on his son's 1960s generation masculinity. While averring that he is "not unsympathetic" to his son's views on the Vietnam War, he caustically adds that "from the way you wear your hair and from the way you dress I do find it difficult to decide whether you or that young girl you say you are about to marry is going to play the male role in your marriage—or the female role" (*CS*, 3). The remark anchors the story in the generational battles of the 1960s, but takes on further resonance when the narrator later recounts the details of his own failed first marriage, one in which conflicting career goals and the division of gender roles were key points of contention.

The narrator's letter is in large part a guilty attempt to explain and justify to his son the reasons for the divorce, but like most of Taylor's narrators he reveals far more that is harmful to his case than he intends. At the root of his conflict with his first wife, Jack's mother, was her deferred desire to have a career in college teaching, as the narrator does. Though they had met in graduate school and taught at the same school early in their marriage, she gave up her work when they had children, though not without resentment. "I had not realized how much her plans for a career had meant to her. But now she accused me of being an antifeminist, accused me of trying to isolate her in the kitchen, even of trying to cut her off from all intellectual life" (25).

The narrator's admission of this split over the nature of the roles in the marriage, an issue that eventually became the focal point for their decision to divorce, has important connections to his experience of his father's and his grandfather's enactment of their own roles in the workplace and in the family.[2] He spends almost as much time telling Jack about the marriages of his grandfather and father as about his own, and it is clear that the male conduct that he had observed within those marriages affected his own conduct. But the relationship of generational experiences is not that of simple imitation. He did not place his career ahead of his wife's, and thus ahead of his marriage, simply because that is what his father and grandfather had done. In fact, something nearer the opposite was the case. Their failures in the larger public world made the strongest impression on him, for these failures drove them back, as he perceived it, into a kind of defeated and enforced domesticity. It is not their autocratic patriarchalism that he imitates, but their defeated domesticity that he rebels against. But in his attempt to set a different course, he simply lives out a new variation on the pattern they have set.

The narrator focuses his memory on an argument with his first wife one Sunday morning, after which he left the house in a huff and spent the morning alone in his office. The significance of this particular argument was that after he arrived at his office, he recognized that he was reenacting a scene from the marriage of his father and mother, and another that he had been told of from the marriage of his grandfather and grandmother. In each of these scenes the husband storms out of the domestic confines of the house to the completely male sphere of the workplace, withdrawing from both dialogue and responsibility. And in the narrator's case and that of his father, the dispute originates in his sharp or hurtful words to his daughter, words that prompt his wife to say "I would be ashamed of myself if I were you" (5, 11).

For the narrator, the remembered scene is connected with a certain continuity of masculine behavior about which he is mildly guilty but which he attempts to understand as an important clue to his own later decision to pursue his career at the cost of his marriage. But it is also linked to another and more profound source of guilt, his loss of contact with his son as a result of the divorce. It is as if he feels himself the last in a male line, connected with his father and grandfather and the product of their experience but utterly shut off from his son, with whom he tries to reestablish a connection. "Perhaps it is a story about you and me—about men" (4) he says hopefully at the story's beginning, clearly indicating his need to reaffirm his lost bond with his son.

Since the narrator reads his own marital experience in the context of his father's and grandfather's, it is important to note the way their lives both cohere and differ. The striking similarity is that in all three cases the men are betrayed, or feel themselves betrayed, by colleagues in their work. The narrator's grandfather, an aspiring politician, was persuaded by a group of his associates to give up an almost sure seat in the United States Senate in order to run for the governorship of Tennessee. But after stepping aside from the nomination to the Senate, he did not garner the expected support for the governor's race, and his promising political career came to an end. The narrator's father was betrayed by his close friend and business associate Lewis Barksdale, who apparently used an insurance company's money fraudulently, implicating him in a scandal, and then failed to take any action to help explain the situation or clear his friend's name.[3] The narrator undergoes what he feels is a somewhat similar betrayal when a group of his academic colleagues fail to support him in a dispute with the college president, and he feels that as a result he must resign his position.

In the case of the narrator's grandfather and father, the effect of the betrayals was to drive them into a withdrawal from the active participation in public life that they had known before. His grandfather "withdrew almost entirely from all male company, seeing men only as his rather limited law practice required him to do. He lived out his life in a household of women and children" (15). Although his father's withdrawal was not as severe, he nevertheless "made no real life for himself in his practice" and "seldom saw other members of the firm away from the office," effecting an almost complete separation between his necessary professional duties and his home life. "His real life was all at home," the narrator says, "where, as he would point out, it had always been" (23).

Yet as the narrator indicates, these were not happy or satisfying patterns of life; each withdrawal represented in important ways a defeat. His grandfather was an embittered man who became "a coarse-tongued old tyrant" of his domestic world. He retired "to the bosom of his family," the narrator tells us, "where, alas, I cannot say he was greatly loved and cherished" (15). His father, while always "affectionate" and possessed of a "reasonably cheerful disposition," nevertheless struck the narrator as "lonely and bored" through much of his later life. "I remember sometimes, even when the family was on a vacation together—when we had taken a cottage at the shore or were camping and fishing in the mountains—the look would come in his eye. And one was tempted to ask oneself, What's wrong? What's missing?" (23-24).

In both cases the refuge of domestic life proved unsatisfactory. Both men, wounded in pride, used the retreat into domesticity as a means of preserving their dignity, so their retreat remained, in a certain sense a public act. The narrator does not articulate this perception directly, but it seems to play a role in his reaction to his own betrayal and thus shapes his conduct as a husband and a father. After discovering that his colleagues would not extend the support he sought during a faculty meeting at his college, "[I] went back to my study, and typed up the final version of my letter of resignation" (35).[4]

This resignation, as it turns out, seems from one perspective to be a good move. The narrator finds another job at a state university, a larger school where he can remain relatively aloof from campus politics and where, most important, his wife also has the opportunity to teach. "I felt it would be possible to pass unnoticed for years, in the university and in the city. I met my classes, I attended department meetings, I made revisions on the galley proofs of my book. It seems to me I spent a large part of every day taking Susie back and forth to school on the bus. And I spent hours in the park with you, Jack" (36). The narrator's more domestic life, that is, echoes that of his own father after his withdrawal from the world of business.

Although it is clear that the narrator takes a certain feeling of wounded betrayal with him into this new life, it also appears that, as he says to Jack, his new circumstances will be conducive to a fuller domestic life and a more egalitarian relationship with his wife, who is hired by his new university as a part-time instructor. But the move seems to have a quite different effect. The narrator comments that after he told his wife of his betrayal by his colleagues at the faculty meeting, she had "burst into tears and threw herself into my arms" and tried to console him for his defeat. But, in a puzzling remark, he explains his own reaction: "As she held me there, it was all I could do to keep from weeping myself. And somehow, for all her tenderness at that moment and despite all the need I had of it, it came over me that this was the beginning of the end for us, that our marriage would not survive it" (34). Thus despite all the optimism of a new beginning, he goes to his new job not with a sense of promise or renewal but with a persisting conviction that his marriage is doomed. "I never for a moment believed our marriage could weather this new turn my life had taken," he tells us, even though, as we have seen, the conditions of the new job would seem to promise just the opposite. "I don't know why. As my mother would have said, the Old Nick himself seemed to have got in me. I *wouldn't* be consoled, I *wouldn't* be comforted, though I consistently made an effort to seem so" (36).

Although he is at first able to conceal it, the narrator clearly reenacts the emotional withdrawal of his grandfather and father, both of whom turned to their families as a refuge from professional trouble but each of whom, in quite different ways, was unable to reconcile himself happily to a domestic fate. The narrator's professional betrayal thus poisons his marriage rather than strengthening it. When he receives news later that he is being considered for the position of dean of men at a different college, he pursues the offer, in the face of his wife's avowal that she will not go with him.

Even though he is extremely successful in his new administrative career, his decision has to be read as a kind of failure. In an interview with Hubert H. McAlexander, Taylor described the narrator as having "sold out to become Dean" (*Conversations*, 119). This refers in part to Taylor's view of the value of teaching and writing weighed against that of academic administration. But in a deeper sense the narrator reveals his weakness of character by placing his professional pride above his family and by refusing to accept his responsibilities as a husband and father. He enacts in his own way a family tradition of unhappy splits between career and domestic life, deliberately, even eagerly, choosing the path that will end his marriage and effectively end his role as a father. He does remarry, apparently with success, but it is this first failure, involving his relationship with his son, to which he returns with a kind of uneasy need for self-justification.

Taylor thus constructs the story as both a psychological analysis of his narrator and a broader commentary on the seemingly unbridgeable divide for men between work and family. Although the two realms can be used in opposition to each other—family providing a refuge from work and vice versa—a real sense of fulfillment would seem to lie in some sort of reconciliation and harmonious interweaving of the two. But the men described in the story consistently refuse to build such lives for themselves, viewing domesticity as a kind of punishment for professional failure. "A man must somehow go on living among men, Jack. A part of him must," the narrator says in conclusion (38). But living among men is not the chief problem for him, nor was it for his father or grandfather. Living as a father and as a husband is the much greater challenge.

As "Porte Cochere," "The Gift of the Prodigal," and "Dean of Men" make clear, the father-son relationship is rife with problems of emotional entrapment and mutual victimization, the pitfalls of being the son inevitably translated into the failures of being the father. Taylor treats the relationship with particular depth and subtlety in "In the Miro District" (1977), observing there that such struggles can extend beyond a single generation. This "father-son" story tells of a grandfather and grandson forced together by a seemingly absent generation between them. The story transcends this single characterization in its commentary on changing social perceptions, however, for it shows the marked change across three generations of the meaning of the "South" and of the Southern identity.

The narrator, pondering his childhood in a pattern typical of Taylor's later narrators, wonders why "in that quaint Tennessee world I grew up in, it was so well established that grandfathers and grandsons were to be paired off and held answerable to each other for companionship" (*MD*, 161). Paired off with his crusty maternal grandfather, Major Basil Manley, the narrator finds himself psychologically captive to the different world and different values that his grandfather represents. The story details his complicated attempt to free himself from a bond that, as he finds, is as constrictive on his grandfather as on him.

Even though he tells us that the persistent memories of his grandfather began to come to him only after he "first got to be a grown man" and "first managed to get away from Tennessee" (159), we come to realize that his escape has not been as clean as he may indicate. Thrust into his grandfather's company as part of his parents' strategy to domesticate the crusty Major into their comfortable upper-class life, the narrator explores his growing need to reject his grandfather as part of his own "escape" to maturity. His attempts at this escape during adolescence constitute the comic and dramatic core of the story, with these moods tightly interwoven.

The story is structured around three confrontations between the narrator and his grandfather which, in the rising order of their intensity, constitute the narrator's declaration of an independent identity. He feels that he must demonstrate his independence by doing something to prove his difference from his grandfather. "Until I made him grasp that, I would not begin to discover what, since I wasn't and couldn't be like him, I *was* like" (190). His grandfather represents a world of experience that has been denied to him, and although their separate historical situations largely account for the difference, it is felt by the narrator as a measure of personal inadequacy. He feels that he lives in an impoverished time, and his grandfather, who carries the heavily significant name of "Manley," is an impossible standard of masculine maturity against which the boy must measure himself.[5]

The three increasingly intense confrontations result in the end of the grandfather's immediate emotional hold on the narrator, although the word "immediate" needs to be given due emphasis here. As in such stories as "The Old Forest" and "Venus, Cupid, Folly and Time," the retrospective narration of the story is itself the chief evidence that the emotional tie has not been completely or permanently broken. The significance of the opening sentence should not therefore be forgotten: "What I most often think about when I am lying awake in the night, or when I am taking a long automobile trip alone, is my two parents and my maternal grandfather" (159). The haunting quality of these memories is an indication of unresolved conflict.

In one of the most effective turns of the story, the confrontations that separate the narrator from his grandfather also end Manley's resistance to the "busy, genteel, contented life" of his children in Nashville (159). Taylor remarked that the story "shows a certain defeat in the grandfather's life when he gave in to the mores around him and moved into town" (*Conversations*, 27), and David H. Lynn has noted that the story recounts "two comings of age": the boy's entry into independent maturity, and Major Manley's reluctant surrender to "the dependence of old age."[6] Exactly how and why Manley's surrender to his children is connected with his break with his grandson is a more difficult question.

The formative event of Manley's character, the subject of repeated stories that the narrator hears from his earliest years, was his escape from a lynch mob after he watched the hanging of his friend. He wandered in the swamp ten days, afraid to show himself for fear that the lynchers would find and kill him too. One of the most frightening aspects of Manley's experience was the hallucination that he was continually pursued in the swamp by "hooded men mounted on strange animals charging toward him like the horsemen of the apocalypse." Moreover, his escape was made in the area of Reelfoot Lake, which had been formed by the great New Madrid Earthquake of 1811, a terrifyingly apocalyptic event in which the town of New Madrid had "crumbled down the bluffs and into the river," and people had disappeared "into round holes thirty feet wide" (183).

The narrator has heard his grandfather's tales of both the escape from the lynch mob and of the earthquake, and these narratives have merged into a picture of the threateningly chaotic nature of experience. For Manley, the quake became the natural analogue of the evil human intention that the hooded nightriders had enacted. His confrontation with them was an exposure to a world absolutely stripped of order, a natural correlative of the great earthquake, which had made even the Mississippi River run backward in its channel. During his flight Manley imagined greater evils than even the hooded nightriders who pursued him; at times he believed that the earthquake "had recurred or commenced again, or that he was living in that earlier time when the whole earth seemed to be convulsed and its surface appeared as it must have in primordial times" (184). Those hellish days brought him "a glimpse into the eternal chaos we live in, a glimpse no man should be permitted" (184).

Although he was finally able to return and obtain justice for his friend's murder, the experience marked him with a profound skepticism about the solidity of social arrangements. This skepticism conditions and complicates his relation with his children. He holds their "busy, genteel, contented life" (159) of bridge parties and country club dinners in mild contempt and adamantly refuses to play the role of the ornamental Confederate veteran who would confer a decided status on the house. His aloofness is a measure of his belief that the life of the Nashville upper crust is a flimsy house of cards, a convenient but fragile conspiracy to deny "the eternal chaos we live in" (184). That belief is therefore something of a fundamental philosophical commitment that holds him aloof from his children, their home, and their social circle. He sees in them a settled complacency to which, because of his own experience, he cannot assent.

His skepticism is borne out by his refusal to accept the available social approbation for his Civil War experience, the ceremonies of "Decoration Day," an indication of his general belief that such ceremonials mask the fragility of "civilization." In a similar vein, he refuses to discuss his war experience with his family. The shaky foundations of that cultural order and the inherent evil and violence in human nature were revealed to Manley during his escape at Reelfoot Lake, and thus he holds himself apart as a measure of how deeply that vision registered in his psyche.

The structure of Manley's past experience is only gradually revealed to us as the narrator, intensely focused on his own difficulties with his grandfather, recounts the series of confrontations by which he seemingly freed himself. But his account of these incidents reveals his conflicting desires: he wants to be free of his grandfather, but he also hopes that he can somehow forge a closer connection with him. He believes he has never actually established the bond that would make the relationship fruitful and enduring.

This is suggested in the first of the incidents, when Manley discovers the narrator and his friends in the midst of an adolescent drinking bout. Although this scene, like the two later ones, is initiated and sustained by the element of surprise in Major Manley's sudden and unannounced appearance at the Nashville house, it is also clear that deliberate exposure of his misdeeds has to some extent been part of the narrator's plan. "I stood there in silence for several moments, waiting for him to begin the kind of dressing-down which he had never given me and which if he could have given me then might have made all the difference in the world in our future relation—and perhaps our lives" (171-72). But Manley retreats into a mildly disgusted aloofness, and the narrator's disappointment that he is not severely reprimanded indicates that he has tried to gain his grandfather's approval through flamboyant misbehavior. Understanding Manley's contempt for his modern, citified, effeminate life, he has sought to prove his masculinity by exhibiting his contempt for social restraints. Manley's overt disapproval would have signaled recognition of the gesture and accepted a paternal bond with his grandson through the discipline.[7]

The narrator's desire to emulate his grandfather has thus been expressed as a resistance to him, but Manley refuses to be engaged. "At some point I could see that he was no longer listening and that, after all, the victory of this engagement was somehow his. Finally I was silenced by his silence" (177). The military metaphor, appropriate perhaps for the old Confederate, establishes the state of conflict that the narrator has now come to feel, and he projects his own sense of emotional exclusion onto Manley: *"Why have you never waited and allowed me to speak for myself?* I knew he was thinking, but didn't say. *And why is it you've never opened your mouth to me about yourself?"* (176). The narrator's conviction that his grandfather has "always thought that I was hiding something" (176) may perhaps be accurate, but its real significance is its expression of his own feeling about his grandfather.

This first skirmish is escalated some six weeks later when Manley discovers his grandson and several of his friends in bed with their dates early one morning while the parents are away from home. The indiscretion is of course larger here than in the drinking bout, and the comic consequences of the discovery are correspondingly greater. The narrator is "at once electrified and paralyzed" by the sound of Manley's car in the driveway at seven in the morning while he and his friends are scattered through the bedrooms of his parents' house, each with a girl. The Major strides up the stairs, opening the door to each of the bedrooms until he finds his grandson, lying on his stomach, unwilling to get up to face him. "I felt the first blow of the walking stick across my buttocks," he remembers, and then realized that his grandfather was striking the girl beside him as well. "By the time he had struck the girl a second time she had begun screaming." Amid the commotion, Manley leaves the room with this order: "I want you to get these bitches out of this house and to do so in one hell of a hurry!" (186-87).

As one might imagine, it takes little more persuasion on the Major's part to clear the house, but one turn of events proves to be especially galling to the narrator: "As they went out through the wide front door the four girls called out, 'Goodbye!' in cheerful little voices. I opened my mouth to respond, but before I could make a sound I heard grandfather answering, 'Goodbye, girls.' And it came over me that it had been to him, not me, they were calling goodbye" (189). Although Manley has completely usurped his grandson's masculinity, the narrator's humiliation is mixed with an odd elation as he describes his reaction to the blows Manley administered with his cane. "At last he had struck me! That was what I thought to myself. At last we might begin to understand one another and make known our real feelings, each about the other" (187).

The blow represents a form of recognition that the narrator has desperately sought, a sign that his grandfather's usual aloofness has given way to some expression of emotion, even anger. The gesture of punishment seems to make his grandfather, for once, emotionally accessible to him, the first requirement of his larger need to develop an independent identity. The hope of some breakthrough of recognition fades quickly, though, when the narrator realizes that his grandfather is striking his date as well. "Already," he confesses, "I had begun to understand that his striking me didn't have quite the kind of significance I had imagined" (187). His grandfather was striking not at his grandson but at the situation, at the mess he found, and so even this confrontation failed to yield the breakthrough that the narrator had hoped for.

That breakthrough would come a few weeks later when his grandfather again paid an unannounced visit to Nashville. In the story's comic-dramatic climax Manley finds his grandson hiding his naked girlfriend in the wardrobe closet of the bedroom reserved for him during his visits to Nashville. This encounter marks the turning point of their relation and becomes one of the key events of his grandfather's later life. The narrator tells us that he has used his grandfather's bedroom and his grandfather's bed the whole weekend, and has done so with a certain defiant premeditation. When he shows his girlfriend into the room, he catches a glimpse of himself in the mirror and thinks "with a certain glee in that moment of my grandfather" and feels "a certain premonition of events" (193). He expects, even hopes, to be discovered, and hopes that his use of Manley's room will affront and offend him. Thus when Manley does arrive the next day, sending the unclothed couple scrambling for cover, the narrator steers his girlfriend into the wardrobe with this remark: "'Over there,' I said, 'if you're sure you want to. But it's his room. He's apt to find you'" (194).

The fact is, however, that Manley is very little concerned about the invasion of his room, having consciously refused to settle in it in any permanent way. His children had bought the house with the specific intention of providing him with a room, and it had served no other purpose over the years. But the little-used furniture and empty drawers and closets are signs of his rejection of the role that his family hoped he would play for them. The narrator's invasion of it is thus another fruitless attempt to penetrate his grandfather's shell. He does, however, strike home in a different way, one that he perhaps does not fully recognize at the time: he has finally committed an act that signifies his difference in values from those of his grandfather.

The girl that Manley finds in the closet is "a Ward Belmont girl . . . whom my parents, as an indication of their approval of my courting a girl of her particular family, had had to dinner at our house several times and even on one occasion when my grandfather was there" (191). She is, that is to say, of an appropriately marriageable class for someone of the narrator's social stature, whereas the girls that he and his friends entertained in the previous escapade were what he had termed "girls of the 'other sort'" (186). Readers of "The Old Forest" will recognize both the nature of this distinction and its importance in dictating the attitudes and behavior of young men of the upper class. The narrator has declared himself to be deeply in love with her—all the more so, he remembers, when, as he closed the wardrobe door, he saw that she "wasn't by any means shedding tears but was smiling up at me. . . . And I think I knew then for the first time in my life how wonderful it is to be in love and how little anything else in the world matters" (194). Part of this rush of feeling, we are inclined to believe, is due to her unwitting role in the narrator's half-conscious plot against his grandfather. When she hides in the wardrobe, she commands him not to let Manley find her there. But when Manley arrives, the narrator not only tells him openly and somewhat defiantly that she is there but offers little resistance to his grandfather's discovery of her: "With almost no effort," he says, "he pushed me aside and opened the wardrobe door" (198).

The reaction is sharper than he, or the reader, might have imagined, after the earlier scenes. "He turned on me a look cold and fierce and so articulate that I imagined I could hear the words his look expressed: 'So this is how bad you really are?'" (198). Manley has recognized the girl and therefore understood his grandson's violation of the values of his social class. The irony is, however, that although Manley has seemingly held the Nashville world of his family, the very embodiment of this code, in mild contempt, despite his nonconformist manners he is deeply concerned with order and its preservation. The previous acts of his grandson posed no threat to order as Manley understood it; this act does.

To understand Manley's reaction fully, we must recur to his experiences at Reelfoot Lake, where his hallucinatory visions of the nightriders and the earthquake exposed him to a world that had lost all order. His escape and return to put his prosecutors on trial was a struggle to restore a measure of order to what had been revealed to him as a chaotic world. The effect of this experience was to impress him with the fragility of all order, especially order imposed by humans through their social codes. That was why he looked with skepticism on his daughter and son-in-law's easy and unthinking assumption that the world had been established to conform to their expectations. Yet though he rejected their genteel domesticity, his scorn for his children's complacency is not a rejection of the social order that he shares with them but a sign of how much more profoundly he understands its tenuousness. That is why he regards his grandson's fornication as a threat.

In this final confrontation Manley is, as Taylor commented, defeated.[8] When he leaves the house in Nashville, the narrator presumes that he is returning in a huff to his farm in Hunt County. But in fact he stays there only briefly, returning instead to join his daughter and son-in-law at the resort where they are vacationing. And he comes back a different man, having discarded his tan gabardine coat for a black serge suit and string tie, the appropriate dress for an aging Confederate veteran: "From that day I never saw him in any other" (199), the narrator recalls. Within a year he moves into the Nashville house and lives there "for the rest of his life, participating in my parents' lively social activities, talking freely about his Civil War experiences, even telling ladies how he courted my grandmother during that time" (202). Finally, it would seem, the narrator has the grandfather he always wanted, and his parents their ornamental veteran. But in fact the incident seems to seal off any future contact between Manley and his grandson, and their relationship is more distanced than ever.

That Manley's domestication is a response to the discovery of his grandson's girlfriend in the closet is clear, but a certain ambiguity in his reaction deserves further comment. The narrator tells us later that he came to understand his grandfather's surrender to domesticity as a response less to his grandson than to a long struggle with his children. "It had, after all, been their battle all along," he says, "his and theirs, not his and mine. I, after all, had only been the pawn of that gentle-seeming couple who were his daughter and son-in-law and who were my parents" (200). This battle had centered on Manley's distrust of his children's complacent domesticity, which he found naive because of his experiences at Reelfoot Lake. He had not taken his grandson's earlier rebelliousness as indicative of any real difference from his parents and did not regard it as a serious threat to the social values that he implicitly shared with his children.

He is shaken, however, by the narrator's final act of defiance because he recognizes it as his grandson's misguided emulation of his own seeming social rebelliousness. When he discovers the girl, his cold stare comments not only on the narrator's character but on his own as well. His grandson confronts him with an image of the evil he had faced most directly in his hallucinations at Reelfoot Lake. That "glimpse [into chaos that] no man should be permitted" (184) was a glimpse into the nature of human evil and, more important, into himself.

It is clear that with the narrator's third rebellion, something breaks in Manley, that he no longer feels capable of sustaining the stance toward experience that he has cultivated over the years. His grandson's act flouts the public order, an order that Manley had seen shaken at the moment of his deepest fear, when he faced the lynch mob. He thus embraces his children's domesticity in order to contain this troubling vision of the antisocial evil within himself and within human nature itself. His angry withdrawal from his grandson is in fact an act of fleeing from himself, a belated admission that the crusty, nonconforming persona he has cultivated flirted too much with the serious danger that he felt he had both witnessed and temporarily mastered at Reelfoot Lake.[9]

The narrator is ultimately a victim of this moment of his grandfather's frightened self-realization—not, of course, an entirely innocent victim. The defiant act that finally does break him free of Manley and thus moves him toward an independent maturity has come at some cost, for he feels himself completely broken away from the past. Adrift in a rootless modern world, he continues to remember his grandfather with puzzlement and guilt, and to feel that he does not fully know himself.

A Summons to Memphis, Taylor's acclaimed novel of 1987, offers a particularly complex version of the father-son bond and is in many ways his culminating and definitive treatment of this central theme. Here he explores the psychological cost of a son's resistance to his father's domination, depicting the attempt to escape from victimization as itself a furtherance of that victimization. It is Taylor's most detailed and most uncompromisingly harsh indictment of a father-son relationship become a destructive force. Phillip Carver, the narrator, confesses late in the novel that he had always "repressed" his feelings about his father's domineering conduct, a fault that has cost him deeply, as he has come to recognize. "I had found no voice within me to protest. (But I knew I ought to have found the voice and having spoken out at the proper time ought by now to have forgotten all seeming injustice. Probably his own conflicts with his father he had protested and forgotten. That was the essence of maturity in a son)" (*Summons,* 133). Right and insightful as this sounds, it is one of many revelatory flashes that seem to come to nothing for Phillip. George Carver holds a prominent place in the gallery of aging, willful, but fascinating fathers that populate Taylor's fiction. Like Basil Manley he is a man of force, accomplishment, and deep experience, experience that his son struggles to understand as he sorts out his own troubled life. Instead of confronting his father, Phillip bent himself to his father's will as a young man and then seethes with angry remembrance in middle age. His unresolved conflict with his father has left him bereft of any achieved and stable identity.

Taylor deftly balances the novel between a depiction of Phillip's gradual and positive coming to terms with the causes of the "ruin" of his life, and the exposure of Phillip as a weak and passionless phantom, forever chained to a past not of his own creating. On the one hand the novel is a positive portrayal of the cultivation of an understanding through memory, but on the other it is an almost merciless exposure of a life of cowardly failure. Do we finally sympathize with Phillip through watching his battle to accept his father—and himself as his father's son? Or do we find the very process of his own self-analysis the means by which we come to distance ourselves from him as a character whose only remaining passion is an aborted vengefulness? Taylor will have it both ways, insisting on the necessity of both compassion and judgment.[10]

   Phillip's self-delusion—or is it duplicity?—is most evident in his early declaration that he felt "a surge of happiness that I had got away [from Memphis] so long ago" (13). In his present life as a Manhattan publisher and rare book collector, his past is never very far behind him, and it is brought back to him with resounding force when he receives a summons from his sisters, Betsy and Josephine, to return to Memphis and help them prevent his elderly father's remarriage. This summons from Memphis comes at a time when Phillip and his lover Holly are temporarily estranged and she has moved out of the apartment that they have shared for twelve years. He mentions this as one of the reasons why the call from his sisters affected him so strongly, but he is quick to tell us that the breakup was only temporary, and "after only a few weeks' separation, she and I have lived in relative contentment since" (8). What is striking in his commentary on his life with her is the placid contentment that he emphasizes, in contrast to the emotional cauldron that he reveals as he discusses his past. "Our orderly life together here—Holly's and mine—is still as different as it could conceivably be from the life of my family in Memphis, or, for that matter, the life of Holly's Jewish family in Cleveland" (8). Phillip's characterization of his relationship with Holly as "orderly" suggests evasiveness or profound emptiness, and his reticence about it reinforces that impression. Holly appears to be no more than part of the trappings of his Manhattan life, which has a feeling of temporariness about it. The only valuable thing about Manhattan to Phillip is that it is not Memphis; he lives there to try to prove to himself that he has escaped from his Tennessee past.

   But the operative summons of the book, we gradually discover, was his father's original decision to leave Nashville for Memphis when Phillip was thirteen years old. Phillip labels the move "a trauma he would in some way never recover from" (133), an act that broke the lives of his sisters and mother and withered his own as well. It is the first of a series of expressions of parental authority against which he cannot quite bring himself to rebel, though his resentment of them festers painfully in his arid midlife.

   The move from Nashville to Memphis obsesses Phillip's memory as the quintessential expression of his father's crippling authority. While his father did not make his decision maliciously, he failed to understand its impact on his family. "How *could* the man have known?" Phillip asks. "His experiences and mine were so utterly different at that moment in life!" (133). This seems like a sincere attempt at forgiving and reconciliation, but much of the novel's tension concerns Phillip's attempt to achieve the emotional understanding that the statement implies. "How could he *not* have understood?" is the subtext of his comment. His obsession with his father's sense of justice indicates deep psychological wounds that have not yet healed, but Taylor also shows us that Phillip's complaint matters, and matters to others as well as to himself. If a wounded man, he is capable of feeling his pain and determined to locate its source in the past, particularly in his relation with his father. If a passionless man, he is so because the great love of his youth was thwarted by his father's interference.

Phillip's explanation for the trauma of the move is based on an important regional discrimination in which Nashville represents the more polished culture of the upper South and Memphis the "cotton and river culture of the Deep South" (4). The 220 miles between the two cities were long ones, and the Carver family felt the move as a significant displacement. In Nashville, one was "two hundred twenty miles nearer to Richmond, to Charleston, to Savannah" (42). The move brought particular pain to Phillip and his sisters, for whom the interconnected domestic and social worlds of Nashville were paramount, but was initially accepted more cheerfully by Phillip's mother, who found Memphis a liberation from her Nashville past and the shadow of her mother's code of genteel propriety. But what began as a happy adjustment soon changed, and Phillip offers one important clue to that change: "For the short time that she kept her health it seemed that she was going to develop an entirely new personality, despite Father's rather constant effort to restrain her and remind her of what she was 'really like'" (25). Although we have to screen this comment through our knowledge of Phillip's conflict with his father, it rings true enough when considered in the context of his father's other acts of control. His mother's reaction to this control offers a suggestive parallel to Phillip's own later life. She awoke one morning "with a strange headache in her right temple," and "for thirty years afterward she seldom got into her daytime clothes" (28). While Phillip has not literally taken to his bed to avoid the control of his father, he has lived in hiding, as an emotional invalid.

George Carver's heavy-handed dealings with his children's love affairs are the worst effects of his domineering personality. After the family's arrival in Memphis he is worried about the ease with which his daughter Josephine seemed to be "settling in" and making new boyfriends. Her new suitors "seemed countrier to him—more Mississippian" (42), and his attitude seems to be that his family must be in Memphis but not of it, a reflection of his own inner conflict about a move that he felt was forced on him.

Having lost control of his professional life, he redoubles his efforts to control his family.[11] "Both girls were made to feel that their conformity, their obedience, their moral support was the then most important matter in their father's life." And, as he adds, they took that responsibility seriously: "They did conform, they obeyed, they supported—they did not marry" (56). As a result, they remain emotionally frozen in a permanent state of adolescence.[12]

What prompted this fateful move to Memphis that proved to be so shattering for the Carver family? As we noted earlier, Taylor offered an explanation rooted in his own father's experience of betrayal, the same narrative source from which he constructed "Dean of Men." George Carver's life in Nashville revolved around his work as an attorney for the growing business empire of Meriwether Lewis Shackleford, a man to whom he was bonded as both a business associate and solid friend. The self-made Shackleford was drawn to George Carver because he saw in him something of a Southern agrarian aristocrat. But Shackleford failed Carver by compromising his reputation in an unethical business transaction. When Shackleford's misdeed was discovered, Carver's own financial security and personal integrity came under question. When Shackleford failed to clear the situation, Carver moved to Memphis to establish a law practice from the ground up.

The pain of George Carver's failure is intensified when we consider that he had battled his own domineering father, thirsting for an identity different from what his father had bequeathed him as a prominent citizen of the small town of Thornton. He regarded his life in Nashville as the sign of his achievement of that identity and was beholden to Shackleford for his emotional independence as well as his financial security. Shackleford's betrayal therefore struck at the core of his identity. He left Nashville for Memphis, we surmise, not only an angered and humiliated man but a frightened one.

One of the novel's most vivid scenes is Phillip's recollection from childhood of the family's initial move to Nashville from Thornton after the death of George Carver's father, representing George's final release from a paternal authority. Phillip remembers the entire family's sense of elation as they arrived at the Shacklefords' driveway deep in the night, and the Shacklefords' excited bustle in response. Their welcome was profuse, and as Phillip's mother observed, "We were like travellers in the Tennessee wilderness a hundred years back being welcomed at the isolated cabin of a pioneer family" (175). Phillip's reconstruction of the moment is significant because it establishes so firmly the sense of familial security that the eventual move to Memphis interrupts. More particularly, it suggests the sense in which the move was crucial to George Carver's attempt to regain the sense of established identity that he thought he had won in his Nashville life. The demise of his success in Nashville must have represented to him a paternal rebuke from beyond the grave.

The novel records Phillip's gradual comprehension of these heretofore dimly understood events, a reexamination caused by the possibility of his father's remarriage in very old age. But this work of comprehension is limited by his resentment of his father's having sabotaged his intended marriage to Clara Price, his first and most intense love, an act that has haunted his entire adult life. However limited we find Phillip's perspective, it is hard to overlook the tyranny of the father in this affair—or the son's fundamental weakness in responding to it. Phillip remembers that after his first sexual experience with Clara "we were truly lovers and imagined ourselves bound to each other for life" (95), and we are never provided with any reason, other than a misguided authoritarianism, for his father's opposition to the match. George Carver, resistant to his own father and himself betrayed in one of his closest emotional ties, seems intent on enforcing a kind of emotional bondage on his family to assure his continuance in the one role in which he feels secure, that of father. He simply refuses to let his family go, and smothers them in the process of holding on.

In a reversal that is fundamental to the novel's structure, Phillip finds himself granted the power to enforce the same kind of imprisonment on his father. When he first receives his sisters' call to return to Memphis and help them prevent his father's marriage, it is difficult for him to share Betsy and Josephine's alarm, a good deal of which seems to be connected with their concern over his estate. He returns reluctantly, ambivalent as always about what course of action he will take, caught between the pressure of his sisters and what he knows will be his father's iron will. Should he prevent the marriage and become his father's keeper, reversing their lifelong relationship?

His decision is made for him when he sees his father waiting on the landing strip at Memphis to meet his flight from New York. After he first discovers, with surprise, that his father has come to meet him—"He was a man who never ran any such domestic errands" (135)—the full force of his own situation strikes him. He has been asked to defy this man, when he has never been able to do more than attempt to escape him. His original move to New York had been arranged by his sisters so that Phillip could entirely avoid any direct confrontation with his father. They had never confronted each other directly about his father's interference in his love affair with Clara Price. A lifetime of avoidance rushes into Phillip's consciousness as he sees his waiting father.

The details of George Carver's immaculate dress remind Phillip of his father's mastery of the world, and the clothes themselves trigger Phillip's memory of the wardrobe closets that his father moved to Memphis, which he associates with his father's power and control, emphasizing his feeling of psychological enclosure. "It was as though someone had thrown open the double doors to one of those wardrobes of his and, figuratively speaking, I was inhaling the familiar aroma of his whole life and being. Only it wasn't like an aroma exactly. For one moment it seemed I was about to be suffocated" (142).

But this fear, even revulsion, should not be misunderstood. It is part of a complex of emotions that seems to invert itself as quickly as Phillip understands and communicates it. Phillip's resistance weakens when his father asks him to serve as best man at his wedding. His father's warm greeting, his absolute assurance that Phillip will gladly so serve, the way "he smiled at me and pressed my hand made him seem irresistible" (143). Phillip is indeed a child again but now a happy one, his father's son.

George Carver's planned remarriage does not, in fact, occur. Phillip's sisters have interfered sufficiently in the situation to assure that. But Phillip learns that in this instance, at least, he has either lacked the will to defy his father or found the compassion to accept his father's choice. Had the novel ended here, we might be inclined to take the more positive view of Phillip's character, and assume that he has mastered the motivation for revenge on his father, and come, however belatedly, to a healthier reconciliation with his fate.[13] But this initial return to Memphis is a prelude to another return a few months later, in which he is again thrust into the affairs of his father and encounters the man that he regards as the ultimate author of his disappointments: Lewis Shackleford. Phillip is summoned by his sisters to a family vacation at the Owl Mountain Inn, out of their concern for their father who has seemed "frail" and in "low spirits" since the demise of his plans for remarriage. Although scorned for years by Betsy and Josephine with their Nashville condescension, the resort, "an old-fashioned watering spot in the Cumberland Mountains" (183), is held in particularly high esteem by Memphians. A place of traditions and deep connections with Memphis social life, it provides the Carvers with the setting for a surprising confrontation with the past.[14]

It is a placid and uneventful vacation until, on the Sunday of his departure, Phillip notices his old flame Clara Price in the resort's dining room. Dumfounded at the encounter, he is trying to sort through his characteristic indecision about whether to speak with her when another surprise meeting upstages his recognition of Clara: his father sees Lewis Shackleford in another corner of the dining room. The stunned Carver children watch as "the two tall and very straight old men [throw] their arms about each other in . . . an ardent embrace" (190). The embrace signifies a reconciliation with the past for George Carver, but his children cannot accept it, as their lowered eyes signify—and Phillip, his healing process incomplete, finds that he is incapable of greeting Clara.

Phillip makes no bones about his displeasure at Shackleford's presence, admitting that he "hated the skinny old man walking there beside father" (192). Any measure of acceptance and self-understanding Phillip might seem to have achieved is certainly compromised by this admission of blind and essentially self-deceptive hatred. To lay the blame for his balked emotional capacity on Shackleford is self-delusion of the most egregious sort; it illustrates his failure to accept responsibility for his own shortcomings and to deal directly with his father about their past conflicts.

But it also suggests an element of jealousy still present, a resentment of his father's capacity to forgive and receive forgiveness from his old friend, and perhaps a deeper desire to deny his father the satisfaction of that reconciliation. The motive of revenge, we realize at this point, may not yet have been entirely extinguished in Phillip. That is made clear when he receives still another summons from Betsy and Josephine some six weeks after this encounter. The crisis as they perceive it is a growing reconciliation between George Carver and Lewis Shackleford,which is so successful that Carver is planning an extended visit at Shackleford's home near Nashville. Betsy and Josephine justify their opposition to the visit on the basis of their father's precarious health, but it is clear that they resent the reconciliation and want to scuttle it.

Phillip returns, as always, with ambiguous motives. His charge from Holly is to go back and "assist in his [father's] escape," a sign of her own sense that one must accept the past as represented by one's parents and not prolong an essentially fruitless struggle against them. In wrestling through her own problems with a similarly domineering father, Holly has argued that "our old people must be not merely forgiven all their injustices and unconscious cruelties in their roles as parents but that any selfishness on their parts had actually been required of them if they were to remain whole human beings and not become merely guardian robots of the young." George Carver, as we have seen, had his measure of "injustices and unconscious cruelties," and although Phillip claims now to have "accepted Holly's doctrine" (194), the reconciliation with Shackleford puts his acceptance to a severe test.

It is by a characteristic act of indecision that Phillip presents us with the evidence that he has not accepted Holly's doctrine emotionally, whatever his rational assent. He arrives in Memphis just as his father is making preparations to leave for his visit with Shackleford—much against the wishes of Betsy and Josephine—and he has asked his chauffeur, Horace, to bring the car around from the garage. When Phillip and his friend Alex drive up from the airport, Alex parks his car, inadvertently, in a place that blocks George Carver's car from leaving the premises—under the porte cochere.[5]

Phillip tells Alex to take the keys out of the car (195), thus making it impossible for Horace to move it and begin the trip. He describes his command as an instinctive reaction, claiming to have become consciously aware of his intention to prevent his father's escape only after giving Alex the order.[16] When his father pointedly says, "I am afraid your car is in my car's way," Phillip looks out the window and "after a moment I said: 'Yes, I'm afraid it is.' . . . . I said: 'We'll be moving it shortly,' not knowing, myself, whether I meant it or not." On such small decisions entire personalities are judged in Taylor's fiction. Phillip's decision to move the car becomes, therefore, a measure of his achievement of a mature acceptance of his father, a victory over his desire for revenge. But he is left, as we are, unsure of his achievement by a turn of fate that punctuates this crisis. "For a moment I debated saying that I would take the keys out to Horace so that he could move the car if he wished. I don't know whether I meant it or not. But I hadn't yet decided about this when we heard the telephone ringing in the back part of the house" (197-98). The call brings the news that Lewis Shackleford has died during the night, thus leaving Phillip suspended in his indecision, unable to complete an act of revenge *or* of forgiveness.

The aborted test of wills between Phillip and his father, read its probable outcome how you will, has one ironic result. He and his father have one brief exchange about his motives for the return to Memphis which Phillip calls "the nearest we had ever come to communication directly on any serious matter" (201). This small breakthrough is followed by a new phase in their relationship, marked by periodic long-distance telephone calls in which the events and people of the past, even Lewis Shackleford, are discussed freely and at length.[17] Perhaps Phillip feels secure enough to make these calls because of his safe distance from Memphis and his knowledge that with Shackleford's death his father has no emotional alternative but to depend on his children. This breakthrough, however slight, sheds some light on the Phillip's earlier moment of indecision by making us see that his father regarded it as an act of defiance and an expression of independent will which at some level he admires, even though he is the victim of it. Phillip's motives were unworthy, signaling his own entrapment in a fruitless struggle against the past, yet the attempt to block his father's visit to Shackleford represented his first direct resistance, something that George Carver had never before seen in his son.

After the news of Shackleford's death canceled his father's planned visit, Phillip observed the seemingly small impact on his family's emotions. At breakfast the next day Betsy and Josephine "seemed to me as fit as a fiddle," and "even Father seemed to have recovered his good spirits and was not dwelling at all on Mr. Shackleford's death." It dawns on him that for his sisters "this was just another inning" in their continuing contest with their father (199-200). Through this direct contest of wills they have achieved a relationship with their father that Phillip never has. His half-intended delay of his father's departure and the belated reconciliation that this seems ironically to have produced indicates the much greater opportunity that escaped Phillip earlier in his life, when defiance might have meant more than petty revenge. Thus we have to take skeptically Phillip's closing assertion that he and Holly, now pursuing their orderly Manhattan lives as before, are "serenely free spirits" (209). The compulsion with which he tells the story is alone enough to belie that self-characterization. *A Summons to Memphis* is if nothing else testimony to Phillip's inability to forget; far from being serenely free, he is condemned to remember.

Mothers and Sons

Although Taylor made the bond and conflict between father and son a pivotal concern of his fiction, he also centered two of his most compelling narratives on the relationship of mother and son. Both his first novel, *A Woman of Means* (1950), and the late novel *In the Tennessee Country* (1994) focus on the motherhood of a strong woman, weakened by the psychological consequences of her own upbringing. In each case, this flawed strength has a profound impact on a son who is deeply dependent emotionally on her but must struggle against her to effect his own transition into maturity. These novels also present problematic father-son relationships, but here the figure of the mother—often in the background of such narratives as *A Summons to Memphis*—is central; these flawed fathers seem of secondary concern. Taylor instead describes a son struggling to form a sustaining relationship with his mother only to lose it (*A Woman of Means*), or battling against the smothering imprisonment of his mother, and eventually crippling himself emotionally (*In the Tennessee Country*).

What these narratives share with Taylor's depictions of conflict between fathers and sons is an understanding of the fragile process of personality development, in which a child is both dependent upon parental nurture and vulnerable to its abuse or excess. Such representations of failed or conflicted parental relationships connect emotional and psychological development directly to the familial context and provide an important setting for Taylor's portrayals of the treacherous process of striving for maturity, the subject of chapter 3.

Although *A Woman of Means* has been comparatively little remarked by Taylor's readers, it is one of his most astute character studies and most emotionally moving narratives, advancing in important ways his earlier depictions of the social and relational basis of individual identity.[1] Quint Dudley, whose mother dies at his birth, is left to be raised by his concerned but self-absorbed father, Gerald Dudley, a man struggling to forge his own identity as strenuously as is his son. Quint recounts the events that immediately precede his father's courtship of and marriage to Anna Lauterbach, the formation of his own deep bond with his stepmother, and the tragic unraveling of the marriage in her nervous collapse. Central to the narrative is Quint's recognition and acceptance of the new identity that his stepmother confers upon him, and his growing sense of the need to maintain it in independence.

Quint begins by describing his complex relations with his new step sisters, Laura and Bess, who would sometimes "let me stay in the room while they wrote in Diary, and ask me for a man's opinion on something" (*WM*, 2). Quint tells us of the diaries partly to indicate his initial progress in becoming a part of this new family. The diaries contain unknowable secrets, but Laura and Bess's teasing openness about the existence of such secrets provides the occasion for a friendly rapport with their new step-brother, rapport of the kind that he has never had with his father. The beginnings of family feeling that the discussion of the diaries represents extends also to the girls' relationship with their stepfather. Coming downstairs to leave on a date, Bess and Laura would "kiss their stepfather good night," hug him and whisper in his ear, "You're a sweet thing," or "I love you." Embarrassed at first by this attention, he gradually grows "accustomed to their familiarities and confident of their affection for him" (5). A family has begun to take shape, and Quint, though never entirely secure about its stability, begins to feel a part of it.

Quint's sense that there is the possibility of a familial trust and intimacy is particularly important because of one complication in his father's marriage: Anna is a divorcee of extreme wealth. Because of her wealth and social position, Quint and his father carry the nagging fear that they may be regarded by Anna's family as interlopers; indeed, Quint's father is never entirely able to overcome Anna's fear that he married her because of her money.

One measure of Quint's growing sense of belonging is his fear of loss, a sign that he feels he has gained something of profound value in his new family. "It was because I felt we were so very well off and so happy that I would worry sometimes about accidents," he remembers. At other times, dismissing the thoughts of accidents from his mind, he would wander through the house, contemplating his sense of happiness and well-being. "I would hunt up my father in the library or in the upstairs sitting room in order to put my arms around his neck in a silent expression of gratitude.

'You like it here, son?' Father would say then, and I could not make an answer" (10).

His father's query indicates one of the factors that have conditioned the marriage, his sense of responsibility to Quint, which he defines in much more specific terms than remarriage alone. His father had shared his son's upbringing with Quint's maternal grandmother, Mrs. Lovell, leaving him with her for summers on her Tennessee farm. The boy was inclined to turn to his grandmother for maternal affection and guidance, but his father consistently intervened. He feared that Quint might become the farm boy that he had been, an identity that he has struggled to escape in his pursuit of a business career. He surrendered Quint to Mrs. Lovell during the summers with reluctance: "I prefer that Quint play close about the premises of the house, Mother Lovell. . . . He's mostly a city boy, not on to country things like the others" (28). But his attitude was less motivated by caution than by his desire to form Quint, even as he was reforming himself, as modern and urban. "If I ever get to be anybody," he tells Quint after one of his business trips, "we'll live in St. Louis all the time" (11).

Gerald Dudley's prescription for his son's upbringing arises from his lingering sense of inadequacy about his own background, which fuels his professional ambition and accounts for his remarkable rise from salesman to company executive. The intensity of his ambition, which is also focused on Quint, is suggested in a pointed exchange with Mrs. Lovell, who frustrates him with her general tendency to ignore his specifications about Quint's behavior. She pleads with him to leave Quint with her so she can raise him in the country: "It's what people need." "Not any more, it isn't," Gerald returns, "and hasn't been for a long time. Quint needs other things." When Mrs. Lovell offers the reply that we might expect—"He needs a mother!"—Gerald's frank response has a particular resonance when we hear it from the perspective of his eventual remarriage: "He needs a mother who has never seen a farm. He needs to go to city schools where they teach you something, and he needs money" (29-30).

But despite his obvious self-absorption and misguided view of Quint's needs, it would be a mistake to think too negatively of Gerald. Quint loves him passionately, as he does Quint, and his ambition for himself and for his son seems intense but never overweening or unscrupulous. Noting one evening his father's handsome elegance in the billiard room of his new wife's opulent house, Quint is moved to an extraordinary declaration: "He inspired me not with filial respect but with the sort of fleeting admiration I sometimes felt for movie stars. My own father was a picture of youthful virtue justly rewarded" (7). But his father's complex blend of vulnerability and force, of self-absorption and profound parental concern, complicate Quint's own process of character formation. His love for his complex and driven father augments his already profound desire for a mother.

In interceding so determinedly to limit Quint's relationship with his grandmother, Gerald effectively cut his son off from a potential mother figure; in marrying Anna, who eagerly wants a son, he provides him another. Yet the pleasure that Quint takes in his new mother and his new family is clouded by the enormous gap between his old life and his new one and his felt necessity to abandon the old in order to accommodate the new. This pull of conflicting loves and loyalties is dramatized in Quint's account of a crisis occasioned by his twelfth birthday party. He receives from his grandmother the unexpected gift of his maternal grandfather's engraved watch, a gift that he understands as both a tribute to his maturity and a reminder of his continuing bond with his mother's family. Initially, he takes pride in the watch, showing it to his stepmother and stepsisters and carrying it with him all day.

But his attitude changes when schoolmates from his new and exclusive preparatory school come to his birthday party and see the watch displayed among the other birthday gifts. One boy remarks, "That's the niftiest alarm clock I've ever seen. You could almost carry it in your pocket" (24). This comment is regarded as uproariously funny by the group, and Quint himself joins in fun, but the humor strikes at his most vulnerable point, his guilty inner conflict about abandoning his grandmother and the farm, and his general feeling of social inadequacy at the new school. "I could still hear their laughter after I got in bed that night, and though I kept telling myself that I had got off some of the very best cracks about the watch myself, I said, 'Why am I so dumb, God? Why didn't I see it was only an old piece of junk from the start?'" (24).

As Quint wrestles with his humiliation that night, he drifts back into the memory of his grandmother and his life on her farm, remembering his guilty acquiescence in his father's intercessions to prevent him from being a real part of his mother's family. He first views his father's marriage with deep apprehension, realizing that it will mean the end of any real connection with his grandmother and may even alter his relationship with his father. He is at the farm the night his father informs him of the marriage, and his reaction upon hearing the news is to hide. "I felt that I was nobody and nothing and that I did not exist," he says, "and that all the decisions that the rich widow and her daughters and my father might make could not affect me" (54).

Quint gradually comes to see his father's remarriage as his own salvation, but not without guilty remorse for the loss of connection with his grandmother. Taylor is careful to demonstrate that Quint's acceptance of his new mother involves the formation of a bond of both trust and intimacy between them, through which he can construct a new social identity as Anna's son. He is pushed toward this by a revealing slip of the tongue: his headmaster refers to him one day as "Anna Lauterbach's boy" (55). Although he quickly corrects himself, the error elates Quint: "This was the moment at which I had come into practical possession of a mother. I thought of the peculiar happiness of loving her as I did, and I thought of the firmness with which I was established in her heart" (56). Having been deprived of the experience of maternal love, Quint now embraces it ardently. The social sanction of that relationship suggested by the headmaster's identification is vital to him because it represents the assent of the world from which his stepmother comes, a world with which he still feels only tentatively connected.

Quint's attainment of the "practical possession of a mother" occurs, however, just when tensions in her marriage with his father begin to surface. Like Quint, Anna has staked her identity on her newly created family but has also been haunted by a fear that Gerald may have married her for her money. Her security and sense of self-worth have always been undermined by her wealth; while she attended school in Switzerland, she confesses to Quint, "I soon found out that even those I was most friendly with always spoke of me as 'the millionairess' behind my back" (39). The failure of her first marriage and her lack of authority over her daughters after the divorce have augmented the fundamental insecurity she brings to her marriage with Gerald Dudley. Although Quint is in some measure the beneficiary of Anna's insecurity in that he is showered with her devotion, he comes to recognize his own vulnerability, even as he ardently accepts his stepmother's affection and the new identity she confers upon him. He becomes her son but recognizes intuitively that he must also begin the process of formulating his own independence.

The first step toward such an identity originates in Quint's "pose as The Southerner" (82) at school, an adaptation to being teased about his accent. "I began to see that [the teasing] gave me a unique personality, made me a *character*" (80), he explains. But the source of that identity is his experience at the farm, where he had been teased by the other children for his city-boy awkwardness. Quint believes that he "allowed that shame to turn me against my grandmother and to make me submit to being taken away from her forever" (81). His pose as "the Southerner" thus intensifies his inner conflict, a conflict so deep that it makes even his growing affection for Anna a source of guilt: "I should have loved my grandmother as I actually loved my stepmother" (82).

Thus Quint feels that he must abandon his artificial identity as "the Southerner," replacing it with a drive to excel that is in may ways similar to his father's and born of the same sense of insecurity. "It was as though a great store of energy had suddenly been released from within me, and I never knew, myself, what undertaking it would prompt me to next" (82). Quint's new energy and ambition eventually result in his being awarded the school's "Dartmouth Cup" for "best-all-round-boy in the Middle School" (83), a measure of his success both academically and socially.

This signal honor, an indisputable recognition that he is no longer an outsider but the school's central personality, seems to be the answer to Quint's doubts about belonging. Yet it too is a source of discord, bringing to the surface his conflicting feelings about his emotional dependence on his stepmother.[2] When he is presented the award at the school's assembly, he admits to "a feeling of annoyance and even of resentment" against the presence of his stepmother, a sense that "she was an intruder." He checks his initial impulse to present her with the cup as a gesture of love and gratitude and instead returns to his own place, avoiding her at the close of the ceremony and trying afterward to "forget" himself in his schoolwork (83–84).

Quint's conflicting impulses of gratitude and resentment, and his attempt to repress them, repeat in his relationship with his stepmother the same dynamic that marked his relationship with his grandmother, suggesting that his guilt over the failure of the earlier relationship has colored the later one. But his refusal to make a public display of his filial affection for his stepmother also signals something more positive, that the painful but important process of establishing his psychic and emotional independence has begun.[3] As he returns home the day of the award ceremony, exhausted by his inner conflict and his effort to repress it, he is overcome by an unexpected surge of joy, a feeling "that I had never been so happy, that my happiness belonged to me alone and was not connected with anything else that had ever happened to me" (84).

Quint's joy signals his momentary release from the psychological tension that his new life has generated, and it also suggests the beginning of a new stability for him through his capacity to find a "happiness that belonged to me alone." It is important to note that this capacity comes to Quint at the moment of his most complete integration into his new world. Yet his possession of new independence is shadowed by the inherent risk that it may eventuate in a self-absorbed and narcissistic isolation. The unsettled quality of Quint's early life with his father and the competing demands for affection that he has attempted to balance have given him something of the quality of a performer, a trait that has added to his success and popularity at school. By adopting the pose of a self-confident and slightly mischievous boy who takes his social place and its privileges for granted, Quint has attracted the acceptance and even the admiration of his schoolmates, thereby masking his own deep insecurities. He achieves through this manipulation of his personality at least some of the self-confidence that his pose assumed, but he also risks the isolation that derives from showing others only a mask. Therefore, when Quint says that "my happiness belonged to me alone," he is simultaneously asserting a necessary, healthy independence and suggesting his own capacity for a damaging self-absorption.

Quint's conflict about his assertion of independence and his fundamental confusion about the proper source of his happiness are very closely connected with his new identity as Anna's son. His search for himself is also fundamentally a search for a mother. That relationship has promised to confer a secure identity on him for the first time in his life, but it comes during his adolescence, when his assertion of an independent maturity entails a lessening of his dependence on all parental figures. The delicate balance that Quint must quickly achieve between love and self-reliance frames his perspective on the tragic end of the marriage between his father and stepmother and her eventual mental collapse.

The marriage is undermined by two key changes in external circumstances that increase the stress on the already flawed trust between Gerald and Anna. Laura and Bess begin to show an increasing disregard for Gerald's advice or affection, eroding his already fragile sense of paternal authority. And in a nearly simultaneous turn of events, Gerald loses his position as company executive and is forced to begin his career again as a salesman with another firm. With no authority as either parent or breadwinner, he begins to feel acutely vulnerable as his wife's dependent. His withdrawal from her exposes her fear of another failure and rejection and sets in motion a nervous breakdown that centers on her delusion of being pregnant.[4]

Quint is the terrified witness to this drift of events, his push for independence accelerated by the urgent necessity of shielding himself emotionally in the storm of the collapsing marriage. As Anna's mental demise accelerates, she becomes paranoid and delusional, lashing out at both Quint and his father while continuing to insist on the reality of her imagined pregnancy. She is permanently committed to a sanitarium, and at the eventual insistence of her daughters her house is sold, thus completing the absolute erasure of her marriage to Gerald and all traces of her connection with Quint. The new identity that she had conferred on him evaporates even more quickly than it had appeared.

Taylor depicts Anna's collapse as quite abrupt, thus unnecessarily truncating the conclusion of the novel. But he makes it clear that Quint has developed, in part through Anna's help, a measure of mature independence. In a final scene Quint reads of Lindbergh's solo flight across the Atlantic. "And when I read the headlines I was overcome with grief for my stepmother; standing in the center of the room, without even putting my hands to my face, I wept bitterly, aloud" (118). The headlines remind Quint of his own isolation, but his weeping is not entirely for himself; he is "overcome with grief for [his] stepmother," a reaction that confirms both his deep bond with her and his capacity to escape his own situation and feel the pain of another. Even in his grief, or perhaps especially in his grief, Quint demonstrates the achievement of a measure of maturity through tragic circumstances. "I had truly become, with the consent of all parties, my stepmother's son" (109), he has come to realize, even as he is losing his stepmother. But in becoming her son, he has also gained for himself an important independence from his father and a further capacity to exercise that independence, thus making possible more genuine and lasting relationships with others.

Taylor's decision to construct and then dismantle a family structure in order to write a coming-of-age novel is indicative of his own interest in the family's psychological dynamics, particularly its impact on the process of maturing. Clearly, he is compelled to return to the parental relationship with an assured sense of its potential for both nurture and destruction. In Quint and Anna's relationship, one of the few places in which he represents a positive bond of mutual nurture, he is also careful to suggest the vulnerabilities that drive each to depend on the other. Through Anna's collapse he reminds us that any seeming achievement of trust may at any moment vanish.

Taylor's *In the Tennessee Country,* published more than four decades after *A Woman of Means,* returns to the analysis of a mother-son relationship in its portrayal of Nathan Longfort, the story's troubled and troubling narrator. Nathan's suffocating bond with his mother is the book's crucial psychological subject, despite his professed obsession with his mysterious cousin, Aubrey Tucker Bradshaw.[5] Throughout a narrative that is superficially concerned with Nathan's pursuit of a male lineage that has failed him, his struggle with his mother for control of his life remains the central cause of his emotional turmoil. Dominated and eventually completely thwarted by her, rendered incapable of taking any pride in the course his life has taken, he fantasizes an alternative identity in his Cousin Aubrey. He finds eventually that his escapism is self-defeating.

Nathan begins his story by confessing his fascination with stories about men who, under "the urging of some inner compulsion" (*TC*, 3), walked away from their lives, homes, and families, never to return. A generally predictable man himself, he seems to lack that very urge, feeling his lack of desire itself as a defining problem. *In the Tennessee Country* is the story of his pursuit of and eventual encounter with one of these disappearing men and his increasing absorption in the myths of escape that such men represent. He admits that in middle age these stories "would keep returning to my inflamed and strangely excited mind" (30), as if the recognition of his own passionlessness has become his only passion.

Nathan's narrative of his obsession is thus an account of his inability to find self-acceptance, of a lifelong struggle against his own choice of vocation as a measure of identity and fulfillment. At his mother's insistent urging he starts out to be an artist but veers away from that path early in his life, deciding instead to become an art critic and professor of art history. Much of his sense of unfulfilled destiny seems tied up with that decision and his reasons for having made it—reasons that neither the reader nor Nathan himself fully comprehends.

Nathan's vocational decision also reflects important choices about marriage and family life, which in his case seem to have been conventional and, in many respects, happy choices resulting in a long and stable marriage to his first girlfriend, Melissa Wallace, and four children who seem to have matured into creative and independent adults and retain good relations with their parents. Nathan attributes much of his family's cohesion to his stable and successful academic career, which includes stints at Kenyon College and the University of Virginia (colleges where Taylor himself taught). Yet even as he makes himself adept at the process of thriving in the complex environment of the university, he longs for the life he feels he has missed—a life that through his imagination has come to be represented by his mysterious cousin Aubrey, who disappeared from any connection with the family during Nathan's boyhood. The mystery of Cousin Aubrey, the last of the disappearing Tennessee men, is also the mystery of Nathan's own lost identity.

Nathan's attempts at self-understanding and self-explanation inevitably return to his need to justify his life as a professor and his corresponding failure to become the painter or sculptor his mother had wanted him to be.[6] But his relationship with her, full of need and emotional dependence for both, is the determining factor in his development. Harboring her own thwarted artistic ambitions, she has tried to mold in him a deep sense of his destiny as a painter.

The intensity of Nathan's relationship with his mother is magnified by his lack of a strong bond with his father, or with any paternal figure. His most crucial early memory is of his journey on the funeral train of his grandfather Nathan Tucker from Washington, D.C., to his burial place in Tennessee. While young Nathan has little direct knowledge of his grandfather, remembering only the long train trip and the shock of the death to his family, he does know his grandfather through family lore, supplemented as he grows up by his own curious digging into the historical records of his life. Tucker was the last of a series of strong patriarchs, a powerful politician beloved by his Tennessee constituents and revered by his family. To Nathan he is a symbol of the complete public and private man, committed to both family and community but having lived a life of self-direction and complete self-expression, always open to experience.

Nathan's search for his grandfather is closely connected to his fascination with the disappearing men of Tennessee legend, including his Cousin Aubrey. His grandfather is prominent in his consciousness because his father and his two uncles by marriage, men who might have provided him with a sense of paternal continuity, are themselves pitiful shadows of the generation before them, deriving their identities vicariously from their own fathers' lives and feeling that deep experience has somehow passed them by.

All three are "like veterans of some war they never got to fight in" (73), intensely proud that their fathers had ridden in Bedford Forrest's cavalry or fought with Fitz Lee's army but unable to live fully themselves. The early death of Nathan's father, a man who never seemed to gain full independence from his own father, confirms the weakness of his physical constitution and suggests a corresponding weakness of will and character. Uncle Hobart, a fop whose marriage is marred by "his successive affairs with various low women" (75), commits suicide in his thirties. Uncle Lawrence is a physician whose practice is marred by his alcoholism and whose mental instability eventually leads to his being committed to an asylum.

Nathan is thus raised in a paternal vacuum, unlike most of Taylor's other male protagonists. He confesses that after his father's death his actual memory of him faded. "Sometimes I would go and stand before a large 'studio portrait' of him in Mother's bedroom, imagining that if I stared long enough and hard enough my memory of him would come back more clearly" (95). Yet if he cannot recall his father's image, he does remember his father's anxiety that his son might never achieve a real masculinity. "I am just afraid that you will make some kind of sissy of him after I am gone" (65), Nathan overhears his father tell his mother when he is six or seven years old. This may well be his father's personal insecurity transferred to his son, but the comment obviously makes an impression on Nathan.

Since we know that Nathan eventually rejects a career as an artist for one as an art historian, we might surmise that his sense of failure over this choice is related to his inability to overcome his father's early strictures. The pattern of crippling father-son relationships, as we have seen, is a fundamental concern of Taylor's, and his presentation of such conflict usually underlines its profound emotional cost. But Nathan's case is different because of his complicated dependency on his mother, a woman whose strong self-control holds in check a tendency toward passionate emotion. Nathan recalls from his childhood her extraordinary capacity to recite poetry and drama and her complete emotional absorption in such performances. "It made my flesh break out in goose bumps to hear the vigor of her voice" (90), he says about one of her recitations of "Lasca," a highly sentimental narrative poem centering on the death of a lover.[7] During another recitation of it, he says that "it was as if another spirit had entered into her body and taken possession" (78).

This transformation is extremely troubling to the boy, who feels dispossessed by the unfamiliar poetic spirit that overtakes his mother. He withdraws in extreme fear and disorientation, trying to distance himself from the unusual passion he senses in her performance: "I had the image of myself as an invisible being while still in the room with the visible others," (79)—a striking description of the depth of his alienation and of his tendency toward self-loathing. His equilibrium is restored only when he returns to "my mother's warm bosom" afterward. "And immediately," he remembers, "it seemed that my mother's real self had reentered her body" (80). His infantile clinging to her arises from his fear of the passionate and sexual persona she adopts in her recitations. He is secure only with "the placid sweet, comforting mother that I knew" (78).

Much later in his life Nathan discovers that his mother had almost eloped with Cousin Aubrey in her early adolescence, and her recitations recall the passion that was thwarted by his final reluctance to marry her. Even though Nathan could not have known these facts in his youth, his bond with his mother seems strong enough to allow him to sense intuitively the presence of this other life in her and to recognize it as a threat. The depth of his need for her and the corresponding insecurity that it engenders become significant factors in the formation of his personality. Seeing in him her missed opportunity for an artistic life, she raises him to be an artist, and his relationship with her is conditioned by that expectation. What might have been the path—a career as an artist—whereby Nathan could have established his own manhood through resisting the will of his father, is thus complicated by the opposing will of his mother. For in helping her to fulfill vicariously her artistic desires, he is responding to what is for him an alien and alienating side of her. His mother's artistic passion can only serve to remind him of that part of her life that did not, and could not, include him.

After his graduation from college at Sewanee, Nathan enrolls in the art school at Columbia, eagerly taking this opportunity to pursue his painting. He is "incredibly productive, and shipped two canvases out to Mother in Nashville." But this initial rush of enthusiasm does not last long. "I suppose my high spirits lasted until about Thanksgiving. I took a train down to see Mother at Thanksgiving and found her ecstatic about the turn my life seemed to have taken. I was doing what I was born to do." Then, after this visit, his enthusiasm for painting mysteriously evaporates. Despite having garnered his mother's unqualified approval for his artistic endeavors, he returns to Columbia with his mood "altogether changed" and finds himself suddenly "bored with the instructors and with my friends among other students as well as with my own efforts to paint" (129).

At this juncture Nathan falls into the activity that will permanently alter the course of his life: visiting New York museums and libraries to become an observer and judge of art rather than a producer of it. "Soon I had reams of notes, and before long I was writing articles which I submitted to the art magazines and the learned quarterlies. I did it almost without contemplating what I was doing. I told myself only that I was doing it out of boredom and I hardly knew what to make of it, when I began receiving letters of acceptance and even adulation" (130). We may doubt that the shift was as accidental as Nathan claims, noting that the abandonment of his painting follows very closely on his mother's expression of profound approval for it. His comment "I was doing what I was born to do" seems in its context as much his mother's description of his life as his own. In some measure, at least, Nathan's change represents his rebellion against his mother's will for his future.

By early manhood, Nathan's inner life has twisted itself into an inescapable paradox. He had intellectually equated art and freedom, staking his own sense of maturity and autonomy on the pursuit of this apparently expressive and unconventional way of life, but he had also come to see it as an act of conformity to his mother's will, an acceptance of the fate that she had declared for him. When he ceases to be a painter and starts to become a scholar of paintings, he breaks free from the expectation that has shaped his life, but at the cost of a sense of fulfillment, for he has internalized that expectation so deeply that it is inescapable. He remains haunted by the idea that painting represents real emotion, while scholarship is a pale, rational evasion of it.

Nathan's emotional entanglement with his mother also impinges on his courtship of Melissa Wallace, whom he eventually marries, and his brief affair with Linda Campbell, an actress whom he meets in New York. In both these relationships he shows himself to be naive, somewhat passive, and clearly emotionally vulnerable. He meets Melissa during his senior year at Sewanee and proposes to her three days later. Their relationship is marked by Melissa's firm refusal of his passive desire to turn over to her every important decision of his life, even his choice of vocation. He recognizes this important and defining difference in her: "The three of us— Mother, Melissa, and I—talked endlessly about nothing but plans for the future. Mother was ever insistent that I had to be a painter. In private Melissa continued to maintain that the decision was mine alone" (128). But although he admires Melissa's clear insistence that he think for himself, he also wishes that she would relieve him of this burden. The stronger and more decisive part of him finally wins out, as his eventual marriage to Melissa indicates, but only after his detour through an affair of sorts with Linda Campbell.

He meets Linda a few weeks after his arrival in New York, while he is still committed, though not officially engaged, to Melissa. He describes her as "beautiful," noting that she is a "rather famous Broadway actress" and "a woman much older than I" (131). But her appeal to him is intensified when, shortly after they meet, she begins to quote from "Lasca," the poem he identifies so strongly with his mother. Their relationship is "platonic" (135), with Linda taking a friendly, somewhat maternal interest in him but showing no physical attraction. Nathan is attracted to her precisely because she is so much like his mother, both in her deep aesthetic sensibility—"she had fallen in love with art at an early age" (136)—and in her self-assured independence. And, like his mother, she sees him only as the young artist: "She was only interested in whatever I might say about my painting and sculpture—however casual it might be" (136).

Nathan's fascination with Linda and dependence upon her grow during his first months in New York, but the relationship ends when she becomes involved with another actor. Their parting is a blow to Nathan, intensified by her somewhat condescending parting words. After advising him "in the very gentlest way" to marry Melissa, she adds a stinging analysis of his character. "Whatever I did with myself, she instructed me, it was my business to remain dependable"—advice that might not have offended Nathan had she not gone on to add a more personal comment: "'For you, my darling Nathan, you along with everyone else were born to be reliable, to be dependable.' I felt that she had censored her speech in midsentence and had come very close to saying 'if nothing else' instead of 'along with everyone else'" (139-40). Nathan's understandable resentment does not, however, prevent him from following her advice exactly. Once the affair is over, he marries Melissa and begins to alter his plan of life toward a "dependable" academic profession, the move that seems to be the source of so much of his unhappiness and self-doubt yet also his great source of pride.

It is important to recognize that the end of Nathan's relationship with Linda Campbell corresponds to his break with his mother over his career choice, a parallel that reinforces the already strong similarity between the two women. One other surprising turn of his narration also focuses attention on his relationship with Linda: her sudden, accidental death in a plane crash immediately after their breakup and her marriage, followed by his journey to Tennessee to identify her body. "The face of the actor-husband looked very familiar to me, but the face of the dead Linda Campbell seemed strangely unfamiliar. Like the face of someone I could not place in the receding past of my boyhood" (140).

The scene has close similarities one in "The Witch of Owl Mountain Springs" (see Chapter 4), whose narrator is called upon to identify the bodies of Sarah and Tim, the couple whose elopement and subsequent acting careers initiate the withdrawal from society of Lizzie Pettigru, the mysterious "witch" of the story. In both cases, the necessity of identifying the bodies entails an uncomfortable self-reflection, confronting each narrator with a past that continues to haunt him. Moreover, these scenes stretch the realistic contours of the narratives in which they appear, each having a certain element of vengeful wish fulfillment about it that makes us as readers pause to consider whether we have crossed some border from actual events into fantasy generated by the narrator's subconscious. Although we are in no position to say definitely that Linda was the product of Nathan's imagination, or that his affair with her did not happen as he described it, we can say that both her remarkable similarities to his mother and the terrible death that follows immediately on Linda's "betrayal" of him push the boundaries of coincidence. Through the character of Linda, Nathan reconfigures his mother as an object of romantic and sexual passion and exercises violent revenge on her by consigning her to a sudden death.[8] We are almost entirely dependent on Nathan's account of the events of his life, and as the story unfolds, we recognize him as at best an unstable source of truth.

Nathan's account of his development centers on these pivotal months in New York during which he becomes immersed in art and then abandons it in defiance of his mother, sees the beginning and end of his relationship with Linda Campbell, and, finally, marries Melissa Wallace and begins his academic career. But all these events, as he recalls them late in his life, are framed by his intense and growing fascination with his disappearing cousin Aubrey. When we come to consider Aubrey in the context of what we know of Nathan's emotionally complicated early life, it becomes clear that this fascination is in large measure a kind of escapist fantasy: Aubrey's ability to walk away from the life he had known haunts the narrator as a possibility that he himself has not been able to choose.

Fascination with escape thus accounts for the fact that Nathan's narrative of his past is woven around a series of encounters with Aubrey, most of them fleeting and mysterious, which augment the haunting quality of Aubrey's possession of his imagination. His first memory of his cousin is that during the long ride on his grandfather Senator Tucker's funeral train, he sensed Aubrey's deep resentment of Nathan's secure place in the family and assured future. As the illegitimate child of the senator's brother, Aubrey has been given a marginal place in the family, but he recognizes that with the senator's death even that place is no longer secure. Following the graveside ceremony Aubrey does not rejoin the funeral party for the return from the cemetery, and after a futile search "it was reported that he had altogether disappeared" (60).

Aubrey reappears over the years at family funerals, where Nathan sees him but his mother and aunts do not—or will not admit that they do. Much of the narrative is imbued with suspense in which we are unable to judge whether Nathan has actually seen his cousin, has had hallucinations, or has been visited by a specter visible only to him. Nathan does not explicitly know during these years of the failed early romance between Aubrey and his mother—she tells him of it much later—but he senses that these strange funeral reappearances are somehow connected with a fundamental emotional instability in his mother; they thus affect his own sense of security.[9] Her emotional vulnerability is suggested most strongly in the last of the funeral scenes, when his grandfather's body is moved from Knoxville and reburied at a cemetery elsewhere in East Tennessee. This is a distasteful event for his mother, one made more painful by her odd "fantasy-fear," developed at her father's original funeral, that "it was not Senator Nathan Tucker's body locked in the casket but that of someone known to her but whom she could not quite recognize, someone whose identity somehow eluded her or, rather, whose identity she could not quite bring herself to acknowledge." This fantasy is, Nathan tells us, shared by "other mourners besides herself" (21) and is again brought to the surface when a chain breaks during the removal of the body from its original burial place, dropping "one end of the coffin back into the slime of the grave" (142). Almost exactly at this moment Nathan sees Aubrey, who hurries away before Nathan can speak to him.

The scene clearly leaves the suggestion that the senator has been somehow reincarnated in the disappearing Aubrey. This ghoulish transfer helps to explain Nathan's irrationally deep fascination with Aubrey. Deprived of his grandfather and lacking any other satisfying paternal bond to help free him from his mother's emotional grip, Nathan directs his need into his compulsive search for Cousin Aubrey.[10]

The preoccupation with Aubrey that began in Nathan's childhood continues and intensifies through his adolescence and middle age, becoming an obsession in his later years. His pursuit of this lost father figure intensifies, that is, as he himself experiences fatherhood and develops an especially intense relationship with his youngest son, Braxton, who shows a decided bent for painting. In encountering his son's artistic ambitions and talents, Nathan is forced to relive his own struggles with his vocation and his sense of failure.

The last section of *In the Tennessee Country* recounts both the discovery of Aubrey and Brax's development to maturity, events that are closely intertwined in Nathan's psyche. As we might expect, Brax is the particular favorite of his grandmother, the boy who may fulfill her thwarted ambition for Nathan and for herself: "'It is because of Braxton's naiveté,' she would say to me more than once, 'that he will become an artist. It was apparent in him early'" (141). What she calls naiveté, Nathan labels a certain "narrowness" of vision which caused Brax "to embrace with a passionate intensity one view or another [to the exclusion of all others] on the successive steps of his program as an artist." As Nathan realizes, his own success as a critic has grown from the opposite capacity, "the enthusiasm I was quite capable of developing almost simultaneously about the various schools and modes of painting" (144-45).

Although his analysis of his son's artistic nature is in part an objective description of their differences, a measure of envy lurks beneath the surface. Nathan sees that his son has the passion and the talent that he himself lacked. It would be wrong to overemphasize the effect of Nathan's envy, since he keeps it for the most part well under control and seems to maintain a close and supportive relationship with Brax, yet it is an important reminder of his still-unresolved conflicts about his own choices in life.

Those conflicts are intensified by his mother's clear partiality for the boy. When she leaves all her money to her grandson, Nathan's inner conflict comes more clearly into focus. He realizes that although it is "a relatively modest sum," it "would support [Brax] as an artist for the foreseeable future!" The bequest has, therefore, freed Brax from any economic dependency on his father, thus undermining Nathan's stature and influence in their relationship. Further, he recognizes that the bequest "represented my mother's renewal of hope for the kind of artist I had never become. It meant that she had cherished that hope till the end" (183). His mother's "renewal of hope" for an artist in the family could also be described as her stubborn refusal to relent in the emotional pressure that she has placed on Nathan at least since his adolescence. It is her final rebuke to him for the exercise of his own will in choosing an academic career. Even though Nathan declares a sense of relief in the turn of events, "a wonderful feeling of being let off the hook once and for all" (183), this calm recounting of his disinheritance is perhaps most impressive for the force of will it suggests in his suppression of rage. The question remaining for him is how to prevent that rage from destroying his relationship with the son who has achieved what Nathan feels that he himself has failed to do.

Brax is the one member of the family who recognizes his father's concern with the fate of Cousin Aubrey as a serious and potentially harmful obsession. Nathan comments with some puzzlement on Brax's "persistent opposition to me in the matter of Cousin Aubrey" (171), one of the "many contests of will " (173) between them. Brax, looking at the story from the point of view of a young man, intuitively identifies with Aubrey. A strong-willed "child of the sixties," as his father notes, who "*must* be allowed to do his own thing in his *own* way" (171), he views his father's curiosity about Aubrey as a form of prying, a possibly unwelcome attempt to intrude upon the life of another: "It seemed to him that the case of a missing person, whether down in Tennessee or elsewhere, was a private matter not to be looked into. It was a man's own affair if he wished to disappear!" (177).

It is Brax who finally discovers Aubrey after noticing the old gentleman several times near his Washington apartment. Although he does not at first know who he is, he is drawn by Aubrey's eccentric charm. So even in this odd and intensely personal quest for his past, Nathan is bested by his son, who seems to have not only the artistic talent but the artistic sensibility that Nathan berates himself for lacking. Discovering later that Aubrey has become dangerously ill, Brax notifies his father and arranges for his long-desired meeting with his mysterious cousin. But the meeting turns out to be somewhat anticlimactic in one very important sense: whereas Nathan has hoped to recover something of a father in Aubrey and perhaps establish a bond with him, he finds that Aubrey is cool toward him. He offers to take Aubrey in, even to pay his hospital bills, but Aubrey rejects the gesture. "I do not wish to be drawn into such family ties," he explains (216). Besides, he tells Nathan, he will soon marry a woman who can take care of all his needs.

There is no great revelation to be had at their reunion; no crucial bond is formed, and the novel ends with a gently ironic deflation of Nathan's expectations and those of the reader, who has been subtly pulled into Nathan's misguided quest. Taylor paints the scene with a restrained humor, contrasting Nathan's earnestness with Aubrey's aloofness and letting us see enough of Aubrey to realize that he has been something of a flamboyant bon vivant and ladies' man, living largely on his charm and cultivated sophistication. After Senator Tucker's death, Aubrey claims he set out to become "the very opposite number" (208) from what he had been before. He made himself "as sophisticated a human being as I could imagine" and learned "to appeal to women especially in a way I had never before done" (208). And Aubrey notes, appraising Nathan after his long separation from the family, "You have so exactly turned out as I had thought you would do" (206)—a comment that surely carries an edge of contempt. Nathan has found nothing in their meeting except perhaps the end of his illusions. Insofar as Aubrey served him imaginatively as a kind of alternative identity, the failure of his attempt to forge a bond with his cousin when he finally finds him only emphasizes to the reader, if not to Nathan himself, the extent to which Aubrey was a means of evasion for Nathan's unresolved inner problems.

Taylor structures the end of the novel to emphasize both Brax's similarities to Aubrey and Nathan's dissimilarities to both of them, but such correlations do not necessarily imply judgments of value. Nathan's deepest problem is not that he has failed to be, like Aubrey, a disappearing man who has dramatically remakes his identity, or that he has failed to have his son's intensity of focus and singleness of purpose in pursuing art. His problem is, rather, that he has not allowed himself to accept the life that he has chosen and pursued. Tortured by a relentlessly romantic inner demon, he is condemned to regard his one act of identity-creating rebellion, his rejection of painting for an academic career, as a cowardly failure. The result has been a self-admitted feeling of "haunting emptiness just outside the satisfaction I took at having *done* my career so satisfactorily," a lack of fulfillment conditioned by his ever present awareness of "the particular painter or sculptor I had set out to be and that my doting mother never forgave me for not being" (187-88). And yet, assessing his life in the terms in which he presents it, can we doubt that his pursuit of painting would have been one long exercise in self-loathing?

The meeting with Aubrey, perhaps because it is a mildly humorous anticlimax, does nudge Nathan somewhat closer to self-comprehension. A few days after the meeting Melissa asks him if he has "solved any problems" and whether he wants to bring Aubrey home for a while. Her questions, approaching as they do the edge of his obsession with Aubrey, prompt him to meditate briefly on his inner life. He says that he has shared every experience with her except one: a recurring dream in which he sees an "ever-vanishing figure" whom he has never quite been able to identify. He has kept this to himself out of a dread that this "fearful, faceless figure" would upset "the surface of our rational life," and that its significance was too large for him to face the task of explaining it. But he understands in part its source, even though he lacks the courage to confront it completely: "The possibility that that faceless figure was somehow my own self only made it the more unthinkable and unmentionable a matter for me" (212-13).

Although Nathan is able to connect this haunting figure with his own struggle for identity, his articulation of the insight reveals his still unresolved inner conflict. By terming the figure "my own self," he suggests that it is the "self" he should have been, the artist that his mother had wanted and that he had set out to become. To state the problem this way is to reconfirm his troubled sense that there was only one "self" that he legitimately could have become, and it invalidates everything that has constituted his adult life, the "self" that he in fact did become. It undercuts his career, his marriage, and his role as a father, things that we know he has valued deeply, however problematic they have been.

The fading figure of his dreams is fused not only with his abortive artistic career but with Aubrey and the other disappearing Tennessee men of local and family legend. The pursuit of Aubrey has thus been a pursuit not only of a lost father but of what he has come to regard subconsciously as a lost self. That lost self is both the *sign* of his discontent and the *cause* of it. Nathan's tendency to take a romantic view of what his life might have been, or a morally self-indicting view of what it should have been, is similar to that of Nat Ramsey in "The Old Forest," who seems to regret his failure to try to reestablish a connection with Lee Ann Deehart after she is finally located. In both cases the regretfully lost option in life, the road not taken, does not seem to have been a viable one. Both Nathan and Nat torture themselves not for what might have been but for what most probably never could have been.

In his old age Nathan's inner conflict becomes focused on Brax, who increasingly reminds him of the "self" that he believes he should have been. This helps to explain the tension in their relationship. Although the bond between the two remains very close, and they share both a fascination with painting and an interest in the family past, Brax chafes at his father's desire for control over him, while Nathan recognizes in Brax qualities to which he somewhat resentfully aspires. This tension comes to a point of crisis late in the novel when Nathan discovers, to his surprise and vexation, that Brax has had paintings accepted for exhibit in major museums and that with his accelerating recognition as an artist he is planning to move to New York, out of his father's sphere of influence. But Brax does not tell him any of this directly; Nathan finds Brax's belongings packed for a move, and many of his canvases crated for shipment to the museums where they will be exhibited.

Stunned by this discovery, recognizing it as both evidence of Brax's surpassing him professionally and a signal of Brax's abandonment of him personally, he reacts with a blend of intense curiosity, exultation, and rage. Tearing the wrappings off several canvases and feverishly inspecting Brax's work, he finds an artistic development "almost beyond belief to my very practiced and critical eye" (219). He regains his composure enough to repackage the canvases and, after the initial burst of emotion, remarks that the work is "beyond anything I had ever attempted" and "would forever set us apart" (220).

But why would Brax's artistic accomplishment stand as a barrier between them? The ambiguities of Nathan's comment resonate at the end of the novel. It is the sad admission of a parent who recognizes that the maturity and independence of his child will forever replace the closeness and mutual dependence they once shared. But it is also the embittered remark of a man who holds himself a failure and has made himself the resentful rival even of his own son. Nathan's loss of Brax coincides with his loss of Aubrey and leaves him to face himself without the crutch of evasion or illusion. It is as if the spirit of Senator Tucker had somehow passed on to Aubrey as the true heir and has now passed on to Brax, leaving Nathan out. Nathan had lived his early life without a father; now he will, in a sense, die without his son.

Nathan tells us, as the novel closes, "I think I have come to terms with the way my life has gone" (226), and though we hope this is the case, the confession sounds more like a statement of defeated resignation than one of acceptance. Perhaps the act of the narrative itself, with its hints of frankness and self-comprehension, offers hope that he has forged some deeper acceptance—though the passion with which he recounts the past weighs against that possibility. The difficulty of judging Nathan's progress toward self-understanding through the process of narrative self-disclosure typifies a key interpretive question in Taylor's later fiction. Nathan's case is, in this sense, quite similar to that of Nat Ramsey in "The Old Forest," Phillip Carver in *A Summons to Memphis*, and the narrator of "The Oracle at Stoneleigh Court." Nathan remains, at the end, one of Taylor's subtlest demonstrations of the difficulties of self-understanding and self-acceptance, a man whose intense pursuit of identity becomes the means through which identity eludes him.

❖ 3 ❖
Fables of Maturity

In centering his analysis of family on the parent-child relationship, Taylor brought the process of developing identity and maturity into focus, as well. The stories and novels that we have examined as father-son or mother-son narratives can also be regarded as accounts of the struggle for maturity. Taylor took a particular interest in the problematics of the process of maturing, understanding that his characters, often beset by parental conflict, carry significant emotional burdens into the families they form as adults. Some of his most powerful stories therefore represent failed or balked personalities such as Phillip Carver and Nathan Longfort, whose emotional lives have been frozen in an imprisoning past. In two of his most accomplished and widely known stories, "Venus, Cupid, Folly and Time" and "The Old Forest," Taylor emphasizes the interplay of the psychological and social roots of the failure to mature. These are chronicles of growth that has been thwarted, condemning a character to replay an unsuccessful struggle against parental authority and thus poisoning his (they are almost always male) adult relationships. Taylor's work demonstrates repeatedly how an incomplete or thwarted maturing process results in a seriously damaged capacity for constructive relationships, and these stories often represent marriage as the arena in which such conflicts are played out.

Tolliver Campbell, the central figure of Taylor's 1976 story "The Captain's Son," exemplifies this recurrent pattern. The son of prominent and well-to-do Memphis parents, Tolliver migrates to Nashville in a pattern that the narrator labels typical for the region: "A young man of good family out of Memphis, for whom something has gone wrong, will often take up residence in Nashville" (*MD*, 5). Yet in Tolliver's case the term "good family" must be taken in the narrow sense of social prominence and wealth, for it becomes clear as the story progresses that Tolliver's parents' alcoholism has wounded him quite profoundly.

The initial manifestation of this wound is his oddly boyish behavior after he marries the narrator's older sister Lila. Rather surprisingly, the newly-weds decide to take up residence with Lila's parents rather than establish their own home, and the narrator describes the family's growing uneasiness with Tolliver's disinclination to pursue any work or profession, preferring instead to spend his time lolling around Lila's family's large house, seeking out and enjoying its most comfortable spots. "I had never really realized what great opportunities for comfort our house afforded or how many cozy corners we had," the narrator comments dryly. "It was as if Tolliver Campbell had become more at home in our house than we were ourselves" (13).

But the initial comic tone that Tolliver's avoidance of purpose gives to the story is gradually supplanted as we discover the depth of his inability to engage the world in any effective way. That failure is revealed most dramatically in Lila's shocking confession that after more than two years she and Tolliver have not consummated their marriage. "He's only a little boy," Lila explains to her mother. "What he wanted of us here was a mama and a papa and a little sister and maybe a little brother" (25). Tolliver's sense of having been deprivated of a stable family life has made him seek one out through his marriage into Lila's family, where he has tried to reconstitute himself not in the role of a father but as a child.

Tolliver's aborted progression to maturity has even deeper consequences when he begins to drink and pulls Lila into a deepening alcoholism with him. Her appalled parents, seemingly as concerned with the appearance of their daughter and son-in-law in Nashville society as with their well-being, try to keep them hidden away as much as possible and eventually nudge them to move back to Memphis, where their problem will at least be out of sight. "Sometimes Lila would come home for a one-night stay," the narrator remembers. "No more than that though. From then on, Lila and Tolliver lived always in Memphis" (35). Lila's bond with her family is permanently damaged by her degeneration into alcoholism, a social embarrassment that her parents apparently cannot bear. Thus, although the story centers on Tolliver's troubled family situation and its obvious manifestation in his failure to mature, it subtly illuminates a less obvious but nevertheless severe shortcoming in Lila's family, and her own resulting inability to assume an independent maturity. Tied helplessly to Tolliver through the prolonged boyhood of the early phase of their marriage, she also follows him without resistance as he lurches from boyhood to failed adulthood.

Taylor's most vivid portrait of the obstructed progress toward maturity is "Venus, Cupid, Folly and Time," a story that also stands as one of his most precise social dissections. By showing how a personal crisis and a crisis of the social order coalesce in Louisa and Alfred Dorset's last party, Taylor weaves psychological portraiture and social critique into a narrative of submerged tension and building suspense. Both in the Dorsets, the elderly brother and sister who host the party, and in Ned and Emily Meriwether, the adolescent brother and sister who attend it—seemingly quite different pairs—Taylor represents parallel cases of trouble or failure in the process of maturing.

In Chatham, Tennessee, the social hierarchy has evolved a curious means of self-perpetuation in the parties that the Dorsets give annually for the select youth of the town. While they are the most unlikely of "social arbiters" (*CS*, 295), the Dorsets are nevertheless accorded the role as electors of the town's "best" youth. Their personal oddities are striking to their conservative neighbors. They dress oddly in public, "the cuff of a pajama top or the hem of a hitched-up nightgown showing from underneath their ordinary daytime clothes." That Alfred Dorset washes his car in "a pair of skin-tight coveralls . . . faded almost to flesh color" and that his sister comes outside "clad in a faded flannel bathrobe" generate a certain revulsion in their neighbors (291-93). Tom Bascomb, who later plays a central role in the Dorsets' social downfall, tells of having seen Miss Louisa "pushing a carpet sweeper about one of the downstairs rooms without a stitch of clothes on." Tom's description of how she "dropped down in an easy chair and crossed her spindly, blue-veined, old legs and sat there completely naked" (293) epitomizes the fascinated disgust with which Chatham observes the Dorsets, who serve as a convenient objectification of the sexuality that the people of Chatham cannot entirely suppress within themselves.[1]

The Dorsets are, as they see themselves, sexually innocent. As bachelor and spinster they "have given up everything for each other" (295). But are they sexless? Although the story offers no confirmation of it, the suspicion of incest hovers over them, emphasizing the discomfort their neighbors feel. Even so, their annual party for the town's affluent adolescents functions as an imprimatur of caste, an initiation into society roughly similar to the coming-out of a debutante. Through these parties the Dorsets have been able to overcome their social ostracism and become social dictators.

The Dorsets have achieved this position largely through the conviction that they have an innate capacity to recognize and receive initiates into their class. "Why, *we* know nice children when we see them" (319), Miss Louisa protests as her final party is broken up, attempting to preserve the illusion under which she and her brother have lived. Despite their severe economic decline they have not surrendered their sense of belonging to a natural social elite, which they affirm through their parties.

Superficially they are asexual, having renounced both world and flesh to preserve the purity of their devotion to an ideal of innocence. Yet behind the Dorsets' superficial innocence lurks an obsession with sexuality (the extent of conscious subterfuge on their part remaining debatable) which manifests itself unmistakably at their annual parties. "Before our turn to go ever came round," the narrator recalls, "we had for years been hearing what it was like from older boys and girls. Afterward, we continued to hear about it from those who followed us" (297). Whatever their parents' motives in sending their children to the parties, it is the fascinating hint of sexual decadence that accounts for the Dorsets' hold over their young guests.

On these occasions the hosts cast their dowdiness dramatically aside. "The most violent shock of the whole evening" is Miss Louisa's astonishing attire: a gown, new every year, "perfectly fitted to her spare and scrawny figure," long, newly dyed hair, dark rouge, suntan powder. She has become a threateningly sexual figure. Mr. Alfred almost matches his sister's transformation "in a nattily tailored tuxedo" (297-98). The parents who send their children, and "never pretend[ing] to understand what went on at the Dorsets' house" (297), can of course sense the air of the sexually forbidden which imbues the festivities. They "are not very nice affairs to be sending your children to," says Ned and Emily's father as his children prepare to leave. His objection is met by their mother's "but we *can't* keep them away." Tacitly conceding his wife's sense of the social necessities, he replies, "It's just that they are growing up faster than we realize" (302).

There is nothing overtly wrong with the parties, which combine "light refreshments (fruit Jello, English tea biscuits, lime punch)" (304) and a tour of the house. The guests listen to a version of the Dorsets' life story and see a series of curious decorations arranged to accentuate certain works of art that have erotic themes. Although the parties are laden with sexual symbolism, they are also arranged so that the Dorsets can display before this captive audience their own version of their innocence and their sacrifice. This enactment of self-justification is of primary importance to them.

The ritual enactment of their innocence takes the form of "an almost continuous dialogue" between the two of them, "all about how much the

Dorsets have given up for each other's sake and about how much higher the tone of Chatham society used to be than it [is] nowadays" (305). The dialogue centers on their reaction in their teens to the death of their parents, an event that clearly traumatized them and resulted in their lifelong refusal to accept adulthood. Forced to struggle against "wicked in-laws" who wanted to sell their house and "marry them off to 'just anyone,'" they were eventually disinherited by their grandparents and further threatened by "a procession of 'young nobodies'" (305) hoping to steal one of the two in marriage. The Dorsets dealt with their loss by retreating into mutual self-possession, finding in their sibling relationship and their family home a haven from threatening change. They have attempted to freeze their emotions at preadolescence, and the parties bring before them fresh images of the innocent youths they have tried to remain. "Ah, the happy time," they say to the young guests, "was when we were *your* age!" (308). For them, each party is a pantomime of return, a vicarious recovery of both their youth and their social place.

But the Dorsets also create an environment in which sexuality looms as a beckoning, threatening force. "A strange perfume pervad[ing] the atmosphere of the house" (298) contributes to the impact of a series of visual displays involving masses of paper flowers and replicas of works of art. Three are mentioned in the story—Rodin's "The Kiss," "an antique plaque of Leda and the Swan," and "a tiny color print of Bronzino's 'Venus, Cupid, Folly and Time.'" Each has sexual subject matter, and the way they are displayed—partially concealed by the flowers, yet illuminated with odd and compelling shafts of light—seems consonant with the Dorsets' sexual confusion. The displays function as traps set to capture the maturing sexual curiosity of the young guests. The children, warned beforehand by previous guests, stand "in painful dread of that moment when Miss Dorset or her brother might catch us staring at any one of their pictures or sculptures." (299). The children are at least mature enough to understand that they should attempt to maintain a facade of innocence: "We had been warned, time and again, that during the course of the evening moments would come when she or he would reach out and touch the other's elbow and indicate, with a nod or just the trace of a smile, some guest whose glance had strayed among the flowers" (299). The children wander through this maze of sexual signals, compelled on the one hand by their fascination with the displays, but equally repelled by apparent attempts to implicate them in a suspected corruption.

The central symbol of the party ritual, and the evening's high point, is the dance Alfred and Louisa perform in a dimly lit room, with "grace" and "perfect harmony in all their movements." After the dance we see Mr. Dorset "with his bow tie hanging limply on his damp shirtfront," hair askew, and "streaked with perspiration" (307). This pantomimed sexual intercourse, the most direct suggestion of incest, is followed by the most desperate plea of innocence. It is then that the Dorsets call the age of their guests "the happy time" and urge them to enjoy their freedom. "With many a wink and blush and giggle and shake of the forefinger—and of course standing before the whole party—they each would remind the other of his or her naughty behavior in some old-fashioned parlor game or of certain silly flirtations which they had long ago caught each other in" (308). The Dorsets believe they have conquered the "naughtiness" that sexual maturity represents by insulating themselves from the adult world through their sibling relationship. They repress their sexual identities only partially, however, and their attempt to freeze themselves at preadolescence causes the lingering suspicion of incest even as they parade their innocence.

Despite this ironic result, it seems reasonable to conclude that the Dorsets, however emotionally crippled, are not incestuous. Although the effect is the reverse of what they intend, the whole point of their parties seems to be to provide a forum for protesting their innocence, which they equate with presexuality. Even the suggestive pictures, which appear to be means whereby the corrupt try to entrap the innocent, are better understood as the Dorsets' attempt to assure themselves of their own purity. If they can prove to themselves that even these young people have a sexual consciousness and curiosity, then their own incompletely repressed sexual natures seem somehow validated. The pictures and the children's reaction to them are the assurance the Dorsets need of the legitimacy of their own condition as creatures with sexual desires.[2]

As a portrait of the workings of social pressure and social selection in a Tennessee city, and of the psychology underpinning them, "Venus, Cupid, Folly and Time" firmly achieves the regionalist's objective. The Dorsets' odd parties have an unusually strong pull on the people of the town because being invited is a way of measuring one's status and of proving that one belongs among the elite. Throughout the story there is the implied satire of the Southern debutante party (one of Taylor's targets elsewhere), a custom that infuses the basic human activity of selecting a mate with questions of societal competition and exclusivity. Brilliant as it is in its social commentary and satire, the story is given added force and subtlety through Taylor's parallel focus on the adolescents who finally disturb the Dorsets' drama. The story's narrator, drawn from the same class and sharing much the same experience as the Meriwethers themselves, cannot treat them with the same interested but distanced objectivity with which he handles the Dorsets. As a result, the reader is drawn into their situation with an engagement surpassing the curiosity that the Dorsets generate.

The children plan a prank through which the Dorsets' social pretensions will be mocked. They bring Tom Bascomb to the party posing as Ned, Ned himself later joining the group without the Dorsets' knowledge. The harmlessness of the jest is belied by the fact that the Dorsets take pride in inviting only the "best" children to their party, fortifying their sense of self-worth by an imagined capacity to know such superior individuals intuitively—and by common assent, Tom Bascomb is not such an individual. It is here that the socioeconomic basis for the Dorsets' social arbitration becomes clearest. Tom has the paper route for their prestigious West Vesey Place neighborhood, and his family lives "in an apartment house on a wide thoroughfare known as Division Boulevard." As the narrator explains, "all of us in West Vesey had had our Tom Bascombs" (304). Each of the privileged children, that is, maintained some contact with an outsider, some friend from a lower economic class; with these friends they could both measure their own elevation and simultaneously feel a sense of connection to the larger world beyond their neighborhood. Tom's anointing as one of the chosen would forever put the lie to the Dorsets' claims to be natural social arbiters.

The difficulty with the Meriwether children's plan is that Tom plays his assigned role too well. He pushes the plan into forbidden ground, shaking the delicate psychological balance of the Dorsets—and of Ned and Emily. If his job is to shatter illusions, he does it with a relish, and though his work of destruction centers on the Dorsets, it pulls the Meriwethers in as well. Their own innocence is the unintended victim of the trick they have conceived.

Whereas the prank is an important gesture of freedom for Ned and Emily, for Tom it is an opportunity to mock a group from which he has been excluded. But the compensation for his exclusion has been a freedom that Ned and Emily covet. The question as Taylor presents it here is not only who belongs and who does not but the psychological cost of belonging—or of breaking free. When Mr. Dorset comes to drive Ned and Emily to the party and Tom looks at "Emily's flushed face" and sees her "batting her eyes like a nervous monkey," a "crooked smile play[s] upon his lips" (301). Tom's Hawthornian smile signals his capacity to be a predator on innocence—both the false or unnatural innocence of the Dorsets and the real innocence of Ned and Emily.

Taylor thus interweaves a narrative of initiation and maturation into his analysis of the social structure of Chatham. We first glimpse this in Emily's reaction as she is walking with Tom to Mr. Dorset's car. "And with her every step toward the car the skirt of her long taffeta gown whispered her own name to her: *Emily . . . Emily*. She heard it distinctly, and yet the name sounded unfamiliar. Once during this unreal walk from house to car she glanced at the mysterious boy, Tom Bascomb, longing to ask him—if only with her eyes—for some reassurance that she was really she" (303). The causes of Emily's crisis of identity and the motivation for Tom's crooked smile are related, as the reader fully understands later when the children's plan is enacted. "The moment Miss Louisa Dorset's back was turned Tom Bascomb [in the role of Ned] slipped his arm gently about Emily's little waist and began kissing her all over her pretty face" (310). Tom's kisses, intended to mock the Dorsets' suspected incest, also free Emily—frighteningly—from the innocent self of her youth.

In the odd triangle that emerges at the party, Ned is also deeply affected. Although he has helped to plan the trick, even Tom's kissing Emily, he finds himself "not quite able to join in the fun"; he stands "a little apart . . . baffled by his own feelings" (311). Each time "an explosion of giggles filled the room," we are told, Ned "would look up just in time to see Tom Bascomb's cheek against Emily's or his arm about her waist" (312). The suggestion of incest which was meant to shock the Dorsets backfires, reminding Ned of his own subconscious sexual drives and producing a symbolic exchange of identities: when he sees Tom, posing as himself, kiss Emily, he sees an enactment of his own unacknowledged desire, a recognition that is acutely painful to him. This sexual awareness will inevitably cast a shadow over his relationship with Emily.

Although the destruction of Ned and Emily's innocence is the chief tragedy of the story, its prelude is the tragedy of the Dorsets, forced by Ned to confront their own sexual identities, which they have tried to suppres. After each burst of laughter they exchange "half suppressed smiles," which last "precisely as long as the giggling continue[s]." Then Tom and Emily mock the Dorsets by squeezing themselves "into a little niche . . . in front of the Rodin statuary," where Tom kisses her "lightly first on the lobe of one ear and then on the tip of her nose." Emily remains "rigid and pale as the plaster sculpture behind her and with just the faintest smile on her lips" (313). Ned observes this, and also the Dorsets "gazing quite openly at Tom and Emily and frankly grinning at the spectacle" (313-14). What we may at first take as their knowing acknowledgment of the kisses' suggestion of incest is more probably their attempt to affirm their youth by joining in the children's laughter. Because the Dorsets have maintained their self-conception as children, they can look at this mirrorlike reflection of themselves without conscious recognition of its implications for them.

But for Ned, whose sexual awareness has been made acute by Tom and Emily's kissing, the Dorsets are a dark self-image that he must reject for his own psychic survival, and he rejects what he sees by naming it to the Dorsets: "'Don't you *know?*' he wail[s], as if in great physical pain. 'Can't you *tell?* Can't you see who they *are?* They're *brother* and *sister!*'" (314). Ned's outburst is of course not a part of the original plan, and it turns mockery and subtle satire into open confrontation. He is met first with stunned silence, while the Dorsets continue "to wear their grins like masks" (314). But the masks fall, and we realize that Ned's outbreak, whatever its cost to him, is also searing for them. "Miss Louisa's face, still wearing the grin, began turning all the queer colors of her paper flowers. Then the grin vanished from her lips and her mouth fell open and every bit of color went out of her face" (314-15). This shock becomes rage as the Dorsets turn on Ned: "What we know is that you are not one of us. . . . What are you doing here among these nice children?" (315).

The phrase "nice children" punctuates this moment of emotional crisis with ironic humor, but in the terms of the symbolic identities that have developed during the evening, the question is pertinent. When the Dorsets ask, "Who is he, children?" Ned confirms their sense that he is an "intruder." "Who *am* I? Why, I am Tom Bascomb! . . . I am Tom Bascomb, your paper boy!" (315). This is, of course, in line with the plan, but it has a deeper importance for Ned because it signifies the turn in his relationship with Emily. He has seen a dim reflection of himself in watching Tom kiss Emily during the party. In proclaiming his identity as "Tom" he both accepts the sexual desire that Tom has enacted and rejects his identity as Emily's brother, a complex negotiation with the forbidden that constitutes part of the difficult self-construction of his maturity.

Ned flees from the party, but in an interesting twist to the story's action he flees *up* the stairs into the second story of the Dorsets' house. The entire house is densely symbolic territory, and to penetrate the second story is to enter further than anyone ever has into the Dorsets' psychological secrets. Mr. Dorset pursues Ned up the stairs and finally corners him and locks him in a room. The scene is chaotic, though not without a comic aspect—Miss Dorset continues to serve lime punch while she waits for a policeman to come drag away her presumed paperboy. But through it all, Emily remains mysteriously passive, standing "oblivious to all that [is] going on." Tom's report that "her mind didn't seem to be on any of the present excitement" (316) does not trivialize those events but rather underlines the profound impact of the entire encounter. Emily, like Ned, has been rushed into a confrontation with sexual desire for which she is not prepared. Ned's reaction is the more dramatic, but Emily's abstracted withdrawal bespeaks as profound a change.

"Venus, Cupid, Folly and Time" is a story of lost illusions, and the Dorsets are the first victims. They are dealt a blow not only by the suggestion of incest in Ned's outburst but by the exposure of a weakness in their capability of social discrimination. They have taken Tom to be the "nice" boy and Ned the intruder, and not until Ned's parents arrive are they forced to recognize their mistake. Emily tells her father that Ned is locked upstairs, but Miss Louisa insists that the boy upstairs is an intruder: "Why, *we* know nice children when we see them." Her insistence becomes a plea as she begins to realize the implications of her mistake. "We knew from the beginning that that boy upstairs didn't belong amongst us. . . . Dear neighbors, it isn't just the money, you know, that makes the difference." This article of faith is echoed by her brother: "People *are* different. It isn't something you can put your finger on, but it isn't the money" (319). But as they find, it *is* the money, or the presumption of money, that has always guided their choice of "nice" children, and that false belief in their ability to make social discriminations on some vague basis of personal superiority is exposed in their mistaking Tom for Ned. When Mr. Meriwether finally finds Ned upstairs and confirms the Dorsets' mistake, the party ends, and with it the Dorsets' position as social arbiters. They are broken, retreating afterward into an almost complete isolation from their neighbors.

The narrator devotes greater attention, however, to Ned and Emily, the real protagonists; their tragedy, not that of the Dorsets, is the burden of the story. The narrator reports that "nowadays" (well over two decades since the events of the party) "Emily and Ned are pretty indifferent to each other's existence." That indifference apparently arose the night of the party, at least according to Ned's wife, who has heard the story repeatedly. The party "marked the end of their childhood intimacy and the beginning of a shyness, a reserve, even an animosity between them" (322). If freed from the social structure represented and enforced by the Dorsets' parties, Ned and Emily have paid a price for that freedom. The shattering of the Dorsets' self-conception of innocence and superiority paralleled their own sudden confrontation with sexual maturity. By feigning to be the Dorsets' secret selves, Ned and Emily unnaturally forced their own unacknowledged desire into momentary consciousness, and that consciousness cost them their sibling relationship.

As we listen to the narrator's final ruminations, however, one other loss impresses us. In the final pages of the story he ceases to be a quasi-objective voice and emerges as a character from whom the readers must establish some distance. The status of these parties as part of the communal consciousness of Chatham has allowed the narrator to assume a near-omniscient point of view, relying on the texture of legend, tradition, and gossip that make up the town's shared knowledge. But as he recounts the history of the Dorset family and their rise to prominence in the social structure of Chatham, his personal stake in the tragedies becomes apparent. The Dorsets "were an obscure mercantile family [from the English midlands] who came to invest in a new Western city" (324). Wholly mercenary and wholly rootless, they left Chatham as soon as they had made their fortune there. But their financial success created their social prominence: "For half a century they were looked upon, if any family ever was, as our first family" (324). These facts amplify the significance of Louisa Dorset's last plea: "Dear neighbors, it isn't just the money, you know, that makes the difference" (319). Alfred and Louisa Dorset, abandoned when the rest of their family forsook Chatham, were left with the social distinctions that money had made but without the money itself.

This historical background demonstrates the fundamental emptiness of the superficially dense social world of Chatham. The narrator knows the emptiness of its social discriminations: "If the distinction was false, it mattered all the more and it was all the more necessary to make it" (323). And he knows even more deeply that this emptiness has cast a shadow over his own life. For when the other Dorsets left, everyone in Chatham with any pretensions to social prominence had to pretend, with Alfred and

Louisa, that "it isn't just the money." Unable or unwilling to leave, "we had to stay on here and pretend that our life had a meaning which it did not" (324).

In their extraordinary strangeness, Alfred and Louisa Dorset mirrored not only Ned and Emily but all their neighbors in West Vesey Place. Even as we can surmise that Ned and Emily recognized something of themselves in the Dorsets, so we can understand that the whole social group of which they were a part also dimly saw themselves in the Dorsets. They paid them homage and made them social arbiters because in so doing they tacitly honored themselves. It took only one outsider, Tom Bascomb, to bring down this house of cards. The narrator is presumably one of many who still feel the aftershocks of the collapse. Alfred and Louisa Dorset, abandoned souls whose tragedy is their inability to face in adulthood a world very different from the one they knew as children, are ultimately complex analogues of the narrator, whose inability to mature is less dramatic but finally no less painful than that of the Dorsets.

In the Dorsets, Taylor represents an extreme case of the failure of the maturing process—characters who have never accepted the necessary transition into new stages of life and have therefore denied crucial aspects of their own personalities. But Taylor rarely offers such extreme cases, focusing more typically on characters who *have* made the transition to adulthood but have done so at some painful cost. Indeed, maturity and pain are almost synonymous in Taylor's work. To grow up is to choose repeatedly, but to make choices is also to abandon other possibilities, which leave their imprint on the memory.

In "The Old Forest" Nat Ramsey begins the description of his struggle for maturity with an explanation of why, when he "was already formally engaged," he "sometimes went out on the town with girls of a different sort." Nat has much to say about that "sort" of girl in the course of the story, remembering that these women were "facetiously and somewhat arrogantly referred to as the Memphis demimonde." The casual social brutality of the phrase designated "a girl who was not in the Memphis debutante set" (*OF*, 31). Such labeling marked out those women's lack of the right social status for marriage but also gave them an air of the exotic in the eyes of Nat and his friends, whose lives were otherwise absolutely predictable.

The women of the "demimonde" represent important challenges to the assumptions by which Nat and his friends have led their lives. He remembers them as interesting and stimulating companions, "bright girls certainly and some of them even highly intelligent," who "read books, . . . looked at pictures, and . . . were apt to attend any concert or play that came to Memphis"—not "the innocent, untutored types that we generally took to dances at the Memphis Country Club and whom we eventually looked forward to marrying" (31-32). As Nat comes into closer contact with these women, his sense of their strength and complexity grows. He discovers that in addition to a "physical beauty and a bookishness," qualities that we might associate with the traditionally feminine, they also have "a certain toughness of mind and a boldness of spirit" (59). They are modern women who, though still restricted by the persisting division of sexual roles, are in the process of transforming those roles.

Nat's struggle for maturity is in part a struggle against the patterned life laid out for him by his family and social class, although he is by no means in open rebellion against his privileged life. In fact, "The Old Forest" describes his desperate attempt to preserve this life when its survival is threatened, an attempt in which he is, in important respects, fighting against himself. Nat comes to identify as a symbol of this conflict the Old Forest, "a densely wooded area which is actually the last surviving bit of primeval forest that once grew right up to the bluffs above the Mississippi River" (38). A week before his marriage to Caroline Braxley, a Memphis society girl, Nat is driving near the forest with Lee Ann Deehart, one of the "demimondaines," when his car collides with a skidding truck on a frozen road. Nat is mildly injured in the accident, but before anyone can arrive to give assistance, Lee Ann walks away from the car and into the Old Forest. Her four-day disappearance raises the threat of scandal and endangers Nat's engagement to Caroline. In his attempt to find Lee Ann, he confronts her world and begins to learn the limitations of his own.

Nat's relation with Lee Ann and her friends, whatever its overtones of sexuality or class difference, is a crucial part of his ability to see beyond the world of his comfortably situated parents and their friends. He associates Lee Ann with the Old Forest because he dimly recognizes that it represents what is beyond the control of his ordered life. "Here are giant oak and yellow poplar trees older than the memory of the earliest white settler" (38). Surrounded by the manmade city, the forest has not submitted to that power. In escaping into the forest, Lee Ann unwittingly proves how tenuous Nat's control of his life is.

The recognition of his powerlessness is a lesson that experience contin-ues to repeat for Nat. Almost casually dropped in the middle of his reminis-cence is a stunning list of personal tragedies: the loss of two brothers in the Korean War, the death of his parents in a fire at his home, and the acciden-tal deaths of two of his teenage children (42). One might suppose that the incident with Lee Ann would pale to insignificance when weighed against those pains, but in fact, these instances of loss and grief have augmented its importance: in the Old Forest, Nat began to learn his mortal limitations. As he remembers it, "life *was* different" (42) in the Memphis of 1937. It is not life that has changed, of course, but his perception of the boundary of the possible. "Our tranquil, upper-middle-class world of 1937 did not have the rest of the world crowding in on it so much" (43). But the remark tells us more about Nat's maturing consciousness of tragedy than about the degree to which persons of his class were insulated from experience. Lee Ann's walk into the forest proved how fragile Nat's world really was.

Immediately after the accident, Nat's sense of vulnerability begins to grow as he realizes the gravity of his situation. The forest looms in his mind, embodying the threatening forces that delimit his social world. "More than the density of the underbrush, more than its proximity to the Zoo, where certain unsavory characters often hung out, it was the great size and antiquity of the forest trees somehow and the old rumors that white settlers had once been ambushed there by Chickasaw Indians that made me feel that if anything had happened to the girl, it had happened there" (44).

Nat is ironically right that "something" has happened to Lee Ann, though not the violence that he feared. Walking into the forest is an asser-tion of independence from the grips of Nat's world, which will attempt to exert a benevolent but nonetheless firm claim on her in the aftermath of the wreck. Her disappearance, though we eventually find it to be considerably more complex, carries the resonance of women's resistance to paternalistic authority of which Nat finds himself a rather reluctant emissary. He recog-nizes the symbolic threat of the forest to the world made by his male ances-tors and realizes with some discomfort that his own fear is similar to that of generations of men in Memphis, who "have feared and wanted to destroy [the forest] for a long time and whose destruction they are still working at even in this latter day." That destructive impulse is the push to moderniza-tion, the drive behind the steady development and conquest of the land. "It has only recently been saved by a very narrow margin from a great highway

that men wished to put through there—saved by groups of women determined to save this last bit of the old forest from the axes of modern men"
(53).

As a persisting wilderness, the forest thus represents a counterforce to
masculine control and, in a larger sense, to all forms of social control. Nat's
meditation on the symbolic connotations of the forest is punctuated by stories of "mad pioneer women, driven mad by their loneliness and isolation,
who ran off into the forest" to be later "captured by Indians" (53). The Old
Forest reminds Nat that "civilization" is male civilization, and he begins to
discover how deeply implicated in that civilization he is.[3] As the Memphis
city fathers reach out in a show of concern for Lee Ann's welfare, they also
enact their own insecurity about the viability of their social structure and
their guilt over its basis in oppression.

Nat is worried about more than Lee Ann's fate. He wonders "if all this
might actually lead to my beautiful, willowy Caroline Braxley's breaking off
our engagement" (45). But the story's heightened tension on this point is at
least superficially without basis. Nat describes Caroline early in the story as
his wife of many years. Our knowledge that the incident did not end his engagement emphasizes the particular burden of Taylor's retrospective narration. By minimizing the tension over the consequences of the accident, he
has focused it instead on Nat's tone as he recalls those events. The question
is not whether he *will* marry, but what the marriage will mean to him.[4]

As Nat flounders in the exigencies of Lee Ann's disappearance,
Caroline demonstrates a capacity to meet the gravity of the situation. Her
stature grows as the story progresses. When she eventually takes over the
search, Nat docilely cooperates with her. So, it seems, his life continues for
most of the next forty years: Caroline's "good judgment in all matters
relating to our marriage has never failed her—or us" (36). But despite Nat's
persuasive depiction of his concern that his engagement might be ruined,
he undermines our faith in his absolute contentment in his relation with
Caroline when he describes the courtship customs of upper-class Memphis.
Engagement "was in no sense so unalterably binding as it had been in our
parents' day," he explains, adding that "it was not considered absolutely dis-
honorable for either party to break off the plans merely because he or she
had had a change of heart" (45). Even more ominously, Nat admits that
"the thought pleased me—that is, the ease with which an engagement
might be ended" (46).

Afraid that he will not be able to marry Caroline, he is also afraid that he will marry her. Even while visiting with Caroline and her parents, he is privately "indulging in a perverse fantasy, a fantasy in which Caroline had broken off our engagement and I was standing up pretty well, was even seeking consolation in the arms, so to speak, of a safely returned Lee Ann Deehart" (46). This suggests Nat's attraction to Lee Ann, but it tells us more about his vague sense of confinement in the world that he inhabits. If Caroline represents a secure place in that world, Lee Ann represents escape. During his crisis Nat is caught between the two worlds. His dreams of Lee Ann are indeed fantasy (she has earlier treated the possibility of their marriage with humorous contempt), but like all fantasies they are revealing. They suggest the stirring of Nat's resistance to the predictable course of his life. He never directs that resentment toward Caroline, for whom he has profound respect. He resists instead the sure movement of the machinery that will take him through a "good" marriage and into a settled life in his father's business. One of the story's ironies is that the crisis transforms what might have seemed a marriage of convenience into a meaningful and durable relationship.

The accident and Nat's reaction to it accelerates a process of maturing that had been already signaled in a very small way by his persistent study of Latin, an activity valuable to him precisely because it is neither useful nor expected of him. The accident and its consequences force him into a much franker relation with Caroline than he seems to have had before, impressing upon him her strength of character and resolve. When he finally tells her that Lee Ann was in the car with him, he is surprised to find that she already knows this. Her reaction convinces him to go ahead and tell an "uncensored version of the accident" (47). Caroline's capacity to take command of the situation impresses Nat, who is characteristically in a state of indecisiveness. "'You do know, don't you,' she went on after a moment, 'that you are going to have to *find* Lee Ann? And you probably are going to need help'" (48). Caroline understands that Lee Ann's disappearance may force an end to her engagement. In recognizing her relative powerlessness in the situation, a fact that is only beginning to dawn on Nat, Caroline finds the source of a surprising strength. Nat's eventual comprehension of her complex and courageous reaction to the events is an essential aspect of the maturity that he achieves.

Caroline might have been expected to play an unsavory part in the story as a spoiled and manipulative rich girl, attempting to assert the requisites of privilege. But Taylor's deft touch allows her to capture our sympathy and seize the moral momentum of the story, supplying the drifting Nat with both a will and a purpose in finding Lee Ann. Her motives are not disinterested, but her courage in the face of possible disaster contrasts favorably with Nat's fantasy-punctuated passivity. Nat has just begun to awaken to the ways that Memphis Country Club life insulates him from experience; Caroline seems more keenly aware of those limits and of their concomitant restrictions on her capacity for choice. As Nat eventually comes to understand, Caroline's social position carries a burden with it, a knowledge of "what was going to be expected of [her] in making a marriage and bringing up a family there in Memphis" (48). Lee Ann represents a threat to those expectations, a threat of competition for the husbands that are required for the survival, as it has been defined to Caroline, of women in her position. Although it is the narrowness of this definition of success, rather than girls of a lower social standing, that is the real threat to Caroline and her peers, Taylor builds a measure of sympathy for her. He depicts her as a woman trapped in a value system as it crumbles. Her quest may seem superficially an attempt to protect her privilege, but it is much closer to an effort to overcome the vulnerability that Nat's accident has revealed to her—the restricted scope of her possibilities for self-definition. The story thus develops around the hunt for Lee Ann, but its actual fuel is this struggle for self-definition that the hunt initiates, not only in Nat but also in Caroline.

Having been insulated from experience by their social class, Nat and Caroline experience their search for self-definition in versions of humiliation, as the perspectives and protections of their upbringing are stripped away in their dealings with Lee Ann's circle. Her friends have a good-natured scorn for Nat and his friends, and in order to communicate with them at all, Nat and Caroline must repeatedly meet that scorn. It leaves their inherited view of the world, already shaky, impossible to sustain. As they surrender that view, their move toward self-understanding advances. Nat first searches for Lee Ann in the company of Memphis police, making the rounds of her friends and inquiring of her whereabouts, and is thus immersed in the world of these women. He finds himself fascinated by their freedom "from old restraints put on them by family and community." He recognizes them as "liberated" women who have both a "strength of character" (63) and a freedom of sexual expression that signals an important shift in the nature of the social world.

The question of Nat's possible sexual involvement with Lee Ann is always present to the police, who ask him at one point if she is pregnant. Even after he has told them she is not, he finds himself later asking one of her friends, Nancy Minnifee, the same question, thereby opening himself to the deepest humiliation of the search. "Nancy's mouth dropped open. Then she laughed aloud. Presently she said, 'Well, one thing's certain, Nat. It wouldn't be any concern of yours if she were'" (62). Nat's blunder reveals the kind of overbearing attitude that provides Lee Ann and her friends with fuel for their resentment, and at least a part of the motive for Lee Ann's defiant flight.

Nat's second day of searching is in the company of his father, the mayor, and the newspaper editor, representatives of the Memphis establishment and members of the last generation "to grow up in a world where women were absolutely subjected and under the absolute protection of men" (67). Nat sees in retrospect—and perhaps began to see at the time—that they were protecting a patriarchy which they sensed was being threatened from within. "They thought of these girls as the daughters of men who had abdicated their authority and responsibility as fathers" and saw themselves as "surrogate fathers," acting to hold together the fabric of the society they knew. "It was a sort of communal fatherhood they were acting out" (67). Although Nat has been formed by his father's world and clings to it with part of himself, he is also stifled and finds in himself some resistance to it. But the very structure of authority that has molded him is beginning to change, making his ambivalence even more complex. As Nat recalls, "I actually heard my father saying, 'That's what the whole world is going to be like someday.' He meant like the life such girls as Lee Ann were making for themselves" (67-68). Lee Ann represents, to Nat, a future both attractive and frightening.

Nat's relations with Lee Ann and her friends have been one expression of his tentative reluctance to follow the expected course of his life. Another small mode of resistance has been his persistence in studying Latin poetry, a subject in which his interest is less than passionate and his skill minimal. That persistence baffles his family, and he himself professes not to understand his motivations fully. But it is precisely because the study is extraneous, even an encumbrance, that he persists in it. When Caroline finds him at home after the accident, a copy of his Latin text nearby, her greeting is revealing: "I hope you see now what folly your pursuit of Latin poetry is" (41). This petty defiance of the expected has been an attempt at self-possession, and although he drops it, his initially mild nonconformity grows in more meaningful ways during the crisis.

Nat's fascination with Lee Ann grows in proportion to her defiance of the Memphis order. Dating the "demimondaines" has been a flirtation with the forbidden, a safe way to test the limits of the social restrictions. But as Nat begins to search for Lee Ann, the gravity of conflict in those relations becomes clear. Lee Ann's friends telephone to warn him to leave her alone, but their calls only add to his determination to find her. Yet he is simultaneously pushed toward a closer intimacy with Caroline. After the day of searching with his father, Nat and Caroline tell "each other how much we loved each other and how we would let nothing on earth interfere with our getting married" (70). The pledge reassures Nat somewhat, but he is still plagued by the phone calls that he has kept secret, and eventually he tells Caroline of them and "all [he] knew about 'that whole tribe of city girls.'" That Nat trusts Caroline deeply enough to be frank, and that she accepts his "confessions" with a nonjudgmental resolve to make good use of them, is an indication of the growing strength of their relationship. For Nat gives her not only "an account of my innocent friendship with Lee Ann Deehart" but also "an account of my earlier relations, which were not innocent, with a girl named Fern Morris" (72).

As Nat's relationship with Caroline grows deeper, so does his confusion about his feelings for Lee Ann. In their frank discussion he held one thing back from Caroline, a growing sense that in his search he was "discovering what my true feelings toward Lee Ann had been during the past two years." He had begun to feel, he admits, "that she was the girl I ought and wanted to be marrying" (72). The story's central question is whether this feeling is merely an example of Nat's tendency toward escapist wish-projection. Is he attracted to Lee Ann because she is what he cannot have, or is he belatedly learning the truth of his own feelings? Even as he entertains them, he realizes "the absolute folly of such thoughts and the utter impossibility of any such conclusion to present events" (72). While this at first seems like a confession of Nat's weak inability to resist the pressure of conformity, other evidence suggests that the impossibility of the fantasy, and thus its essential safety, is part of its appeal.

One remark about his relationship with Lee Ann is particularly significant. He notes that he "had never dared insist upon the occasional advances I had naturally made to her," feeling a kind of protective sensitivity toward her because of her "delicate" and "vulnerable" nature. Moreover, he had sensed that she was "too intelligent for me to deceive her about my intentions or my worth as a person." Yet he was not frustrated or disappointed with the chaste nature of the relationship but rather "relished the kind of restraint there was between us because it was so altogether personal and not one placed upon us by any element or segment of society, or by any outside circumstances whatever" (72). But of course the contours of their entire relationship had been determined by the class barriers between them. Nat was destined to marry a woman from his social set, and he and Lee Ann understood this from the outset of their friendship. There would never have been such a friendship except for the distance that social structures had decreed between them. The impossibility of marriage had the effect of freeing them from some aspects of sexual tension. But to recall that freedom as an indication that no "element or segment of society" had placed restraints on them is the kind of obtuseness that marks Nat as still seriously immature. Caroline's emergence as a central figure in the story is the result of her capacity to replace Lee Ann as an embodiment of reality for Nat. In her presence "my thoughts and fantasies of the day before seemed literally like something out of a dream that I might have had" (73). Nat grows toward a more mature self-knowledge through his rejection of immature fantasy.

Nat's explanation of his relations with the "city girls" and his sexual affair with Fern Morris provides Caroline with the information she needs to negotiate successfully the hostile territory of Lee Ann's network of friends. To act on the information, Caroline must again go through a certain humiliation, parading her vulnerability before these hostile women and openly struggling to regain what she once might have regarded as hers by right—her coming marriage. Caroline's humiliation undermines the perspective from which she has hitherto seen the world, and thus makes a fuller self-development possible.

She must finally appeal to Nat's former lover, Fern Morris, who offers her a clue to Lee Ann's location. That clue is Lee Ann's possession of a snapshot of a woman whom Nat has known as the proprietor of a nightclub: Mrs. Power, a woman with "a huge goiter on her neck" who "was never known to smile" (66). This sinister figure is Lee Ann's grandmother, to whom she returned a few days after the accident. But Lee Ann had tried to keep her connection with Mrs. Power a secret because of the social embarrassment that it might cause her, and her motive for hiding now is not to avoid the scandal of having been caught with Nat, or to make herself an obstacle to Nat's marriage. Caroline deduces the complex motivations behind her disappearance when Nat tells what he knows of Lee Ann's past at a number of boarding schools away from Memphis. " 'They kept her away from home,' Caroline speculated. 'And so when she had finished school she wasn't prepared for the kind of "family" she had. That's why she moved out on them and lived in a rooming house'" (79). Lee Ann's reasons for disappearing thus turn out to be very different from those that Nat first surmised. Her flight is less a defiance of the social order than an indication of her fear to be exposed to it. It is primarily to avoid social embarrassment that she has tried to protect her past from discovery and publication.

Caroline's discovery of Lee Ann's whereabouts initiates a process of self-confrontation in Nat that forms the climax of the story. When she and Nat finally locate Lee Ann at the apartment above her grandmother's nightclub, Caroline tells Nat to stay in the car while she goes up to talk to Lee Ann. Although we may suspect that her gesture is in part motivated by a jealous insecurity, its operative motive is Caroline's recognition that Nat may inhibit her communication with Lee Ann. But Lee Ann's near presence prompts Nat to a painful moment of self-analysis. As he waits in the car, he imagines his separation from her as a sign of his closure to experience. Should he accept that closure? To leave the car and enter the apartment, against Caroline's instructions, would be the culminating act in Nat's growing defiance of the expected course of his life. "I suddenly realized—at that early age—that there was experience to be had in life that I might never know anything about except through hearsay and through books. I felt that this was my last moment to reach out and understand something of the world that was other than my own narrow circumstances and my own narrow nature" (79-80).

This interpretation of his complex emotional tie to Lee Ann is an advance over his earlier feeling that he might be in love with her, as he recognizes. "The notion. . . that I was in love with her and wanted to marry her didn't really adequately express the emotions that her disappearance had stirred in me" (79). As Nat has come to understand something of Lee Ann's suffering, he has come to see her as a symbol of experience, an alternative to his own sheltered life. His decision to stay in the car, ending his pursuit of Lee Ann, is thus an important moment of self-definition. "It may be that the moment of my great failure was when I continued to sit there in the car and did not force my way into the house where the old woman with the goiter lived and where it now seemed Lee Ann had been hiding for four days" (80).

Certainly Nat has his regrets about the incident, and it is possible to see his failure to act here as a confirmation of his essential passivity and lack of courage. Ann Beattie, referring to this moment as indicative of his whole personality, observes that "it seems an understatement to say that he remains conservative to a fault" (109). Yet though we may grant that Nat's feeling of crisis is genuine and that it locates an essential element of his personality, it is not hard to see that his impulse to burst into the house—an action that represented for him at that time an active grasping of experience—would have been a ludicrous mistake. Whether from good judgment, loyalty to Caroline, or simple cowardice, Nat remains in the car. In this case, his inaction is an act of wisdom—or at least an avoidance of folly. What could he have said to Lee Ann that would have constructively addressed her situation? What could he have said that she would not have rightly rebuffed? His feeling that it is within his power to reestablish some connection with her, if that is what his impulse to enter her grandmother's house means, is a sad overestimation of his capacity to exert control over experience.

Nat's mistake is not that he does not burst into Lee Ann's room, grasping for the experience of life that she represents for him; it is in labeling as a failure an act that is, under the circumstances, the only decent one he can take. Although he does indeed grow in recognizing the narrowness of his own experience, he has not yet achieved a full acceptance of the limits from within which he must pursue experience. His failure to act is thus appropriate. His real failure, and one that he seems to labor to understand as he recalls the incident many years later, is not to recognize the appropriateness of the decision.

There is some evidence, although by no means conclusive, that Nat may have grown in some measure toward an acceptance of the limits of experience and thus learned in a small way to meet it more constructively. He recalls his "extraordinary decision" to leave his career in business at age thirty-seven and "go back to the university and prepare myself to become a teacher" (80), a decision that breaks the established pattern of his life. Nat qualifies its impact with frank self-assessment, recognizing that his move into teaching during middle age was an attempt "to comprehend intellectually" a world that he had failed to know by "direct experience" (80).

Nat is a victim less of his inability to act than of his tendency to romanticize some vague notion about the grasping of real experience, a flaw revealed also by Taylor's narrators in other late works.[5] There is a Proustian flourish in

Nat's romantic sense of his failure to grasp experience and his retreat into the intellectual life to analyze that failure. Insofar as this bespeaks immaturity, the story charts an arrested self-development. But without exaggerating the significance of his vocational change—which occurs after his father dies, leaving him financially secure—we find that Nat does eventually alter the course of his life, in a delayed but seemingly genuine effort to understand. His accident with Lee Ann at least shook the foundations of his comfortable ignorance and accelerated a process in which recognition of his narrow personal and social experience became a stimulus to self-development.

But the story resists a linear reduction to any thematic certainty. One strand works against this building indictment of the past—Nat's nostalgia for the lost world of Memphis. Nat himself is no complete convert to modernity; part of him continues to yearn for the world that his accident shattered. His desire for the past, despite the lessons of his experience, is itself problematic for any definitive reading of his character. Consider his account of dinner with the Braxleys the day after the accident. During the evening a call comes from his father, and Nat is shown to the telephone by one of the Braxleys' African American servants. "As he preceded me the length of the living room and then gently guided me across the hall to the telephone in the library, I believe he would have put his hand under my elbow to help me—as if a real invalid—if I had allowed him to" (43). The suggestion of infantile dependency accurately reflects the weaker parts of Nat's character, but the social trappings of the Braxley house—particularly the brief image of the plantation South that his dependence on the faithful servant evokes—suggest precisely the kind of life that has restricted Nat and Caroline's vision of the world and against which they must struggle to attain a mature identity.

Nat is quite explicit about his attraction to this now extinct world when he recounts being driven home by the same servant, Robert. Nat has fallen asleep on the brief drive home and must be awakened when they arrive.

I remember how warmly I thanked him for bringing me home, even shaking his hand, which was a rather unusual thing to do in those days. I felt greatly refreshed and restored and personally grateful to Robert for it. There was not, in those days in Memphis, any time or occasion when one felt more secure and relaxed than when one had given oneself over completely to the care and protection of the black servants who surrounded us and who created and sustained for the most part the luxury which distinguished the lives we lived then from the lives we live now. [46-47]

That modern lives are indeed different is, at least in part, a lamentable fact for Nat, even though he goes on to admit the injustice of the arrangements that made his former luxury possible. "They [the servants] did so for us, whatever their motives and however degrading our demands and our acceptance of their attentions may have been to them" (47). There remains some part of Nat which has not been weaned from the comfortable and ultimately unjust innocence of his upper-class childhood. That has, of course, made the achievement of such maturity as he has all the more difficult, and it renders the judgment of his character much more problematic. Nat's nostalgia is an oblique affirmation of the very world that his experience has proved to be both crippling and unsustainable.

Although we know much less about it, the change in Lee Ann after the accident and after her talk with Caroline is also significant. A profile emerges of a woman pushed by the circumstances of her past toward a search for deeper self-knowledge. Hiding in the Old Forest, Lee Ann realizes that she has "no choice but to go back to the real world" (81). The forest has been a momentary shelter from the crisis of self-knowledge initiated by the accident. Her return signifies acceptance of her grandmother and, in a deeper sense, an acceptance of herself. Her shame about her family, originating in a sense of social or class inferiority, has caused her to live a life of concealment and denial. Her relationship with Nat, a boy from a social and economic world unattainable to her, has only exacerbated her self-division. Her escape into the Old Forest and her eventual acknowledgment of her grandmother are thus acts of healing and self-integration.

Throughout Caroline's efforts to deal with the crisis, Nat has been largely unaware of the stress she is under; he begins to realize her pain only as they drive away from Lee Ann's hideaway, having solved the puzzle of her disappearance and ensured that there will be no damaging publicity. In this moment of success Caroline discloses for the first time the vulnerability that has impelled her. She asks Nat to drive "as fast and as far" out of town as he can, a revealing gesture of escape from Memphis. She tells him what she has learned of Lee Ann's past and then, he recalls, she "burst into weeping that began with a kind of wailing and grinding of teeth that one ordinarily associates more with a very old person in very great physical pain, a wailing that became mixed almost immediately with a sort of hollow laughter in which there was no mirth" (83).

Caroline's wail is prompted in part by her sympathy for Lee Ann but, more important, by her recognition of the fundamental emptiness of the social forms she has preserved in finding Lee Ann. Caroline confesses "feelings of jealousy and resentment" of Lee Ann and her friends, a resentment arising from her sense of imprisonment within the very social forms that she has striven to preserve. She tells Nat that she was shaken by Lee Ann's "freedom to jump out of your car, her freedom *from* you, her freedom to run off into the woods'" (85).

Caroline's surprising declaration of resentment of her social imprisonment anchors the story firmly in social criticism.

> "*You* would like to be able to do that?" I interrupted. It seemed so unlike her role as I understood it.
>
> "*Anybody* would, wouldn't they?" she said, not looking at me but at the endless stretch of concrete that lay straight ahead. "Men *have* always been able to do it," she said. [85]

Nat has presented Lee Ann and her friends as modern women who have taken control of their lives in ways that were impossible to previous generations. The conflict over Lee Ann's disappearance is one not merely between Nat and Lee Ann but between Lee Ann's generation of women and the male power structure. In her assertion of survival, Caroline has been forced ironically to reaffirm that power structure, and her conversation with Lee Ann has brought that fact home to her. Like Nat, she sees Lee Ann perhaps for more than she is, a figure of freedom whose existence outside the Memphis upper class is a reminder of her own confinement within it. She describes Lee Ann and her friends as women who "have made their break with the past. . . . How I do admire and envy them! And how little you understand them, Nat" (85-86).

Caroline understands her difference from women like Lee Ann, and the achievement of that knowledge, however painful, confirms her strength and intelligence. She has recognized the way her choice has been restricted by her sex and social position, and she resorts to the language of power to explain her motivation. "Don't you see, it was a question of how very much I had to lose and how little power I had to save myself. Because *I* had not set *myself* free the way those other girls have. One makes that choice at a much earlier age than this, I'm afraid" (88). Like Lee Ann, Caroline has recognized that acceptance of even a restrictive past is not only necessary but can be a progressive and affirming step. Taylor later explained his purposes in his portrayal of Caroline in an interview with W. Hampton Sides: "But I said to myself, it would be more interesting to see if I can make this society girl appealing as a human being and see what her life is. I wanted to see human beings set in certain historical situations from which they can't escape" (*Conversations*, 136). Throughout his fiction Taylor suggests that the past cannot be ignored, that the attempt to ignore it is ultimately destructive.

Caroline has come to recognize that "power, or strength, is what everybody must have some of if he—if she—is to survive in any kind of world." In preserving such power as she has through preserving her engagement, she also helps Lee Ann to gain a new power in her restoration to her family on more open terms. Caroline has come to see that power may arise from the very circumstances that have made for weakness. "I know now what the only kind of power I can ever have must be," she tells Nat. "You mean the power of a woman in a man's world," Nat replies (88). Restricted as this power is, Caroline's capacity to exercise it with a knowledge of its limits is her source of strength.[6] And her explanation of it forces Nat to a deeper understanding that his strength must also come from an exercise of power in a world in which his own situation is limited. Thus he concludes with a recognition of Caroline's "support and understanding . . . when I made the great break in my life in my late thirties" (89).

These are not dramatic victories of self-assertion or the overcoming of adverse events. They are closer to forms of accommodation with experience, assertions of self within limited spheres of action. Taylor's fiction revolves around his analysis of the tragedy of human limits, both psychological and social. But Nat tells a story in which the response to experience, not the negations of experience, bears the emphasis.

❖ 4 ❖
Men and Women

If we understand "The Captain's Son," "Venus, Cupid, Folly and Time," and "The Old Forest" as varied but representative stories about the difficulties of the transition to a psychologically balanced maturity, we should also note the prominence of the theme of sexuality in all of them. Tolliver Campbell's unwillingness to consummate his marriage and the Dorsets' refusal of sexual maturity are extreme examples of sexual dysfunction. The fear of adulthood has for these characters led to a fear of sexuality itself, a fear that, for the Dorsets, wars against a fascination with it. Ned and Emily Meriwether's loss of ability to communicate with each other and Nat Ramsey's somewhat evasive fascination with Lee Ann Deehart are less extreme but nevertheless significant signs of a sexual drive that is in some respects at war with other aspects of the personality and results in severe inner conflict.

Each of these stories reflects the restraints of the sexual code of the early twentieth-century South, and Taylor's recognition that the tension between restraint and desire is a fundamental element of psychic development. Desire often expresses itself, Taylor argues, through resistance to the social channels that have evolved for its expression. Such resistance is usually either covert, as are Nat Ramsey's affairs in the Memphis "demimonde," or subconscious, as are the Dorsets' elaborate celebrations of "innocence" in their annual parties. In either case, such erotic energy is a shaper of character, affecting every facet of an individual's personality and, if severely thwarted, threatening to deform it.

Taylor's treatment of the erotic began with two of his earliest and best-known stories: "A Spinster's Tale" (1940) and "The Fancy Woman" (1941), both published in the *Southern Review,* were instrumental in the launching of his career. "A Spinster's Tale" records a young woman's tragic hardening into isolated spinsterhood after the death of her mother. Although it demonstrates Taylor's early interest in depth psychology and the formation of the sexual identity, it is also firmly rooted in family lore and the Southern tradition of oral narrative: "It was based almost entirely on the stories my mother told me," he later commented (*Conversations*, 79). He also explained that it was written under the influence of Henry James, as its psychologically probing autobiographical narration might suggest.[1] It is narrated by a character who seems to be simultaneously searching for and avoiding self-understanding, a Jamesian mode surely, and one extended brilliantly by Taylor in later works such as "The Old Forest," *A Summons to Memphis,* and *In the Tennessee Country.*

"A Spinster's Tale" provoked a surprising but important reaction from Robert Lowell, Taylor's college roommate at Kenyon and an important figure in setting his course as a writer. "Why do you write about such nicey-nice people?" he asked Taylor. Although Lowell's reaction seems to miss the psychological subtlety that gives the story much of its impact, it nevertheless posed the kind of challenge that Taylor needed to expand his subject matter and concern. "To show him I said to myself, 'I'm going to write a story about a woman who is so corrupt that she can't recognize innocence when she sees it'" (*Conversations*, 79). The result was "The Fancy Woman," the first sentence of which—"He wanted no more of her drunken palaver" (*CS*, 167)—Taylor wrote with no idea of where it might lead.

The move from "A Spinster's Tale" to "The Fancy Woman" was an important extension of Taylor's range, for it led him from an analysis of the interior dynamics of psychological development to a close-grained description of the psychological ramifications of manners and class distinctions mediated by gender divisions. "A Spinster's Tale" has undeniable intellectual force augmented by a carefully worked-out architectonic structure—an impressive display of Taylor's early mastery of the craft of fiction. But it is thin in comparison with "The Fancy Woman," primarily because of the much larger depiction of social reality in the later story. The vaguely early twentieth-century world of "A Spinster's Tale" seems like a stage backdrop compared with the specificity and detail of Tennessee society depicted in "The Fancy Woman." "I didn't think I knew anything about such people," Taylor told J. William Broadway. "But then I began to remember growing up and friends of mine whose parents were divorced or living a riotous life. And the whole thing came back to me" (*Conversations*, 79). The "whole thing" here, I would add, is not only this particular story but the social world that informed Taylor's fiction throughout his career. In this sense, "The Fancy Woman" was a breakthrough story, one that helped chart the course of Taylor's entire career.

Considered together, the two stories explore the interconnection of family relations, sexual identity, and social identity, each focusing on the particularly problematic nature of the role of woman in this equation. "A Spinster's Tale" is on one level an investigation of sexual pathology as Elizabeth, the main character, describes in retrospect the gradual process by which she developed a lifelong aversion to masculine sexuality.[2] The title, crucial in conveying the information that Elizabeth has remained a "spinster," focuses the reader's attention on the question of her sexual awareness and development. Taylor's task is to portray through her perspective the process by which she excluded sexuality from her experience.

The fundamental source of Elizabeth's pathology is her grief for the death of her mother and an accompanying sense of betrayal or abandonment. But her emotional imbalance becomes intertwined with her fixation on Mr. Speed, an old man who periodically stumbles by her house in a drunken rage. Elizabeth's reaction to Speed as a frightening representation of evil, and of masculine evil in particular, eventuates in her rejection of her sexual nature. Elizabeth tells us that she first observed Mr. Speed in October, following the death of her mother the previous spring. Although the connection between the two events is undeniable in her narrative, the time elapsed suggests that the appearance of Speed is less a causative factor of her psychic trauma than a symptom of it. Taylor said he intended to write a story that demonstrated "how the shock of [the discovery of evil] affected a woman's whole life" (*Conversations*, 154), and Speed's fuming, drunken rages are in a sense an exemplification of evil to a protected and impressionable thirteen-year-old girl. But thinking of Speed as a personification of evil tells us less than realizing that he is the objectification of Elizabeth's awakening but unacknowledged sexual awareness and her simultaneous horror of it, a horror intensified by her subconscious feeling of betrayal because of her mother's death.

Just before her first observation of Speed she has been standing before a mirror, searching for "a resemblance between myself and the wondrous Alice who walked through a looking glass." She cannot find such a resemblance, she says, seeing only "my sharp features" and "my heavy, dark curls hanging like fragments of horsepipe to my shoulders." This moment of adolescent narcissism, combining fascination with her body and revulsion to it, is followed by an odd series of gestures that suggest her difficulties in self-acceptance: "I propped my hands on the borders of the narrow mirror and put my face close to watch my lips say, 'Away.' . . . I whispered it over and over, faster and faster, watching myself in the mirror: 'A-way—a-way—

away-away-awayaway." Suddenly I burst into tears and turned from the gloomy mirror to the daylight at the wide parlor window" (*CS*, 143). It is just this moment, when she feels completely vulnerable, that she observes Speed "cursing the trees as he passed them, and giving each a lick with his heavy walking cane." She becomes "dry-eyed in [her] fright" and stumbles away from the window (143).[3]

Elizabeth's repeated exclamation of the word "away" is interestingly ambiguous, a suggestion of the internal tensions with which she is struggling. She later refers to this experience as "something like mystical" (155), indicating its strong impact. "Away" is Alice's means of entry into the imaginative world of the looking glass, and Elizabeth's imitation of Alice is in fact a wish for removal from the world in which she finds herself, an expression of her turmoil and deep unhappiness after her mother's death. But it is also important to note that the words are spoken into the mirror, to an image of herself, and thus constitute an expression of self-loathing aimed in particular at her bodily self, with its increasing sexual maturity, as she views it in the mirror. She wishes her physical self "away." Her grimacing facial contortions, which seem to enact this feeling of disgust, confirm her self-rejection.

Because Elizabeth's physical maturity coincides with her mother's death after childbirth and is thus associated with sexuality, her "away" is also a cry of grief that her mother has gone "away" from her. She remembers this moment throughout her life as a turning point, referring to it again in the last paragraph of her narrative. Moreover, in her grief and confusion Elizabeth develops a pathology in which all men become versions of Speed. He is "the dreamlike projection of some masculine principle that the motherless girl unconsciously fears and resents," as Albert J. Griffith has noted.[4] Elizabeth's anger is thus not entirely self-directed. Her exclamation of "away" eventually signifies her ordering all men "away" from her in the isolation of her solitary life.

Elizabeth's repeated pronouncement of the word may not, of course, include these later implications at the moment she utters it, but it comes to include them as the scene grows in significance to her. It is important to remember that the narration is retrospective, and that Elizabeth is herself seeking to understand and justify the course her life has taken. What seems to give her repetition of "away" particular significance is Speed's appearance just after this the crisis moment, and Elizabeth's linking of her fear of him with her desire for her mother's presence. After stumbling back from the window where she saw him, Elizabeth tells us, "I stood cold and silent before the gas logs with a sudden inexplicable memory of my mother's cheek and a vision of her in her bedroom on a spring day" (143).

That memory refers to an encounter that took place shortly before her mother's death, three days after the family had held a funeral for the stillborn child. Her mother had been lifted from her bed to a chair; she called for Elizabeth and, in a gesture of comfort and tenderness, "with a smile leaned her cheek against the cheek of her daughter." As Elizabeth remembers it, "the furnishings of the great blue room seemed to partake for that one moment of nature's life. And my mother's cheek was warm on mine." This moment of bonding with her mother is of tremendous importance to the frightened, grieving young girl who, in the aftermath of the loss of the baby, fears the abandonment that the loss of her mother would mean. But their closeness is broken when "a few moments later my mother beckoned to the practical nurse and sent me suddenly from the room" (144). Although it seems probable that Elizabeth's mother was overcome with pain or illness at that moment, her withdrawal has a powerful impact on Elizabeth, giving her a subconscious confirmation of her fear of abandonment.

Elizabeth indirectly verifies the importance of the moment by trying to deny its significance when she explains the effect on her seeing Speed. She says that as she "sat before the gas logs trying to put Mr. Speed out of [her] mind" (144), she remembered only the warmth of her mother's cheek on hers. But her mother's warmth has been fused with being sent away; in reaching self-defensively for the memory of her mother's love, she inevitably brings back the memory of her mother's rejection, now compellingly associated with Speed, the embodiment of a frightening masculine world that Elizabeth must learn to negotiate alone.

This psychological situation is of course complicated by the onset of Elizabeth's sexual maturity, in which the sensuous impression of the warmth of her mother's cheek, repeated by the heat of the fire, is confusingly associated with Speed and his angry violence. Once she has seen Speed, her terrified fascination with him grows, affecting her relationship with other men. Late one evening she beckons her drunken older brother into her room after he returns to the house. As she throws her arms around him and sobs, expressing both childlike loneliness and subtle seductiveness, she smells "for the first time the fierce odor of his cheap whiskey" and places her "cheek on the shoulder of his overcoat which was yet cold from the February night air" (150). Her brother is obviously a surrogate both for her mother and for Speed, and the scene represents the fusion of her desire for the restoration of maternal warmth with the awakening of her feelings of sexual desire.

After noting her brother's habit of excess drinking on several occasions, she observes her father drinking in the parlor one Saturday afternoon with his brothers, talking and laughing heartily. This would be to most observers an innocently convivial scene, but it affects Elizabeth differently: "In my brother and father I saw something of Mr. Speed. And I knew it was more than a taste for whiskey they had in common" (157). Her growing disgust with her father and brother is accompanied by an interest in the "forbid-den," expressed in her curiosity about the servants' and men's bathrooms, which she begins to inspect. "The filth of the former became a matter of in-terest in the study of the servants' natures, instead of the object of ineffable disgust. The other became a fascinating place of wet shaving brushes and leather straps and red rubber bags" (162). Elizabeth is increasingly under the influence of her sexual nature while she is also at war with it. As this ten-sion builds within her, she focuses both her disgust and fascination on Speed, whose stumbling passes by her house become ever more central to her psychic economy.

Elizabeth's great dread is that Speed will one day take notice of her and try to enter the house. She watches one afternoon as her brother goes out to retrieve Speed's derby for him after the wind has blown it off. She quizzes him about Speed, and he answers matter-of-factly that the man has "burned out his reason with whiskey" but that he is no one to fear: "You'll get used to him, for all his ugliness" (154). This is a prospect that Elizabeth cannot accept, and she resents the tolerance and sympathy for Speed that she senses in her brother and father.

Circumstance finally does bring Speed to Elizabeth's door; he is caught one day in a heavy downpour and stumbles toward her porch for shelter, "drunker than I had ever before seen him," with his anger "doubled by the raging weather" (164). As Elizabeth later reconstructs it, this is a moment of testing in her life, for she feels that her ability to handle the confrontation with Speed is a gauge of her ability to maintain control of her own life.[5] It is a test of her independence but also her first step toward the isolation of her spinsterhood. Speed is allowed to enter the house by the family maid, Lucy; assuming that the pounding on the porch is Elizabeth's brother, she opens the door to find Speed, "his face crimson, his eyes bleary, and his gray clothes dripping water." Lucy backs away from him in fright, leaving Elizabeth to handle the situation by telephoning for the police.

What follows is a surprising moment in which Elizabeth is brought to the edge of a new awareness of herself and others by momentarily seeing the man in a different light. "Mr. Speed heard me make the call. He was still and silent for just one moment. Then he broke into tears, and he seemed to be chanting his words. He repeated the word 'child' so many times that I felt I had acted wrongly, with courage but without wisdom. I saw myself as a little beast adding to the injury that what was bestial in man had already done him" (165). Elizabeth's brief insight is not only an important reminder of Speed's humanity, a fact that the reader may be prone to forget, but also an indication that she is still capable of attaining a different attitude toward him and thus a more balanced sense of herself and her relations with others.

But the element of choice that comes into play proves determinative of the course of her life. When Speed leaves the house, he slides on the wet porch and falls "unconscious on the steps." Elizabeth is frozen with indecision as she faces the question of whether to aid Speed now that he is no longer a menacing threat but a helpless, pitiable man. As she watches him she also finds herself in a revealing process of self-examination: "I was frightened by the thought of the cruelty which I found I was capable of, a cruelty which seemed inextricably mixed with what I had called courage. I looked at him lying out there in the rain and despised and pitied him at the same time, and I was afraid to go minister to the helpless old Mr. Speed" (166).

Elizabeth's anger, with the decisive help of her fear, defeats her pity, and that "victory" is a conclusive one. Recalling the incident long afterward, she confesses the permanence of her change: "But, despite the surge of pity I felt for the old man on our porch that afternoon, my hatred and fear of what he had stood for in my eyes has never left me" (166). Elizabeth thus remains frozen emotionally throughout her life by the anger and fear that she focused on Speed. Her rejection of pity for him constitutes a rejection of all men, and consequently a rejection of her own awakening sexual drives.

It is, of course, interesting to find this tale of spinsterhood and isolation at the outset of the work of an author primarily concerned with family. What must be remembered is that it is within the context of Elizabeth's loss of her mother, her primary familial relationship, that she develops her isolation. Although Taylor conceived the story primarily as a psychological character study, we can see in it many of the presuppositions about personality formation within family experience that would become characteristic of his developing fiction. Elizabeth's rejection of marriage and the possibility of family becomes, in this sense, a beginning for Taylor's explorations of the dynamics of many unhappy families.

"The Fancy Woman" at first seems to be a reversal of direction from "A Spinster's Tale": Josie Carlson's lack of sexual restraint contrasts with Elizabeth's frigidity, and her scheming for marriage contrasts with Elizabeth's decided isolation. But it is instructive to observe how similar the two women are. Their shortcomings are manifested in different ways but are rooted in the same insecurity that poisons their relations with others.

The roots of Josie's insecurities are suggested in the story's first sentence, which would prove so fertile for Taylor: "He wanted no more of her drunken palaver" (*CS*, 167). Obviously, the sentence reveals her tendency toward alcoholism, a flaw that is repeatedly emphasized in the story. But, perhaps more important, it suggests her domination by her lover, George, and thus establishes the story's central narrative line: Josie's futile attempts to resist or alter that domination and thereby gain a dignity of person.[6]

George is imperious in his dealings with her, treating her like a child or a servant and refusing to recognize her independence or maturity. He insists that she go riding in an attempt to sober her up, but also, it seems, as a sort of punishment for her drinking. When she resists, tearfully and angrily, he laughs derisively and talks to her as one would to an infant in a tantrum: "Boochie, Boochie. Wotsa matter?" (171). Josie understands this scornful condescension well enough, but she is trapped by it, unable to elicit any meaningful response from him and forced into petulant anger and deceitful plotting in her futile attempt to establish some independence.

George's mistreatment of Josie gives us the basis for a measure of sympathy for her, but it is hard to carry that sympathy very far when we see her extend the same contempt to others. Her insecurity manifests itself in a suspicion of the servants in the house, whose disapproval she feels and resents. She reacts to them with hostility and racist contempt, attempting to assert a superiority that she does not actually feel. When George speaks to her of "friend-girls" Josie takes the term as some form of mockery and explodes: "'Friend-girl? You never heard me say friend-girl. What black nigger do you think you're talking down to?' She was looking at him now through a mist of tears and presently she broke out into furious weeping" (171). The outburst suggests Josie's sense of class inferiority and helps to explain her anxiety about the servants' attitude toward her. She is contemptuous of them because she understands her situation to be similar to theirs. Their presence in the house reminds her that she, too, is George's servant, unable to meet and deal with him as an equal.

Josie attempts to overcome her feeling of inferiority by unscrupulously plotting to ensnare George into marriage, coveting his money and status. "George was worth getting around. She would find out what it was. She wouldn't take another drink. She'd find out what was wrong inside him, for there's something wrong inside everybody, and somehow she'd get a hold of him." Josie's scheming reveals her cynicism and corruption, rooted, as Taylor makes plain, in her own history of mistreatment, which has proved corrosive to the better elements in her personality. As a frequent victim of others, she has been in a position to experience the "wrong" inside them; her response now is to try to victimize George himself by discovering his vulnerability. "Little Josephine would make a place for herself at last. She just wouldn't think about him as a man" (175).

Josie's decision to refuse to think of George "as a man" contains an important ambiguity. It means, primarily, that she hopes to find the will to resist the emotional and physical attraction she feels for him, thus giving her the controlling power in the relationship. But it also means that she must dehumanize him in some fundamental way and think of him only for what she can gain from him—to regard him, that is, as he has heretofore regarded her. This coldly calculating side of her is intermingled with an almost desperate longing to belong, to have a secure place, a desire that is inflamed by speculation about George's house, its decoration, and the wife that seems missing from his life. "The wife had left him for his meanness," she imagines, "and he was lonesome. There was, then, a place to be filled. She began to run along the road. 'God, I feel like somebody might step in before I get there'" (175). Josie's "corruption," though real enough, is a direct manifestation of her desperate need for place, identity, and dignity.

Her insecurity is soon increased by a turn of events that transforms the story from a straightforward psychological study like "A Spinster's Tale" to a narrative in which individual psychology is measured as an element in a highly ordered and rigidly defined social world. It is here that the work takes on a notable social specificity, a density of realistic texture characteristic of Taylor's continuing work. Guests from Memphis, longstanding friends of George, arrive for an overnight stay and must therefore observe and pass judgment on George's "fancy woman."

Josie had not previously felt the social distance between herself and George to be insurmountable. She had, in fact, been emboldened by her perception of George's weaknesses, recognizing that his money and status had not given him manners in his dealings with her and surmising that his "meanness" (175) may have cost him his marriage. But this sort of confidence is hard to maintain before his guests, who come from what is for Josie a different world. She recognizes that "these *were* Memphis society people," of an economic class completely different from her own, and she fears that they will recognize that she does not "belong" among them. "What if she had waited on one of them once at Jobe's or, worse still, in the old days at Burnstein's? But they had probably never been to one of those cheap stores" (179). Josie understands that they are the ones who can define her as a "fancy woman," and her insecurity is deepened by a conversation that she overhears among the arriving guests:

> "You'd better get *her* out, George."
> George laughed. Josie could hear them dropping ice into glasses.
> "We'll take her back at dawn if you say."
> "What would the girls say to that?" He laughed at them as he laughed at Josie.
> "The girls are gonna be decent to her. They agreed in the yard." [182]

George's lack of concern about social appearances may at first seem a liberation from convention, but it is better understood as a measure of his callousness. His refusal to send Josie away is an act less of principle than of personal convenience, a measure of how detached he feels from any permanent connection with her.

Taylor's depiction of the gap in social rank between George and Josie eventually leads, however, to an ironic confirmation of Josie's belief that she is George's equal. The guests arrive for an overnight party which begins with dancing and drinking and ends in sexual play: George's friend Phil Jackson visits Josie that night while, she later suspects, George is visiting Mrs. Jackson.[7] This further humiliation for Josie, emphasizing both George's light regard for her and her own lack of self-control, underlines her suspicion that corruption and moral vulnerability are rampant in the upper classes. The witheringly ironic comment of Jackson's wife the next morning confirms the fact of equality among the debauched: "'And how do *you* feel this morning, Miss Carlson?' It was the fact that it was Jackson's wife that got her the most. But then the fool woman said, 'Like the rest of us?'" (189). The comment both mocks Josie as an unworthy social climber and sardonically remarks on the decadence that characterizes these "Memphis society people."

But this is not the worst of Josie's humiliations. That comes later at the hands of George's younger son, Buddy, who arrives with his older brother the next day. Readers of Taylor know that his sometimes surprising yet ut-

terly persuasive portrayals of character are perhaps his greatest achievements as a writer, and he extended this gift of characterization to children
and adolescents with particular grace. Buddy is among the earliest of these
accomplishments, a character who is striking primarily for the sharp contrast he brings into the story. He is in his sentimental innocence like a creature from another world, and this difference is crucial to the process of
Josie's ultimate humiliation.

Buddy, a youthful literary prodigy, is forced by his proud father to recite
poetry that he has memorized to the assembled guests. Although initially reluctant to do so, he warms to the task and circles the table reciting a stanza
from Swinburne's "The Match" to each of the women there with a kind of
innocent formality. "The boy *did* have a way with him!" Josie recalls. "His
eyes were big and he could look sad and happy at the same time" (190). The
Swinburne poem, a blending of medieval courtliness and erotic decadence,
becomes the meeting point for Buddy's aggressive innocence and Josie's vulnerable skepticism. She listens to him with growing suspicion as he gains
confidence and power, realizing that she will soon be the object of one of the
stanzas and believing that what he chooses to recite to her may be significant. "But now the kid was perfectly sure of himself, and he had acted timid
at first. It was probably all a show. She could just hear him saying dirty lim-
ericks" (190). These suspicions seem confirmed when he begins to recite for
Josie, "in his grandest manner," the final stanza of the poem:

> If you were queen of pleasure,
> And I were king of pain,
> We'd hunt down love together,
> Pluck out his flying-feather
> And teach his feet a measure,
> And find his mouth a rein;
> If you were queen of pleasure,
> And I were king of pain. [190]

After the events of the previous evening and Mrs. Jackson's acid comments
on them, we should not be surprised to find that Josie perceives a clever
insult in the choice of the stanza; she "gave the brat the hardest look she
knew how. It was too plain. 'Queen of pleasure' sounded just as bad as
whore!" (191).

But Josie's reaction, though understandable, is eventually proved
wrong. She is unable to recognize Buddy's essential innocence, partly

because of her own cynicism about the inevitable weaknesses of others, and partly because of her feeling of extreme vulnerability among George's Memphis friends. But misreading Buddy's intentions is a mistake that readers are likely to share at the moment, for we have been led through the narrative largely from her perspective, sharing her sense of displacement and insecurity. The eventual confirmation that it was a mistake thus constitutes an important turn in expectations, an ironic surprise to both Josie and the reader.

This turn is the result of her response to a request that Buddy later makes, which she misinterprets in a way that reflects her own cynicism and corruption. The day after the recitation Buddy calls her to his room and asks, "Don't you think it's time you did something nice for me?" Josie, believing herself propositioned by an adolescent, takes the question in jest.

> Josie laughed, and she watched Buddy laugh. Queen of pleasure indeed!
> "I want to draw you," he said.
> "Clothes and all, Bud? . . ."
> "No. That's not what I mean!" [196-97]

Buddy, whose artistic talents have been praised earlier by his brother, has apparently paid a sincere compliment to Josie's beauty by asking her to pose for a sketch. Her misinterpretation of his innocent request shocks him, and, when she realizes her mistake, embarrasses her deeply: "Josie forced a smile. She suddenly felt afraid and thought she was going to be sick again but she couldn't take her eyes off him" (197). She condemns herself, through this mistake, to receiving the same suspicion that she has shown Buddy, and his rejection of her is absolute: "'That's not what I mean,' she heard the kid say again, without blinking an eye, without blushing. 'I didn't know you were that sort of nasty thing here. I didn't believe you were a fancy woman. Go on out of here. Go away!' he ordered her" (197).

It is important to understand Josie's rejection here as the result not only of her moral failure but also of her failure of social perception. She incorrectly interprets Buddy's gestures because she is not conversant with the world that produced him. Buddy terms Josie a "fancy woman," and he is able to do so because he speaks from within the world that Josie will forever only observe. Taylor's presentation of her "corruption" is thus not limited to her character but originates in the complexities of her relation to the world of the "Memphis society people" among whom she has found herself.

Although the story is in this sense a study of Josie's motives and an indictment of her cynicism, it is also an indictment of the corruption of the upper class in the modern South, dramatizing the decay of family structure as symptomatic of a larger cultural unraveling. We see little of George's thoughts or motivations, since Taylor keeps the focus on Josie, but his character is revealed clearly enough through his treatment of her. George's callous sexual aggressiveness and the generally debauched way of life of his upper-class friends reflect Taylor's perception of a larger collapse of cultural cohesion in the modernizing South.

Both "A Spinster's Tale" and "The Fancy Woman" explore the ways that erotic attraction and its denial shape, and sometimes warp, the development of the personality. As Taylor's work developed through the 1950s and 1960s, this concern became enfolded within his developing interests in the psychological dynamics of the modern family and the social transition of the modern South. Writing to some extent against the grain of postwar public cultural assumptions, Taylor presents marriage and the family as points of social stress and psychological conflict, insisting on the complexity and tension lying beneath the presumably placid surface of the American middle class. Writing at a time of enormous upheaval in the South, he describes the presumably peaceful period before it—the 1920s, 1930s, and early 1940s—as actually having generated the energies and instabilities that became prominent after the war.

"Venus, Cupid, Folly and Time," for example, illustrates Taylor's sense of both the psychological and social dimensions of sexual repression but submerges the prominent erotic theme within the discourse on family and generations that characterizes most of the stories from the 1950s and 1960s. In the 1980s, however, Taylor returns with renewed interest to the themes of sexual desire and emotional betrayal, beginning in "The Old Forest" a series of works in which the attainment or failure of love is a central concern.[8] We have examined "The Old Forest," *A Summons to Memphis*, and *In the Tennessee Country* in different contexts, noting their considerations of family and maturity. Each of them also involves failed or frustrated love as a central element of character motivation. Two stories from Taylor's last collection, "The Witch of Owl Mountain Springs: An Account of Her Remarkable Powers" and "The Oracle of Stoneleigh Court," focus more directly on frustrated erotic desire and trace the haunting pathologies that originate in such frustration.

"The Witch of Owl Mountain Springs" is one of Taylor's most unusual and difficult stories, melding motifs of social privilege, sexual desire, psychological abnormality, the supernatural, and criminal violence into a strange and compelling narrative. Taylor makes provocative use of an intriguingly ambiguous first-person narrator whose account of his relationship with a woman named Lizzy Pettigru leaves more questions than answers. The story resists interpretive closure, and the obvious unreliability of the narrator's version of events adds to the elements of surprise and intrigue that create a strong narrative current.

Lizzy Pettigru is twice the victim of betrayal by those upon whom she depends closely. The nature of those betrayals, both of them sexual, is significant, as is the fact that the story's narrator recognizes—consciously, at least—only one of them, being himself the agent of the other. These betrayals result in Lizzy's pain-wracked withdrawal from the world into a life that remains psychologically obscure both to the narrator and to the reader. Taylor chooses to observe the mystery of Lizzy's mind only at a distance and further complicates his portrayal of her with the motif of the occult. The narrator remarks that he eventually came "to accept that perhaps Lizzy Pettigru had, consciously or unconsciously, made a compact with some dark spirit," the source of certain witchlike "powers" that were attributed to her (*OSC*, 143).

Lizzy's transformation from a daughter of the Tennessee upper middle class into a witchlike recluse must first be understood as a reflection of the deterioration of the Southern aristocracy. Lizzy is the daughter of a family that "stretched back into eternity—through Virginia and South Carolina and Cavaliers and Charles the Martyr" (120). Her transformation is in one sense an attempt to deny her class origins, a gesture similar to that of Harry Weaver in Taylor's play *A Stand in the Mountains*.[9] The narrator regards her class affiliation as a crucial aspect of her personality. He is fascinated with Lizzy not as an individual but "as a girl who was from that particular group." Observing "the bonding of such girls," he explains, "has constituted one of the chief delights of my entire life." This admitted preoccupation is disturbingly voyeuristic, since the narrator himself, as a man, would be necessarily excluded from such a bond. His desire is conditioned by his intense preoccupation with social status, for he is fascinated with "their very evident awareness of their own closeness and congeniality and even their exclusiveness" (118). "Exclusiveness" is the operative term here. He is drawn to that which he knows to be unattainable, having constructed his desire in a way that will shield him from the possibility of direct personal relations.

Social place and the history of its evolution function for him as a substitute for intimacy; for this reason he can speak with detailed knowledge of the "stock" from which Lizzy has come and explain how the history of Owl Mountain Resort, where the story principally takes place, lends her and her friends an exclusive identity. That identity, as the narrator reveals to us with apparently no embarrassment, is based in ethnic and religious discrimination. Owl Mountain Resort "had originally been founded as a gathering place for the principal Protestant sects in our region: Presbyterians, Episcopalians, Baptists, Methodists, and Lutherans." Whatever the religious motives of the founders, they were also set on establishing a retreat based in WASP exclusivity. "It was natural that no Jewish people would wish to go there," he reports innocently, adding that the original charter "stipulated for all the world to read that no Roman Catholic could ever own property inside the Grounds." As the narrator explains it, this was "not even vaguely" a resort of the highly fashionable or affluent set but rather a retreat of those who saw themselves "as the special urban remnants of an old gentry out of another time, out of their remotely agrarian past." For him, Lizzy Pettigru is the "very epitome" of this class (119).

But this identification is one that he projects upon her, not one with which Lizzy herself seems entirely comfortable. Coming to know her during his first summer at Owl Mountain, he constantly tells her of his fascination with the girls whose social standing and social graces seem so impressive to him, including her among them. "But it seemed always to be Lizzy's principal aim to make me understand that underneath and essentially she was cut from a different cloth." The narrator's attempts to link her to the group of girls who surround her and her attempt to distance herself from them seem to constitute an essential element of their relationship. It is as important for him to believe that Lizzy is one with the other girls as it is for her to assert a unique identity: "No, I am not like them at all," she tells him; "there was a mysterious essence in her being which she asserted was totally different" (130).

And in fact Lizzy does prove to be quite different, as her reaction to her betrayals will reveal. But the mystery that surrounds her is also exacerbated by the narrator's amazing obtuseness, which shields him from any sense of another person's inner life or any full comprehension of his own. "'You ought to *see* it for *yourself*,' she would tell me. And then she would laugh merrily" (130). That comment signals her recognition of his blindness and her understanding that he would profit greatly by deepening his sensitivity to what is around him.

The narrator's insular resistance to anything deeper than the superficial indices of social lineage and status becomes increasingly clear as his narrative continues, opening a gap that creates one of the story's most important effects. We are drawn increasingly toward Lizzy Pettigru, out of both compassion and curiosity, as the gap grows between her actions and the narrator's capability of comprehending them. But his ignorance functions ironically as a spur to the reader's attention: as Lizzy remains a mystery, the narrator's dullness begins to seem increasingly dangerous.

The narrator's obsession with social status, and Lizzy's denial of it, provide the initial framework of the story as a social allegory. Its close connection in this regard with *A Stand in the Mountains* is important, for in each case Taylor is pursuing a similar cultural narrative of the decay of the very class with which the narrator here so insistently identifies Lizzy. Lizzy, who we come to see as rejected, barren, and perhaps dangerously destructive, represents one aspect of that culture. The narrator, attenuated, sterile, self-deceptive, and also dangerously destructive, represents another. Together they embody Taylor's pronouncement on the fate of the Southern gentry. These significations begin to be made plain when the central event of the story, Lizzy's sexual betrayal, is recounted.

It is difficult to categorize her initial relationship with the narrator, who is younger and less socially sophisticated than she, but it is safe to say that it is something other than a romantic attachment. The summer after they meet, Lizzy is in fact engaged to Tim Sullivan, whose family were "the richest Roman Catholics in Nashville." The Sullivans, barred by the terms of the Owl Mountain covenant from owning property there, were "willing and content merely to lease someone else's cottage in the Grounds during July and August." Tim's acceptance among the young people makes it seem as if religious prejudice has not survived into Lizzy's generation, who regard him "as one of themselves." And, given the Sullivans' wealth, the social barriers that might have been erected do not materialize. "The idea of a marriage of the Sullivan money and the Pettigrus' gentility was widely approved and even applauded," we are told (132-33).

But Lizzy's prospective marriage, the possibility of which depends on the combination of money and changing social attitudes, is destroyed in a scene with special relevance to the story's social allegory of class declension. Her Catholic fiancée abandons Lizzy for her visiting friend Sarah Goodrich, who refers to herself as "Owl Mountain's token Jew" (134). The two of them quite obviously represent groups prominently excluded from permanent residence at the Owl Mountain Resort and, symbolically, from a secure place in Southern culture. Their abandonment of Lizzy and her withdrawal into isolation must thus be read as having more than merely personal significance, allegorizing the sterility of Southern WASP culture.

Tim and Sarah are the stars of the resort's annual play and thus spend much time together in the Pettigrus' parlor, rehearsing their parts. Outside the room during one of these rehearsals, "Lizzy hear[s] Sarah say the word 'Jew' and hear[s] Tim say the word 'Catholic.'" When she enters, she notices that they are regarding each other "with what [are] clearly teasing expressions on their faces," expressions change "immediately" upon her appearance (133-34). This moment, a Jamesian scene of recognition, is a sign that a bond has formed between them, initiated in part by their recognition of their difference from the others at Owl Mountain.

They are left to rehearse in the front parlor while the Pettigrus retire. But Lizzy, now suspicious, returns in the dark to verify her fear. Taylor's description of her discovery is one of the most vividly realized scenes in his fiction, and its iconographic impact on the reader is a crucial correlative to its psychological impact on Lizzy. She finds the door to the parlor closed but sees light under the door and pouring through "the large old-fashioned keyhole to which there had never been a key." Framed by this contrast of light and dark, Lizzy peers through the closed door, a sign of her emotional exclusion and psychic isolation. "In her nightgown and without slippers on her feet she forced herself down on her knees, and through the big keyhole she saw them. Afterward she would feel that in a sense peering through that keyhole was the most degrading part of the whole experience." The scene that she witnesses is, especially under these circumstances, a shock—Tim and Sarah are making love. Taylor communicates part of that shock through the physical detail etched in Lizzy's memory and later communicated to the narrator. "They were on the Brussels carpet and what she first saw were the soles of their feet. She wanted not to see more but she knew that she must, and then suddenly she was distracted from the sight of their actual bodies by their faint animal-like sounds. Now she withdrew almost despite herself" (135).

The impact of this visual image is deepened by the utter exclusion that it signifies for Lizzy. The closed door and her humiliating effort to see through it become emblematic of the course of her life, an exile from human contact and intimacy. Lizzy returns to her room where "she sat the rest of the night" (135). What thus began as a willful resolve to discover the truth about Tim and Sarah becomes a willful resolve to see no more. Lizzy responds to her shock and feeling of degradation with an equally powerful emphasis on self-control. Her long night of pained, solitary contemplation is the prelude to a life that becomes one long act of complete social withdrawal.

Lizzy's stunned witness to this scene of her betrayal is the "calamity" that initiates what the narrator calls "the disastrous fate that would ultimately be her lot" (121). But it is not the final blow dealt her. Finding that Tim and Sarah have left together during the night, leaving a note explaining that they are together committing their lives to the theater, Lizzy seeks out the narrator as a confidant, telling him "all that she had heard and seen last night, sparing [him] nothing" (138). Lizzy's motivation is partly, we suspect, the sheer relief of unburdening confession, and the narrator, who holds her in almost worshipful reverence, is an ideal audience. But she is seeking more than a sympathetic ear. She tells him of her pain at Tim and Sarah's thankless departure: "But I can see that neither of them has ever appreciated the love I was able to give them and *did* give them." The narrator responds by falling back on his sense of Lizzy's superiority, a quality that he has mystifyingly idealized since his first meeting with her. "'Why did you have to waste yourself on them?' I blurted out. 'They were not worthy of you—you of all people'" (138). This is comfort of a very limited sort, more relevant to the narrator with his preoccupations about social status than it is to Lizzy in her pain. Her need is for human connection, not for a false sense of superiority that would justify aloofness. But she hears in the narrator's words a hint of some deeper suggestion and meets it straight on. "'Who *is* worthy of my love?' she asked" (139).

The narrator's response to this question is crucial to our understanding of the story. It not only contributes to Lizzy's fate but also reminds us of the narrowness of the sensibility through which we receive the narrative. "I can't imagine," he tells her. The remark is indicative of his emotional sterility, and its obtuseness masks an evasive aloofness and deep self-deception. "I can't imagine," he repeats, and as his response to her continues, it becomes darker in its implications: "Why, Lizzy, you have had the same wonderful chances that all the other girls have had," he tells her. "You have refused to be what everyone knows you are, the very best of the whole lot. You ought to be glad to be betrayed by what they are. It proves what *you* are" (139). The narrator's pique is directed at Tim and Sarah, the interlopers at Owl Mountain, but its real source is jealousy arising from his thwarted attraction to Lizzy. That jealousy will continue to fester in him throughout his life.

It is necessary to draw back from this detailed reading of the story to notice the structure of its larger development. The social allegory is played out most completely at this moment, with Lizzy representing the abandoned sterility of her class, and the narrator embodying its exclusionary viciousness. Thereafter, the story turns away from social allegory toward psychological analysis, as both Lizzy and the narrator begin to reveal the restrictive and ultimately self-destructive bounds of their individual characters. They continue to represent the decay of the exclusionary Southern upper classes, but they also become studies in pathology as Taylor moves the story to its weird and violent conclusion.

Upon hearing the narrator's evasive answer to her question, Lizzy looks at him "without tears and without belief," then runs away. "And it would not have done," he remarks, "on that day of all days to have Lizzy seen being hotly pursued down Owl Mountain Middle Path by such as I." His concern for manners or seemliness masks his characteristic inertia. Here, then, their relationship ends, for "Lizzy would never again through all the years acknowledge any acquaintance between the two of us" (139). But as we learn, it does not end entirely for the narrator, who makes a lifelong habit of observing her decline. For him, such voyeurism is the substitute for intimacy, and we come to understand that he takes perverse satisfaction in Lizzy's demise.

Taylor's decision to shift the story's emphasis from social allegory to psychological portraiture can be explained in two ways, neither of which entirely exhausts its implications. On one level, he seems to be limiting class status as an explanatory category for human actions—limiting it but not, it is important to note, ruling it out entirely. Tim and Sarah's actions may have had some support in their reaction to social exclusion, and Lizzy and the narrator's reaction to them may have been framed to an extent by those same boundaries. The narrator may use his perceptions of social status to shield himself from authentic emotion. But these considerations can explain Lizzy's decline and the narrator's deepening isolation only partially. Taylor moves beyond the layer of class considerations through which the narrator introduces us to the story's events in order to probe at deeper causes—or mysteries—in human behavior.

I believe there is some element of truth in this explanation I have been laying out, but it is a limited one, making the story seem more controlled and rational in its unfolding than it really is. In "The Old Forest," to offer a contrasting example, Taylor works through a narrator who is in the process of deepening self-discovery, and the story does move through successive stages of revelation.[10] But "The Witch of Owl Mountain Springs" seems to spiral into ever deeper mysteries, connected with both the subject of the story, Lizzy, and with the narrator, who becomes increasingly problematic as the story continues.[11]

The first clues to the nature of his problem can be discerned in his series of images of the aging and deteriorating Lizzy, whom he describes, some forty years after the end of their relation, as monsterlike. "By then her craggy old face and her unkempt hair could remind one of nothing that was human, much less of those long-ago charming girls." There is no compassion in this description, only an utterly self-absorbed remark on how "deeply disturbing and irritating" it was that he "could no longer find that resemblance" (124). This confession, combined with his account of his parting with Lizzy, reminds us that he is obsessed with preconceived ideals rather than actual persons, an obsession that serves to insulate him from reality. But his withdrawal is rendered even more disturbing when he informs us of "moments of amnesia which have recurred throughout the rest of my life in moments of great stress" (127), moments having to do primarily with acts that are embarrassing, inappropriate, or hurtful. These attacks, suggesting the distance between the narrator's conscious self and his inner drives, are of particular importance in relation to his strenuous repression of sexual desire for Lizzy, a repression that is occurring even as he details his early fascination with her beauty.

His narrative is from this perspective an account of a forty-year pattern of voyeuristic observation of Lizzy during summers at Owl Mountain, as she gradually sheds the outer elements of her upper class and enters into "a compact with some dark spirit" (143) that gives her a rumored identity as a witch. As the narrator's obsession with Lizzy twists inward over the years, he offers us a version of her life that focuses on her burning desire to revenge her betrayal and culminates in a weird account of Tim and Sarah's return to the mountain in old age. In this climactic ending, we enter a Poe-like landscape that mixes mental delusion, the supernatural, and maddeningly evasive narration into a tangled but fascinating interpretive coil.

The narrator details Lizzy's increasing isolation over the years, noting in particular the way she refuses to see friends from her childhood who come back to visit her at Owl Mountain. This isolation leads to rumors among the local people about her "powers"; they "wrongly supposed that she had purposely and magically somehow drawn these old acquaintances to Owl Mountain and then had turned her back on them" (142), an enactment of vengeance for her own earlier betrayal. The rumors are augmented by tales about old friends of Lizzy's who encounter bad luck as they attempt a visit. Hearing such rumors, the narrator confesses to "a kind of fear of Lizzy" and "even a kind of hatred for this creature I once idolized" (149). Lizzy's "powers" serve to confirm a quite different and independent identity from the one the narrator has attempted to project onto her, and her divergence from his ideal threatens to expose to him the falsity of his own consciousness. He is particularly disturbed when, observing her in the village one July morning, he sees "a look of peace and satisfaction on her face that somehow frightened me." He finds this look "repelling" and reacts to it strongly: "It inspired me momentarily with inexplicable feelings of bitterness" (149).

By this point in the story his "bitterness" is by no means "inexplicable" to the reader. Lizzy represents to him a life that he once hoped to control and mold, even though he was frightened to be too near it. He had taken unadmitted satisfaction in her betrayal by Tim and Sarah, and used his own rejection of her to express a vengeful envy of her love for Tim. The peace and independence that she has been able to acquire, at whatever cost, are thus a rebuke to him.

The extent to which the narrator is finally able to enact his seething envy is unclear in the story, but Taylor leaves ample room to surmise that he has enacted it in a horrifying way. The story's climax is initiated by the return of Tim and Sarah, who after leaving Owl Mountain became well-known film stars. But in an extreme version of the rumored difficulties that beset would-be visitors to Lizzy at Owl Mountain, they are killed in an auto accident before they reach her.

The narrator's account of the accident is notable in leaving every impression that Lizzy is to blame for Tim and Sarah's demise, that she has used her witchlike powers to lure them back to their destruction. Their car slides off the curving road and down the mountainside in a spectacular crash, the causes of which remain mysterious. "From the sound of screaming brakes it could only be surmised that some wild thing must have suddenly appeared from the wooded slopes above the road—some deer or bobcat or fox—and in braking the car at such speed on the newly spread gravel the driver must have lost all control of the vehicle" (153). A futile effort is made to trace some such wild creature, but "no identifying track could be found." After offering this explanation the narrator concludes pointedly, "yet surely there could have been no other explanation for the frightful accident" (154). His implication is clear: Lizzy used her supernatural powers to cause the accident through some witchlike control of the wild animals of the mountain, or by appearing in the road herself.

But while we consider this possibility, he goes on to describe another scene that has a direct bearing on our interpretation of the accident. He is called to the morgue to identify the bodies of Tim and Sarah and records his "shock" at "the sight of the youthfully smooth and untroubled countenances of the two dead people—their dark heads of hair, the unblemished cheeks, the unwrinkled lids of the closed eyes, the serene expressions on their relaxed faces" (154). The "shock" he mentions and the physical detail of his description bring to mind a previous scene: Lizzy's discovery of Tim and Sarah making love, a scene that the narrator remembers in detail from her account some forty years earlier. These contrasting images of sex and death are the psychic engines of the story, profoundly indicative of the obsessive tendencies of the narrator's own mind. His denial of sexuality results in his fascination with physical deterioration, as in Lizzy's case, and with death, as embodied by Tim and Sarah.

Even the mode of the narrator's confirmation of the identities of the bodies has a macabre significance: "'Yes, yes!' I said, almost without thinking, and turning to the men who had escorted me there." There is more to his blurted assent than simple recognition or identification. His "yesses" can be read to suggest a profound satisfaction with what he surveys, and his reaction is complicated further when he adds, "And I could only think to myself, '*She* did this to them!' It was as if she had done it long years ago on the night they had eloped" (154-55).

The narrator's implication that Lizzy has caused Tim and Sarah's death is key to the most easily available psychological portrait of her as one who has been utterly warped by a need to revenge her earlier betrayal. Enhancing but also complicating this reading are the rumors of her supernatural powers, which, however skeptical we feel about them, add a compelling quality to this portrait, giving her life a mythical or archetypal dimension. In this respect the story can be opened to a feminist reading of a sort, with Lizzy representing a form of gendered victimization, her supernatural powers emblematic of a discovery or recovery of a source of alternative power in witchcraft. Though I believe that Taylor intended this view of Lizzy's character to be an open alternative as the reader moves through the story, it must be said that its credibility is weakened by the nature of its source, the narrator, whom we have begun to recognize as far from a disinterested player in the drama that he recounts.

As should by now be evident, "The Witch of Owl Mountain Springs" is not a story that is easily reducible to a unitary interpretation; Lizzy's character and her role in the events at the end of the story are crucial focal points for several variant readings. One might establish the poles of the possible interpretations as, on the one hand, the narrator's version—a straightforward account of Lizzy's acquisition of supernatural powers, her use of them to kill Tim and Sarah, and her coincidental murder later on by an unknown vagrant—and, on the other, an opposite reading positing the mentally unstable narrator's growing obsession with Lizzy and his final murder of her. The other puzzling elements of the story—the rumors about Lizzy's possession of "powers," the cause of Tim and Sarah's death, the extent to which the narrator is self-deluding—are all open to question. I incline toward an emphasis on the narrator's instability and his culpability in Lizzy's death, but this is not a story about which one can be absolutely certain.

The narrator's credibility is weakened by his comments and actions after he identifies the bodies of Tim and Sarah. Although he says that Lizzy "did this to them," he has even deeper resentments against her originating in his abortive relationship with her decades before. "Why had I come back to Owl Mountain Springs all these years? Why had I been destined to live so long as to see all vestiges of what I could love in Lizzy's face and figure entirely vanish? And at the last I found myself asking myself: was I ever in her mind any different from the others? And did *she* still have some hideous fate in mind for *me*?" (155). These are the thoughts of a man whose obsession is verging on paranoia. Subconsciously bonded to Tim and Sarah all these years through his own unacknowledged betrayal of Lizzy, he begins to recognize that bond when he views their corpses. Looking at them is an oblique form of self-recognition, and it helps to explain his horrified fascination with the superficial youthfulness that he emphasizes in his initial description of their bodies—a view that he has to revise: "Not until later did it occur to me that what I looked upon was the work of dye jobs and face-lifts and perhaps something of a local undertaker's work" (154). The narrator has confronted his own mortality in this scene, has recognized the decay beneath the superficial youthfulness. His shock manifests itself in a sudden upwelling of hatred and suspicion aimed at Lizzy and results in one of his curious blackouts, "another long period of sleep" punctuated by "a troubling nightmare of the kind you cannot afterward quite remember" (155).

He is wakened from that sleep with the news that "Miss Lizzy Pettigru's cottage was on fire" and is soon told by the postmistress that before the fire "Miss Lizzy had had her throat cut" (157).

Although Taylor is most often seen as an inheritor of a fictional tradition represented by Chekhov and James, I referred to Poe earlier to describe the mood of this story. The account of Lizzy's murder carries the mark of Poe even more decidedly, especially when we remember his "Ligeia" and "William Wilson," both narrated by unstable and unreliable characters whose narratives implicate them ever deeper in the violence of the stories. Although Taylor's narrator notes that "the postmistress, and everyone else later on, pronounced [Lizzy's murder] most clearly the work of one of the old vagrants from down in the cove" (157), a number of details point to the narrator: his mysterious sleep and unremembered dream while the murder was being committed, his trembling right hand as Lizzy's body is being brought out, the evidence of a clumsy attempt to cover the evidence by setting a fire, the murder knife wiped clean of fingerprints. None of these constitutes absolute proof, but together they bear the weight of our speculation better than any alternative. And most important, they fit the psychological portrait at the heart of the story of the narrator as a man whose inner and outer lives are so utterly divorced from each other that some sort of violent eruption is always lurking.

The theme implicit in the violence of the story's ending is the danger of evading self-knowledge. Even though "The Witch of Owl Mountain Springs" is unusual in its plot and setting, it shares with most of Taylor's other works a concentration on the problematics of identity. It is an analysis of the individual's success or failure in understanding the process whereby he or she is defined by early experience, family, and the larger culture, and the extent to which it is possible to assert some unique quality of being that works in opposition to that definition. Evasion and self-delusion play a destructive role in the process by feeding on the energy of self-exploration and often diverting it. The narrator, who caries self-evasion to a horrifying extreme, exemplifies its destructive power.

Taylor's purposes in "The Witch of Owl Mountain Springs" are further illuminated in "The Oracle at Stoneleigh Court," a related story whose narrator also seems increasingly unreliable as it unfolds. This story too centers on the failure of a relationship between a man and a woman and is formulated as a narrative of memory much like that of "In the Miro District" or "The Old Forest." In this form, as we have seen, memory and self-exploration can also serve as modes of evasion and self-justification. But "The Oracle of Stoneleigh Court" is further complicated by the narrator's own confusion about his conflicting desires.

Much of the energy of the story derives from the narrator's vivid recollection of Lila Montgomery, who spurns his offer of marriage. His passion for her, recalled here decades after their parting, is still persuasive, and his emotion engages us even as we witness the sad failure of this relationship because of confusion, miscommunication, and pride. Though we come to understand how that failure reveals the weakness of each character, the story centers on the narrator's self-absorbed insensitivity, of which Lila is, at the end, the victim.

Although the relationship between the narrator and Lila is the focus of the story, a different character provides its title and frames and sustains its narrative development. Augusta St. John–Jones, the narrator's Aunt Gussie, is the "oracle" of the Stoneleigh Court apartments in Washington. The widow of a Tennessee politician who died soon after his election to the House of Representatives, Aunt Gussie has forged her identity through her resolve to maintain her increasingly precarious place in Washington society. The narrator, stationed in Washington briefly at the outbreak of World War II, looks up his aunt out of what he admits are "obscure needs quite beyond my own comprehension" (3) but needs that are surely related to a desire to come into better knowledge and more sympathetic understanding of his family past. Aunt Gussie, aged seventy-five when the narrator reacquaints himself with her, claims occult powers that keep her in direct contact with figures from the family history, especially the narrator's grandfather, a Tennessee governor who also served in the United States Senate.[12] "You do look so like your late distinguished grandfather," Aunt Gussie tells him during their first meeting. "And sometimes, you know, he comes here still" (17).

The narrator is curious about Aunt Gussie's profession of knowledge about his past but alarmed by her intense interest in his future, sensing her desire to bind him to a family tradition about which he feels deep ambivalence. His fears are confirmed when Aunt Gussie begins to take an interest in Lila, offering her career help that turns out to be destructive of his romantic pursuit of her. In response to his marriage proposal Lila tells him of her desire for "something other than this life—something else, though I don't yet know what" (38). Later, in their final meeting before he leaves Washington for an overseas assignment, she explains further, "You see, I want to be somebody who matters." Aunt Gussie's Washington connections have yielded her a job offer "that [she] cannot resist" and that promises "bigger and bigger things." She confesses that she is "an ambitious creature" who is "wrapped up" in her future. "I am afraid I can't give myself to anybody else while that is the case" (42). Aunt Gussie has become a rival to the narrator, and Lila's painful and humiliating refusal of his proposal colors their relationship when it resumes under quite different circumstances after the war.

Lila's refusal is devastating to the narrator in part because she represents to him a means by which he can feel that he is an active participant in life rather than a passive bystander. Although we should never doubt his intense physical desire for her and the genuinely romantic spell that he seems to be under in her presence, this attraction wars with the passivity and indecisiveness that are the chief aspects of his personality. The narrator has originally attempted to register as a conscientious objector and believes that this protest accounts for his having been drafted early. Yet his attempt to claim conscientious objector status seems to have been halfhearted, not pursued with particular vigor, and he apparently accepts his military status philosophically. This is typical of his overly self-conscious ambivalence. He accepts the draft as a stroke of fate that relieves him of the pressure to shape his own life.

For Lila the war makes a satisfying Washington career more attainable. "I am afraid the war is my oyster," she tells him, and possibly her "only chance" for the "something other than this life" that she has not yet identified (38). Lila is confused about her direction and motives, but she differs from the narrator in her straightforward ambition to make work and public activity more central in her life.

The narrator's decision to propose to Lila before he goes overseas is prompted by a long discussion with Aunt Gussie about his ancestry, during which she temporarily overcomes his resistance to his family history. The series of "apparitions" she produces for him—including his grandfather as a young orator, then governor, then "in full feather on the floor of the Senate chamber" (35-36), as well as his grandmother and other members of the family—make a deep impression on him. He refers to these "apparitions" variously as the product of Aunt Gussie's "narrative," "stagecraft," and "mesmerism" (35), equating these modes of expression and implying that the imagination, as it manifests itself in narrative or on the stage, is a form of the occult and that the occult, as Aunt Gussie practices it in her Stoneleigh Court apartment, is a work of high art. Aunt Gussie's re-creation of the family is preceded by her reading of the narrator's palm, a sign of her magical command of past and future. Aligning him with her own sensibility, claiming him, in a sense, as one of her own, she declares that after he has "known experience," he "will finally become some kind of artist" (35). The narrator's "visibly trembling" hand signifies his deep apprehension of her prophetic powers and his equally strong desire to place himself passively in her keeping, accepting the family past that she delineates for him as the basis of his "true calling" (34).

That the narrator is indeed under Aunt Gussie's "spell" confirms her power, as a representative of his family past over his future. Her identity as "oracle," one in touch with the future, arises from her intimate knowledge of the family and implies that he must accept a fated or determined course of life that recapitulates the lives of his ancestors. These ancestors, his politician grandfather in particular, are daunting personalities, especially as Aunt Gussie evokes them with her dramatic-occult powers. The narrator is *haunted* by these figures, feeling himself to be a member of a generation in declension from more potent generations of predecessors.

After giving himself over to Aunt Gussie's vision of the past, the narrator realizes the desire for deep experience that his passivity has heretofore denied him. "I had a strong feeling," he tells us in recounting Aunt Gussie's presentation of his family history, "of the richness of life and the pleasure that was to be had in looking back into things that were unchanging and seemingly unchangeable in the world I came out of" (36), a feeling that connected him with the wellsprings of life. He leaves her apartment wanting "to pursue the same rich human endeavors that my forebears had pursued before me," and he fears dying in battle before "taking to wife some truly glorious girl that fate had sent my way" (36). Immediately after the meeting with Aunt Gussie, he seeks Lila out to propose marriage.

When Lila refuses his proposal, therefore, she refuses his entire destiny, as it seems to him, and cuts him off from what appears at that moment to be his most direct path to genuine "experience." Even more painful to him is her confession that Aunt Gussie has been a prime influence in her refusal, since she has encouraged Lila in her ambition to pursue a Washington career. Lila has chosen what she feels will be a life of fuller experience, as her desire for "something other than this life" (38) suggests. When she explains that "I want so to be somebody who matters" (42), she implies that a life as the narrator's wife would *not* matter.

Aunt Gussie's spell, which now seems to extend over Lila as well, has therefore inspired both of them to seek more actively the full experience of life. Aunt Gussie, in some ways denied such experience by the early death of her husband, has sought to regain it vicariously through her influence on Lila and the narrator. She offers yet another example from Taylor's work of the disastrous consequences of intergenerational warfare, her desire for vicarious experience becoming an increasingly destructive force in the lives of Lila and the narrator.

The narrator proposes marriage to Lila just before he is to be sent overseas, and his experience there establishes the framework of the latter half of the story, in which their relationship is reestablished on quite different grounds. The irony of his war experience is that despite his earlier desire to achieve status as a conscientious objector, he becomes a war hero, winning the Medal of Honor for single-handedly capturing two dozen German soldiers during the D-Day invasion of Normandy. But he cannot remember his heroic deeds, having buried the traumatic experience in his subconscious. He is able to recount the events only because others have told him of them, and he lives in a state of perpetual embarrassment over both his acts and his inability to connect them to the person he now knows as himself. He returns to the Memphis home of his parents to recuperate from his wounds, but he is also in full retreat from the world that he had wanted to experience before the war. The shock of the war has incapacitated him for experience or, perhaps more accurately, augmented the passivity that has always obstructed his pursuit of experience.

The narrator's retreat in Memphis is interrupted, however, when Lila accompanies the dying Aunt Gussie back to Tennessee and uses the trip as an opportunity to reestablish her relationship with him. She suggests what appears to be a significant change in her attitude when she steps off the train and gives the narrator "a kiss on my lips of the kind I most assuredly had never before received from her," a kiss that he labels "no less than alarming" (55). Both Lila's kiss and the narrator's reaction to it signal the important changes that have taken place during their three-year separation. Just as she showed very little physical affection to him in their early courtship — "our affair in those early days had been almost entirely platonic" (55), he explains — he had then showed little of the coldness and prudishness that constitute his reaction to her "alarming" kiss. In the aftermath of the war they have traded roles. She is now the pursuer and he the pursued, and the reasons for this change are of great importance.

In one reading of the story, the one that seems to reflect the narrator's version of events most closely, Lila's change of attitude is the result of the fame and public approbation that he has achieved as a war hero—fame, we must remember, from which he seems to flee. He never offers such an explanation directly, but it is the conclusion to which his recital of the events inevitably leads us, and it is bolstered by his sense that Aunt Gussie has had an important influence on the growth of Lila's interest in him. When he sees his aunt for the first time in the Memphis hospital where she spends her final days, she greets him with a very straightforward account of her motives: "You young scamp you, you see I have hunted you out in the wilds of West Tennessee in order to return your 'fantastically good-looking girl' to your safekeeping! I think you will find her worthy of the war hero that you have become" (58-59). As the narrator soon discovers, Aunt Gussie and Lila became firm friends during the war, "read accounts of my own Normandy exploits in the newspaper," and accounted him a "hero" (65).

Clearly, Aunt Gussie's reading of the narrator's fate has come to include his marriage to Lila, but the narrator no longer feels so impelled to seek that fate. His exposure to the realities of the war, an example of what human society at its worst could produce, seems to have strengthened the passive and retiring element of his personality, turning him inward and inclining him against the larger public world that Aunt Gussie and his ancestors have represented and that Lila, too, has embraced. This reemergence of his identity as a "conscientious objector" is ironically punctuated by his actual experience as a war hero, the memory of which he has repressed. And as the story unfolds we come to understand that he is an "objector" not just to military service but to the whole bewildering direction of the modern world in the postwar era.

The narrator's changed attitude is represented by his relationship with Ruthie Ann Sedwick, who seems to offer him the possibility of a life of quiet and withdrawn domesticity in Memphis, as opposed to the public life that Lila has sought in Washington.[13] The narrator has been dating Ruthie Ann when Lila arrives in Memphis, forcing him into a choice between them that is deeply revelatory of his own values and self-conception.

The narrator feels that Lila has changed during the three years she has been working in Washington, a change that might best be described as an increased artificiality in her manner. The "companionable and always impersonal feeling that had formerly marked her personality" when they first knew each other had made her somewhat mysterious but nevertheless genuinely engaging. But when she arrives in Memphis, he notices a "peculiar mixture of rigidity and effusiveness of manner that most distinctly set the new Lila apart from the old." She seems to him to have lost her impressive ability to meet others on the basis of their individuality and now to have "a oneness in her way of addressing people where once there had been great shades and distinctions at hand for everyone" (62-63). Moreover, he comments on the extensive wardrobe she has brought from Washington, a sign of her professional success but also an indication of the superficiality that disturbs him. In a telling later comment he notes that his family reacted to Lila as if she were "a veritable reincarnation" of Aunt Gussie (72). It is as if she has, in searching for the unknown identity that she felt the world of Washington held for her, adopted the one already created by Aunt Gussie. The narrator's new friend Ruthie Ann provides a framework for his new perception of Lila because he believes that "she was always without personal ambition or vanity" and, in contrast to Lila, "seemed content enough to continue always living there alone with her mother" in a life of quiet simplicity (76).

The narrator's portrayals of the two women emphasize the contrast between Lila's seemingly complex artificiality and Ruthie Ann's natural simplicity, a contrast that eventually provides the basis for his choice. Yet it should not be forgotten that this contrast is also a measure of the narrator's perception, colored by his own motives and his felt need to rationalize his decision. Has Lila changed so radically, we might ask, or is her "change" due in part to his perception of her?

The question is most pressing when we attempt to understand the narrator's account of their lovemaking the evening after she arrives from Memphis. As he tells us, it is Lila who initiates the sexual encounter, making two sudden and uncharacteristic changes of mind in the process. He describes his sense after dinner that first night, as he is taking her home, that she is "the same old Lila Montgomery" he knew before; her passionate kiss seems to have faded in significance now. But this perception is momentary: "Then as if she had changed her mind—had had it changed for her by some power outside herself—she relaxed her grip on the door handle and asked, 'Won't you come in for a while?'" The narrator needs little encouragement: "I was out of the car almost at once," he remembers, noting that "her change of heart—or mind—seemed irresistible to me" (69). After the two of them go into the house, Lila seems to undergo "another sudden change of intention" and leads him to her bedroom, where they begin a "brutish love-making" which, despite his apparent eagerness, he finds unsatisfying, a "mechanical and most unnatural performance" that left them more "strangers" than they had been before. He puzzles over his impression that Lila was "driven . . . by some other desire or some other power than her own" (70).

Although the narrator appears not to comprehend the implications of his repeated references to the alien power that seems to have motivated Lila to make love with him, his comments imply that she is under the power of Aunt Gussie, that her actions are an expression of Gussie's will and Gussie's lust, not her own. In the complications and interpretive possibilities of this scene, Taylor's narrative becomes slippery and indeterminate in the extreme, principally because of the increasing difficulty of judging the credibility of the narrator's reports of Aunt Gussie's occult powers and, more generally, assessing the reliability of the narrator in other matters. Taylor's late fiction is characterized by narrators who are, in varying degrees, self-deluded or deceptive, and these stories often use memory and retrospective narration to dramatize the competition between honest self-appraisal and callous self-justification. Within this framework of problematized epistemology, the motif of the occult plays an important role not only in "The Oracle at Stoneleigh Court" but, as we have seen, in "The Witch of Owl Mountain Springs." The elements of the supernatural, reminiscent of Poe and Hawthorne in their ambiguity, may constitute a literal account of the narrated events, necessarily requiring us to accept their reality for the purposes of the story, or they may constitute a way of representing some deeper truth about the working of the mind.

The difficulty of interpreting the narrator's sexual encounter with Lila is augmented by the mixture of fascination and revulsion with which he relates it. Although he responds eagerly to Lila's initiative, he is also disturbed by it, as if it constitutes damning evidence that she is no longer the innocent girl of his dreams. Their "brutish" lovemaking seems in retrospect to be "indubitable evidence" (70) of the sexual experience that he had gained during the war and that she had gained, he believed, in Washington during the war years. It is as if, emerging from the war, each lost an innocence that had been an important aspect of their relationship. Their erotic encounter drives them further apart—or, more accurately, drives *him* away from her. Within a few pages we find him confessing his "great desire"—

even a feeling of "torture"—to "repeat the performance" (74-75), yet further in the narrative he remarks, "I never slept with her again, though. I was spared that" (79). This extreme self-division is evidence of a mind at war with his desires.

The narrator's account of his reunion with Lila seems intended to create the impression that he is a victim pursued by not one but two women, one of whom exerts an odd occult power over the other. This perspective grows as the narrative develops, for the narrator becomes increasingly explicit about the connection between Lila and Aunt Gussie. He notes that his family seems to regard Lila as "a veritable reincarnation" of Aunt Gussie and speculates that "the great change I thought I had noted in Lila" was in fact the "influence" of his aunt (72-73). By representing Lila as the helpless pawn of Aunt Gussie and her occult powers, the narrator simultaneously portrays himself as Aunt Gussie's intended victim, a man whose essential virtue and autonomy are under attack.

The narrator's response to this challenge is to seek a safer haven in his relationship with Ruthie Ann Sedwick. He goes to see her the day after his affair with Lila, not to confess, he tells us, but rather "to stand in her presence and try to discern what my own feelings would be when she and I stood face to face" (75). Ruthie Ann, "a serious amateur horticulturist," is hanging tomato plants upside down in her basement in order to ripen the last of their fruit—a domestic and nurturing activity that emphasizes her contrast to Lila, with her impressive business wardrobe and professional ambition. Ruthie Ann, he tells us, has "an almost perpetual smile on her generous mouth" and a "sense of her own dignity" that does not destroy her spontaneity. Her lack of vanity and her capacity to seem serenely content with her quiet life appeal to him. "When we were talking a while that day among the upside-down tomato plants, suddenly I found myself stepping forward and then leaning among those upside-down plants to embrace for the first time this girl I knew I had fallen in love with" (76). This innocent kiss among the tomato plants is in stark contrast to the "brutish" lovemaking of the evening before, and it seems to clarify the narrator's confused feelings, enabling him to begin the process that will lead to his choosing Ruthie Ann over Lila for his wife. Even though the passion that Lila awakened in him before the war may still be present, it is sufficiently complicated now to prevent his acting on it without reservation. Ruthie Ann offers him a refreshing simplicity, a purity of motive, but her real value to him is that she represents a refuge from Lila.

Drawn to the simplicity of her life with her mother, he takes to heart Ruthie Ann's Thoreauvian comment that they are able to live so happily together "because we want so little." This lack of ambition and material desire allow them "to remain at peace with the world," and he finds them to be conscientious objectors in the purest sense of that term. But he also notes that he met them "just before it would have been too late"—before, that is, "the worldly Lila would have swept me up into her arms and made a national celebrity of me, the unknown war hero," by taking him back to "the great world of D.C." where such status was most important. This comparison of his possible lives with Ruthie Ann and Lila leads him to a decisive moment of insight about his fate, a moment, he claims, of moral clarity: "What I recognized was that there just might be time for me to save myself" (81).

He decides, therefore, that he must marry Ruthie Ann and "do so at once" (82). They hastily arrange a ceremony across the river in Arkansas, without announcing their plans to his family or to Lila. There is no discernible reason why such a quickly arranged marriage is necessary, or why it should be concealed until after it is done. The narrator acts so precipitously, in fact, that we suspect him of acting out of fear, trying to "save" himself, as he has said, from Lila and the life that she offers. He seems to feel that he is warding off some threatening force, and with that possibility we are reminded of the "spell" under which Aunt Gussie may have placed Lila. But the threatening force against to which he is really responding is his own desire. In marrying Ruthie Ann, he saves himself not only from Lila and Aunt Gussie but from himself, a "salvation" whose value has to be questioned.

Although the narrator may prefer that we see him acting from high motives in his choice of a life marked by "uneventful seclusion . . . gardening, reading our favorite fiction, taking turns with the shopping" (88)—having rejected "the worldly Lila" (81) and her ambitious plans—he is actually pushed toward that choice by a combination of insecurity, inner division, aversion to responsibility, guilty desire, and, arguably, resentment. In fact, revenge may be a more accurate word than resentment for this element of the narrator's motivation, and it represents the darkest and most elaborately concealed strand in his perplexing narrative.

The story is, from this perspective, an account of a man whose wounded pride demands that he reject the woman who once rejected him, even though he still desires her. The effect on Lila of his decision to marry Ruthie

Ann certainly augments this darker reading of his character and motivation. Upon hearing the narrator's brother blurt out the news of the marriage, Lila asks to lie down, explaining that she is "experiencing some kind of shock — some kind of electrical shock almost." The narrator, witnessing Lila's reaction in the presence of his family and Ruthie Ann, then offers this revealing comment: "I had the ugly impulse suddenly to burst into laughter." And when Lila proceeds to faint, he continues to be unmoved, feeling "a mixed compulsion again to laugh out loud and to go and try to say something consoling to the poor woman" (85). This is hardly the speech of a man who has only shortly before "saved" himself morally, and his hard-hearted contempt suggests that he has desired vengeance on Lila for a very long time.

The narrator is careful to check his watch for the exact time that Lila faints and tells us later that it coincided exactly with the time of Aunt Gussie's death. He dismisses this oddity as coincidental, but of course his making a point of it indicates his sense of its significance. The clear implication is that Aunt Gussie's death released Lila from the "spell" she had been under and even, perhaps, that Lila's learning of the narrator's marriage was connected with Aunt Gussie's death. That he reports these events adds some viability to a reading of the story that takes its supernatural elements literally, making it a modern version of the ghost tale. The cases for and against such a reading are as complex and finally indeterminate as the debates over the reality of the supernatural elements of Poe's "Ligeia" or James's "The Turn of the Screw." But as in those works, the supernatural motif in "The Oracle at Stoneleigh Court" also opens the story to important psychological insights. Clearly, the narrator remains obsessed to the very end of the story with Aunt Gussie and her relations with Lila, and he feels pursued and threatened by those things that Aunt Gussie, and Lila, may be taken to represent: family, history, the necessity to take one's place in the world. Ruthie Ann seems to offer a way to escape all this, and he takes that opportunity, settling a score with an old flame in the process. But as he reflects on this decision late in his life, one can sense the desire that Lila's memory still provokes in him. He is, like other Taylor narrators, a man who looks back on a life of emotional failure and barrenness, much of it self-inflicted. His narrative reveals that emptiness, even as he consciously turns away from it.

PART 2

❖❖❖

Family and Culture

❖ 5 ❖
Losing Place

The Tennessee society in which Taylor situates his dramas of intergenerational conflict appears on first examination to be tightly ordered and elaborately structured. But in some moments of crisis it reveals itself to be disordered to the point of chaos. Taylor portrays a culture that has, sometimes uncomfortably, intermixed aspects of the plantation South and the frontier West, thus embracing conflicting codes of familial paternalism and extreme individualism. In both cases, as Taylor observes, women are often the victims of restrictive social codes. But even these conflicting elements of Tennessee culture were in a state of rapid flux in the earlier twentieth century as the upper South became more urban and affluent and merged more closely with the dominant stream of modern American culture.

In a 1987 interview with Barbara Thompson, Taylor described his own complicated relation with the shifting culture of the twentieth-century South: "I have always said that there are no more loyal Southerners than those who grew up *just* outside the South or in the Border States. We lived in a little South of our own in St. Louis. We had a houseful of servants from my father's farm in the cotton country of West Tennessee, and the adults— black and white—would talk about the South, about the way things used to be there" (*Conversations*, 139). This houseful of displaced persons understood that an old world was lost to them, and they faced their new America warily, bearing a burden of remembrance and preservation.

Taylor shared that wariness, but he would develop a profound skepticism of Southern regional puffery and cultural self-delusion. The early influence of the Southern Agrarian movement, mediated through Allen Tate and John Crowe Ransom, provided Taylor with an example of a commitment to search out a lost or bypassed culture in hopes of finding there a usable stance toward modern life. But after some youthful enthusiasm for the project, Taylor came to see Southern identity as more a problem than a solution to the challenge of modern life, especially when Southern regional pieties thickened. Nevertheless, he shared the Agrarians' central concern with cultural displacement and infused that problem into many of his stories.[1]

The struggles for maturity and the conflicts between generations that we have observed in the works discussed in previous chapters can be regarded not only as attempts to achieve self-comprehension and personal balance—maturity and integration in a psychological sense—but as explorations of social place. Taylor's characters face perennial difficulty in discovering or confirming where they belong in Southern society and how they should regard their place, be it exalted or humble. His most illuminating dramatizations of character involve depictions of an individual's reaction to a felt loss of place and the wrenching struggle to hold or reassert a fading social identity. This is of course complicated by the shifting nature, and what Madison Smartt Bell has called the "extreme fragility" of the social structure itself.[2] In extremes, the problem becomes the more serious one of accepting utter defeat and facing the enormity of rebuilding a social identity. From these extremes emerge characters whose will and resources are tested to the fullest; those not broken by the experience achieve an enlarged command of their resources and a sense of survival that are the closest things to heroism in Taylor's decidedly unheroic world.

Although the problem of social displacement is shared by both sexes, Taylor's most vivid portrayals of it center on women, who, because of the severity of the definition of their social role, are most vulnerable to social change. Taylor's early fiction is dominated by women characters, whom he portrays with both acuity and sympathy, realizing that to understand their situation is to understand more completely the workings of Southern culture.[3] Harriet Wilson of "A Long Fourth" (1946) recognizes both the end of her motherhood and the end of her false sense of elevation over her African American maid Mattie in a story that details the crumbling of a social role in the face of the pressures of modernity. Aunt Munsie of "What You Hear from 'Em" (1951) faces abandonment by the white children that she has raised in Thornton, as they leave the small town of their birth for more successful lives in Nashville and Memphis. Miss Leonora Logan of "Miss Leonora When Last Seen" (1960) resists the efforts of her hometown of Thomasville to force her out of her house, her belief in education and racial harmony standing as a rebuke to the town's corrupt values. These women differ in their strength of character, from the powerful determination of Aunt Munsie and Miss Leonora to the confused weakness of Harriet. The roles they enact and the values they espouse also differ in important ways. But they share a desire to resist the drift of their culture, rightly or wrongly, and suffer enormously as a result. Each of them perceives this struggle as something of a life battle, for each feels in her own way that she is being asked to surrender a vital element of character, a role in which she has learned to define and cultivate herself and without which her past seems robbed of meaning.

The particular dilemma faced by these women can be better understood by recurrence to the phenomenon of disappearance that plays an important role in two of Taylor's later stories. In "The Old Forest" the disappearance of Lee Ann Deehart is the catalyst for the story's action, signifying a threat to that social structure. The attempt of the town's authorities to find her generates opposition from her friends, who bond together in hostility against Nat and the society that he represents. "Perhaps in old pioneer days," Nat speculates, "before the plantation and the neoclassic towns were made, the great forests seemed woman's last refuge from the brute she lived alone with in the wilderness" (*OF,* 53). Lee Ann's escape into the Old Forest enacts women's rebellion against gendered social roles, transforming her presumably personal act into one with broader social significance.

On the other hand, the narrator of *In the Tennessee Country* explains that Tennessee society had come to accept the disappearance of a man. "In the Tennessee country of my forebears it was not uncommon for a man of good character suddenly to disappear. He might be a young man or a middle-aged man or even sometimes a very old man. Whatever the case, few questions were ever asked" (*TC,* 3). Such disappearances, rather than being seen as a tragedy or a crime or (as in the case of Lee Ann) a threat to the social fabric, were regarded as a necessary safety valve for society, incidents which—however unsettling for those near to or dependent upon the man—were nevertheless necessary and justified.

This difference in the social assessment of a man's and a woman's disappearance demonstrates Taylor's representation of the differing weight of social expectation on women, and thus to the correspondingly greater importance accorded to maintaining defined social roles in the formation and preservation of a woman's identity. This was one of the earliest and most persuasive themes of his fiction. Given the intensity of these social demands, Taylor also recognized that the pressures of social change that unsettle established roles are more likely to be dramatically exemplified in the characters of women.

In "A Long Fourth" Taylor studies the life crisis of a middle-aged woman, Harriet Wilson, linking her psychological trauma to the unraveling of her place within the upper-middle-class culture of the modern South. Harriet's self-definition and sense of security are largely dependent, as Taylor shows, on class and racial distinctions that are fundamentally oppressive to those against whom Harriet defines herself. Yet even though her unthinking acceptance of these deeply flawed values makes her unsympathetic in many respects, her situation is not without its pathos. Nor is her case an unimportant one, for Taylor represents her as a woman entrapped in the deeply gendered divisions of Southern culture.

Harriet is "a pretty woman just past fifty," whose husband (we know him only as "Sweetheart" in the story) remains enthralled by her beauty even after years of marriage. Although he assures her that "you're nobody's fool, darling" (*OF*, 198), much of the story works to prove that she is almost everybody's fool, a woman who has traded both her independence and her self-respect for the comfort of being taken care of. Taylor exposes her self-delusion through his ironic presentation of her attempts at self-justification, a train of thought prompted by her husband's gentle dismissal of her in an early conversation. "But really she had always considered that she was nobody's fool and that she certainly was not merely a vain little woman ruled by a husband's flattery, the type her mother had so despised in her lifetime" (198-99). Taylor plants this suspicion of Harriet's vanity and weakness early in the story and then details the wracking process through which she is finally forced to confront the truth of it. That confrontation is devastating psychologically to Harriet, but it also reaches beyond her particular condition because it entails a much larger social force—racism. Harriet is brought down by the very element in her life that has provided her a false elevation: her privileged social position in a racially divided culture.

The vehicle of Harriet's self-confrontation is her maid Mattie, a long-time employee in the Wilson household who has also raised her nephew, B.T., there. The story begins with Harriet's conversation with her husband about getting B.T. off the place. He has become a nuisance and at times an embarrassment to Harriet, but Sweetheart still retains a sense of paternalistic obligation toward him, and this initial disagreement is the sign of an important shift in social attitudes that makes the story a cultural fable as well as a psychological study. The bond of obligation between master and servant that signified the idealized version of Southern racial relations has clearly begun to erode in the Wilson household, and though Harriet is less willing than her husband to maintain the old loyalties, she is not prepared to face the consequences of racial egalitarianism either.

The Wilson house itself is an emblem of the changing social milieu that the story records. Sweetheart, a Nashville physician, is clearly given to nostalgia, attempting to preserve a version of the Old South in his house and acreage, "eight miles from downtown Nashville on the Franklin Pike" (199). Mattie, a house servant, works in the kitchen, while B.T. plays the role of fieldhand, working in the Wilsons' yard and large garden. As their domestic arrangements signify, the Wilsons are mid-twentieth-century suburbanites still in the thrall of the values and signs of meaning of the Old South. In this situation Harriet has only her role in the family as a source of belonging and personal fulfillment. Albert J. Griffith, noting her complete identification with that role, characterizes her as "a latter-day hearth goddess, a custodian of domestic virtues and values" (31). She and Sweetheart could perhaps sustain their illusion of living in a changeless world indefinitely, but it is not a world that their children can or will maintain. As Harriet begins in middle age to realize that her position and purpose in life have begun to be undermined, she is left with little emotional sustenance and is finally forced to confront the hollow fiction by which she has lived.

Harriet's "long Fourth" is the holiday weekend occasioned by the visit of her beloved "Son," who is returning from his work at a New York publishing firm for a final stay at home before his induction into the army at the beginning of World War II. The visit is momentous for Harriet, who has been "worrying for weeks about Son's going into the Army and how he would fit in there" (201). But its significance is even greater because he is bringing a woman friend, Ann Prewitt, with him. The story follows the contours of the family's preparation for the visit, as reflected primarily in Harriet's household preoccupations and her necessary interaction with her husband, children, and servants. But paralleling the looming crisis of Son's visit and subsequent departure for the Army is a similar crisis in Mattie's life: B.T. is preparing to leave the Wilson household to work in an aircraft factory, and the prospect of losing him is weighing heavily on Mattie.

With the inclusion of Mattie's parallel situation, Taylor opens an important expectation in the story, the hope that Harriet and Mattie will find a bond in their common loss; this would add strength and dignity to both their characters by suggesting that each has opened herself in new ways to compensate for the change she is undergoing. But their shared difficulty is obscured by the Southern racial divide. Even though Harriet sympathizes with Mattie superficially, Taylor makes her essential detachment clear by recording the trivial personal worries that preoccupy her while she listens to Mattie and makes gestures to console her. In truth, Harriet wants B.T. to go, but not before the holiday weekend she is planning, when she will need his assistance. All Harriet considers is her own need to have sufficient "help" during the visit, and she is relieved to find that B.T.'s intended departure is not until after the weekend and will thus not involve any inconvenience to her.

Harriet's hypocritical reaction to Mattie's concern reveals her insularity and insensitivity, but it is important to qualify that description by noting that her insensitivity does not seem constitutional; it is limited quite narrowly to racial categories. Taylor's portrait of Harriet thus explores the larger impact of socially generated racial categories and their power to subsume individuals.[4] Harriet is not a woman who is normally insensitive to the feelings and opinions of others; in fact, she is arguably too sensitive to them, staking much of her self-worth on being able to satisfy those opinions. But her sensitivity is strictly bounded by the racial division that constitutes a key part of her Southern cultural inheritance.

Mattie, stung by her grief at the loss of B.T., is the character through whom we recognize Harriet's thwarted sensibility. Mattie's grief makes her desperately vulnerable and thus less cautious about overstepping the boundaries between black and white, as indicated in her direct appeal to their shared maternal role and expectation of ready sympathy. "Miss Harriet," she says, "it's like you losin' Mr. Son. B.T. is gwine too." But the comparison triggers revulsion and anger in Harriet, who rejects Mattie's appeal utterly. "How dare you? That will be just exactly enough from you!" she retorts (208). The scene reveals not only how deeply Harriet is bound to her culture's racist attitudes but also the location of her deepest emotional vulnerability. She is desperately overprotective of Son and, we come to learn, disturbed not only by his going into the army but by a more frightening suspicion that her love for him is not fully repaid.

Son arrives with Ann not long after Harriet's difficult encounter with Mattie, and it is evident that her reaction to his arrival is in part conditioned by her attempt to deny Mattie's assertion of their shared situation. She tells herself that Son's good looks and gentlemanly demeanor confirm "the justice of her outraged feelings this afternoon." Moreover, she sees Ann, "a ladylike young woman in the black traveling dress and white gloves," as evidence that she has "even underestimated the grossness of Mattie's reflection upon him." But these attempts at self-justification do not succeed; in her sadness and fear she begins to cry, and her weeping becomes "so violent now and . . . so entirely a physical thing that it seem[s] not to correspond to her feelings at all" (211).

Harriet insists so desperately on the difference between Son and B.T. because it reinforces the difference between her and Mattie, a distinction that is important to her not primarily for racial reasons but because of her emotional vulnerability as a mother. Her racial prejudice masks a deeper feeling of emotional insecurity that the maturity of her children, and their disregard for her, has created. Harriet's insecurity becomes more dramatic when she later overhears Son and Ann calmly and analytically discussing her weeping and its possible causes. "I can't imagine what it is," Son says to Ann. "Something seems to have come over her. But there's no visible change. She hasn't aged any. I looked for it in her hair and in the skin about her neck and in her figure." Son's cold discussion of his mother's aging seems to indicate that she has already lost her role as mother: "It hardly seemed possible to Harriet that this was Son talking about herself" (214). When she witnesses his objectification of her, the world that she has known and in which she has had a secure place spirals away from her as an alien thing.

In overhearing Son speak about her, Harriet experiences the same objectification that she has forced on Mattie. This ironic reversal of roles, in which Harriet is injured through the same insensitivity that she has shown to another, also exposes the limitation of her judgment of Son, who strikes us as far from the saint his mother assumes him to be. Harriet's accidental discovery of his detached and clinical analysis of her is perhaps even more painful than a direct rejection, because it suggests that Son's apparent regard for her has been duplicitous and that there is no deep emotional bond beneath his veneer of filial devotion.

The change in cultural attitudes that many young Southerners were undergoing in the 1940s is exemplified in Son, who presents us with the difficult problem of a character whose racial and social attitudes are more progressive than his mother's, even though he appears to have serious personality flaws. He is, as Ashley Brown has commented, a "cold, indifferent observer of other people's weaknesses" (84). His successful career in the New York publishing business has created a chasm between his childhood and his adult life. Harriet senses the change, as her anguished reflection at the end of the story suggests: "It seemed that her children no longer existed; it was as though they had all died in childhood as people's children used to do" (236). But until this visit Son had been very much alive to

Harriet, a "model son" growing up and "so good about keeping in touch" after moving to New York. "What the young people [in Nashville] thought especially fine was that, being the intellectual sort, which he certainly was, he had been careful never to offend or embarrass his family with the peculiar, radical ideas which he would naturally have" (210). Son is relatively successful in keeping his real life and attitudes hidden from his family, but one wonders whether to categorize this as polite consideration or cynical condescension.

The hint of Son's duplicity that Harriet discovers in the overheard conversation is confirmed later in a difficult and embarrassing confrontation provoked by Ann Prewitt. Harriet's assumption has been that Son was bringing Ann home as his fiancée, or something near it, but that assumption is gradually undermined. Harriet's daughter Kate observes to her mother that Son is "not at all" in love with Ann, and that she "never looks at him" (227). This is in part gossipy speculation on Kate's part and, as we eventually find out, only half right, but it puts the nature of the relation in doubt and raises further questions about his relations with others, including his family. Harriet is disturbed by Kate's speculation, for she has been hoping to find the signs of a "normal" or conventional pattern in Son's life, which the visit with Ann at first seemed to signify.

Ann confirms our suspicions about Son's character with a direct and bitter denunciation of him before the entire family. Son approves of people only when they "amuse" him, she says acidly. "He cares nothing for anything I say except when I'm talking theory of some kind." As she sees it, Son has brought her with him to Nashville expecting her to express "disagreeable" opinions to the family, "while he behaves with conventional good taste." Ann's denunciation is an awkward moment for the Wilson family, to say the least. Sweetheart listens "with his hands hanging limp at his sides and his mouth literally wide open." But in contrast with the rest of his family, Son quickly ceases "to show any discomfort," distancing himself from the awkward encounter as an amused spectator. "You are really drunk, Ann. But go on. You're priceless. You're rich. What else about me?" (232). As this scene makes clear, Harriet has invested much of her emotional life in a person who is cold and haughty, and her hope of ever receiving any form of emotional sustenance from him, beyond empty civilities, is very slim. We cannot help but speculate on her part in having made him what he is, but that does not entirely negate her pathos at this moment.

This series of increasingly tense revelations and confrontations forces Harriet into a severe emotional crisis in which she comes to recognize her exclusion from true agency in the world and to find that the social role she has accepted, as Southern wife and matriarch, has evaporated. It is useful to compare Harriet with Caroline Braxley of "The Old Forest" in this respect: each of them faces an erosion of power and thus of identity in the changing situation of women in the modernizing South. "Power, or strength, is what everybody must have some of if he—if she—is to survive in any kind of world" Caroline has realized (*OF*, 88). But Harriet is discovering, too late, that the power she thought she had is empty or illusory.

The story's final crisis, and perhaps its most intense, again involves Harriet's relation with Mattie and returns to the parallel between the two that is its core of significance. After Ann's outburst about Son has played itself out, Harriet retreats to her bedroom, attempting to find some solace in repeating the Lord's Prayer, a last desperate gesture toward a world of stable, traditional values that has seemed to disappear. But Harriet is not allowed even this form of escape. Her prayer is interrupted by "the fierce shout of a Negro woman" (233), a voice she recognizes as Mattie's. Mattie has waited in B.T.'s shack behind the house all evening to drive off the woman that she suspects her nephew will bring back there. Everyone in the Wilson household is aware of B.T.'s habit of bringing prostitutes home with him, so Mattie's decision to attempt to intervene in his life now has to be regarded as a desperate attempt to reassert maternal control over him, even as he prepares to leave. It is a gesture provoked in part by jealousy and in part by her desperate sense of abandonment, an indication that her emotional crisis over the separation is, like Harriet's, of great severity. To intervene in his plans for the evening is apparently Mattie's only available means of resistance to B.T.'s departure, in the face of which she feels helplessly alone.

The shout that Harriet hears is Mattie's confrontation with the woman, whom she does succeed in driving away. But she drives B.T. away as well and thus faces the same sort of lonely vigil that Harriet is suffering. When Sweetheart asks Harriet to try to bring Mattie in and calm her, the two women are brought together at the moment of their most intense vulnerability. Harriet recognizes that just as Mattie has been an element of her own crisis this weekend, she has been part of Mattie's, and that to help her at all she must attempt to reestablish their broken contact. She finds Mattie alone in the cabin, and her offer of conciliation is direct: "'Mattie,' she said at last, 'I was unkind to you Saturday. You must not hold it against me'" (235). Admittedly this is a late apology, but at least Harriet does not attempt to cover over or excuse her insensitivity.

Mattie meets the apology with equal directness, offering "neither forgiveness nor resentment. . . . In her eyes there was grief and there was something beyond grief." She is in control of herself, however: "After a moment she did speak, and she told Harriet that she was going to sit there all night and that they had all better go on to bed in the house." But there is more to this declaration than the simple assertion of Mattie's command over the situation. "Later when Harriet tried to recall the exact tone and words Mattie had used — as her acute ear would normally have allowed her to do — she could not reconstruct the speech at all. It seemed as though Mattie had used a special language common to both of them but one they had never before discovered and could now never recover" (235).

This moment of achieved communication, impermanent and unrecoverable, is the referent by which we can judge the tragedy that the story portrays. Taylor intimates that the shared ground between Mattie and Harriet was important and that their respective crises of abandonment had offered a glimpse of their potential for mutual self-understanding. But the possibility for realizing that shared ground has passed. Harriet, after a silence, leaves Mattie, "but she looked back once more and she saw that besides the grief and hostility in Mattie's eyes there was an unspeakable loneliness for which she could offer no consolation" (235-36).

Taylor is not a writer given to easy reconciliations or a naive sense of the redeeming possibilities of human relationships. The recognition of the missed possibility of some saving communication is the only solace that "A Long Fourth" offers, and the stress must be placed on "missed" rather than "possibility." The story ends with Harriet again in her room, unable to pray, unable to weep, and unable to forget Mattie and her lonely vigil. She is aware only of the dark and "the chill of autumn night about the room" (236).

Harriet Wilson's tragic sense of failure reflects Taylor's repeated concern that those who accept prescribed social roles too uncritically may find themselves abandoned as the social underpinnings of these roles shift. This is especially true for women, who must surrender so much of their autonomy to preserve the social structures of which they are a part. Aunt Munsie is Taylor's most dramatic exemplification of this danger, because as an African American woman she is the most rigidly defined by social roles, and the most vulnerable to changing social forces. Taylor's moving portrayal of her is rooted in his own experience, for as he explained to Barbara Thompson, she was modeled on his own nurse, "the same nurse my father had when he was a baby." "She absolutely belonged to us," he said, "or we absolutely belonged to her" (*Conversations,* 140). Taylor's understanding of the maternal bond and familial responsibility generated in such a relationship is the grounding of the story. But the narrative is also frank about the costs of such a relationship, especially in an era in which traditional social roles deriving from the hierarchy of the Old South were shifting rapidly.

Taylor introduces Aunt Munsie as a somewhat enigmatic and mildly comical character whose question to everyone in her hometown of Thornton is also the title of the story: "What You Hear From 'Em?" It can be correctly interpreted only by the town's old-timers, who understand Munsie's past. Newcomers sometimes take her for a beggar as she makes the rounds of town with her wagon gathering slop for her pigs. "They spoke of her as Old What Have You for Mom, because that's what they thought she was saying when she called out, 'What you hear from 'em?' Their ears were not attuned to that soft 'r' she put in 'from' or the elision that made 'from 'em' sound to them like 'for Mom'" (*CS*, 239). The irony of this mistake is that Munsie is in a sense one of the town's aristocrats, surrogate mother to the Tolliver children, one of Thornton's more prominent families. Her question divides the town, then, between the insiders who recognize her place and can respond to its deeper implications, and recent interlopers who lack the memory to understand.

That division indicates the change that is taking place—a modernization that is erasing the collective memory of Thornton as it replaces old ways with new. Aunt Munsie is the embodiment of the old ways, her slowly pulled wagon a constant barrier and rebuke to the automobiles that are becoming more and more common. "The dark macadam surfacing [of the streets] was barely wide enough for two automobiles to pass. Aunt Munsie, pulling her slop wagon, which was a long, low, four-wheeled vehicle about the size and shape of a coffin, paraded down the center of the street without any regard for, if with any awareness of, the traffic problems she sometimes made" (236). The shift to automobile traffic is the superficial sign of a much larger change that Thornton has undergone, the most serious aspect of which is the erosion of generational continuity by the mobility that accompanies economic opportunity.

What Munsie is really asking the people of Thornton is directly related to that generational change: What do you hear from Mr. Thad and Mr. Will? These are the Tolliver boys, whom she raised but who have now moved to Memphis and Nashville. But she is asking more than that; she is asking when the boys will fulfill the promise they made her to return to Thornton. "All she wanted to hear from *them* was when they were coming back for good" (235). Of course they are not coming back; "They're prospering so, Munsie," Miss Lucille Satterfield remarks (241), and this explanation is a measure of the larger change that has come over Thornton, which is not "what it had been before the Great World War." Many of the town's bigger old homes are now empty, "not because nobody wanted to rent them or buy them but because the heirs who had gone off somewhere making money could never be got to part with 'the home place'" (238). Thad Tolliver with his Ford and Lincoln dealership in Memphis is typical of his generation, unable to pass up the money of the bigger cities but equally unable to admit, at least to Munsie, that he is never coming home.

Munsie's repeated question and the persistence of her habitual rounds of slop gathering are indications that she has not fully comprehended the finality of the changes in Thornton. This is partly due to her age; she was born as a slave and is in her eighties when the key events of the story occur. But her resistance to the change goes deeper; it is rooted in the accommodations she has made within the South's hierarchical culture. As servant to a prominent family she assumed its status, and her role transcended that of servant when she took over the household after the death of Mrs. Tolliver. "Without being able to book read or even make numbers, she had finished raising the whole pack of towheaded Tollivers just as the Mizziz would have wanted it done. The Doctor told her she *had* to—he didn't ever once think about getting another wife, or taking in some cousin, not after his 'Molly darling'—and Aunt Munsie *did*" (244).

This extraordinary demand could have been made only in the context of the racial hierarchy of the South, and Munsie's remarkable accomplishment—we must accord her that—did not come without a price: she formed a closer emotional bond with Thad and Will Tolliver than with her own daughter Crecie. But the changes in Thornton that have called Thad and Will away to the cities have stripped her of the position she filled with such distinction. She measures her life in terms of "those halcyon days after the old Mizziz had died and Aunt Munsie's word had become law in the Tolliver household" (244). Her resistance to Thornton's change stems from her reluctance to relinquish the role she had so admirably performed.

This description of her may seem to imply that she is a nostalgic sentimentalist, but Crecie describes her as "hard about people and things in the world" and says that she will not reminisce about her childhood, her marriage, or even her life with the Tollivers: "Mama's a good old soul, I reckon, but when something's past, it's gone and done with for Mama. She don't think about day before yestiddy—yestiddy, either" (244-45). What Crecie notices in her mother is one manifestation of pragmatism, her capacity to face a task and gear her life to the challenge of productive work. "The Doctor told her she *had* to . . . and Aunt Munsie *did*" (244).

Her pragmatism is further exemplified in the differing views that Crecie and her mother take about the nature of the social structure in Thornton. Munsie does not, in fact, object to the Tolliver boys' making their fortunes; to her "there were things under the sun worse than going off and getting rich in Nashville or in Memphis or even in Washington, D.C." She recognizes the power of money and respects anyone with the willingness and ability to earn it. Crecie, on the other hand, "was shiftless, and like[d] shiftless white people like the ones who didn't have the ambition to leave Thornton. She thought their shiftlessness showed they were *quality*." Munsie, who is in no way bound to the false codes of the old Southern aristocracy, meets her daughter's attitude with derision: "Well, if there be quality, there be quality *and* quality. There's quality and there's *has-been* quality, Crecie" (239). For Munsie, "quality" is an earned state; her difficulty with Thad and Will's absence stems from her intense pride in their accomplishments.

But she does not fully understand the alteration in economic and social patterns that has separated her from the Tollivers, for the range of her experience has limited her to Thornton, a vantage from which she still measures all value. Lucille Satterfield, a white friend of the Tollivers who knows Munsie and her history with the family, urges her to go to Nashville or Memphis to see how well Thad and Will are doing, recognizing her sense of pride in their accomplishments. "They've done well, Munsie—yours *and* mine—and we can be proud of them. You owe it to yourself to go and see how well they're fixed" (241). But Munsie's reaction brings the question back to Thornton and the values that she has learned there in a quite different era. "Why should she go to Memphis and Nashville and see how rich they were? No matter how rich they were, what difference did it make; they didn't own any land, did they? Or at least none in Cameron County" (242).

Land ownership was the measure of wealth preached by Dr. Tolliver, Thad and Will's father, and as Munsie understands, even he was echoing the wisdom of his own father: "Nobody was rich who didn't own land, and nobody stayed rich who didn't see after his land firsthand" (243). The agrarian-based economy from which this wisdom sprang has been superseded by an economy centered on Lincoln dealerships and other such consumer-oriented businesses.

Munsie's refusal to recognize the automobile traffic in Thornton is of a piece, then, with her refusal to acknowledge Thad and Will's wealth as long as they remain away from Thornton. To her, their wealth in Memphis and Nashville, their lives there, are abstractions, postponements of their inevitable return to reality, which Munsie knows only as Thornton. "No, it was not really to own land that Thad and Will ought to come back to Thornton. It was more that if they were going to be rich, they ought to come home, where their granddaddy had owned land and their money counted for something. How could they ever be rich anywhere else?" (243). For Munsie, to be rich signifies much more than the possession of a certain amount of money. Money "count[s] for something" to her only in the broader context of the community relations and family influence that mark the social structure of a small town. She is limited by her experience, but even here her wisdom cannot be wholly disregarded, for the larger implication of her view is that Thad and Will's wealth, if unconnected to the network of relations and influence that Thornton represents, is essentially hollow. They may, that is, have money, but they are not rich.

Munsie's extreme provincialism functions ironically as a source of wisdom, then, a stance from which she—and, by implication, Taylor—can expose the bankruptcy that modern affluence covers over. Although she does not romanticize "the old times," knowing by experience that "nothing about the old times was as good as these days," she cannot surrender her view of Thad and Will as extenders of the Tolliver lineage: "There were going to be better times yet when Mr. Thad and Mr. Will Tolliver came back" (243-44).

The story builds to Munsie's final recognition that the world has changed permanently, as she discovers that her place in it has changed and finally comes to understand that Thad and Will will not be coming home. What brings about this realization is the "plot" that one of the Tolliver boys hatches to get Munsie and her wagon off the streets and thus protect her from what many feel is inevitable injury. The plan also promises to clear up a major obstruction to Thornton's traffic—and thus its progress—as a side benefit. Thad or Will (the perpetrator is never explicitly named) arranges to have the town outlaw the keeping of pigs within the city limits, and the Tollivers buy out the two others who do so, leaving Munsie as the law's sole target. Not surprisingly, Munsie is enraged when she hears the news from Crecie: "They ain't no such law!" she declares. But within a month she has learned "all there was worth knowing about the conspiracy" and Thad and Will's part in it, having gained the final confirmation from the constable himself (245-46). The passage of the law shocks Munsie into understanding the fact of her dispossession in the changing world of Thornton. The restraint that the new law represents and Thad and Will's hand in it signify that her maternal and familial relation with them is a thing of the past. It may be cherished in memory, both by her and by the Tollivers, but it no longer functions in the business of day-to-day life, in the realm that really matters to Munsie.

This is a sobering, even tragic, revelation, but it does not break Munsie. Her strength, in fact, is indicated by the clarity of her comprehension. Taylor portrays it in a scene marked less by intense drama than by mild humor, underscoring Munsie's strength and capacity finally to accept the fact that the old Thornton and its relationships have been forever changed.

The scene is reported by Crecie, who observes her mother the afternoon after her final, confirming conversation with the constable over the passage of the law. Munsie returns home in a rage—"She come down them steps like she was wasp-nest bit" (247), Crecie says—and begins knocking a hole in the fence around her pigsty with an axe, so she can drive her sow with its nine shoats to a buyer just beyond the town line. But before setting out, Munsie pauses to address a curious speech to her collie pup, who seems to get her attention because, as Crecie puts it, the pup "did look so much like Miss Lucille Satterfield." Munsie's speech, then, continues the dialogue begun months before when Miss Lucille urged her to visit Thad and Will at their new homes.

"Why don't I go down to Memphis or up to Nashville and see 'em sometime, like *you* does?" Aunt Munsie asked the collie. "I tell you why. Becaze I ain't nothin' to 'em in Memphis, and they ain't nothin' to me in Nashville. *You* can go!" she said, advancing and shaking the big axe at the dog. "A collie dog's a collie dog anywhar. But Aunt Munsie, she's just their Aunt Munsie here in Thornton. I got mind enough to see *that*." (249)

Munsie speaks not only to her exclusion from the boys' new life ("I ain't nothin' to 'em in Memphis") but also to her own lack of emotional connection with that life ("they ain't nothin' to me in Nashville"). This may be the most painful part of her understanding, for it takes her self-recognition beyond victimization and forces her to admit that her familial bond with the boys is unable to withstand the forces that are changing her world.

Subsequently, Munsie's stoical acceptance is signaled by a change in her demeanor that everyone in Thornton notices. "They said she softened, and everybody said it was a change for the better" (249). What this "softening" amounts to is a greater willingness to play the role that Thad, Will, and all of Thornton have expected of her. "On the square she would laugh and holler with the white folks the way they liked her to and the way Crecie and the other old-timers did," showing a new willingness to recognize the past in ways that she never would before. "When Mr. Will and Mr. Thad came to see her with their families, she got so she would reminisce with them about their daddy and tease them about all the silly little things they had done when they were growing up" (250). Instead of continuing to live as if the old ways still mattered, Munsie has now accepted that the past is indeed past.

The parallel between Munsie's change and that of Major Manley of "In the Miro District" is clear, as Taylor himself has pointed out in interviews (*Conversations*, 125-26); both are, in a sense, defeated by the drift of the new culture. The tragic quality of Munsie's "defeat" by the change in Thornton is also clear, yet it highlights the strength that makes her one of Taylor's greatest characterizations. Munsie cannot control the social forces around her, but she will not delude herself, and her knowing acceptance requires a courage that sets her above the world that has defeated her.

Miss Leonora Logan is one of Taylor's most vivid and memorable characters, a woman whose hopeless struggle to bring civilization to Thomasville, Tennessee, costs her her place in the town. She is the last of the Logan family, prominent in Thomasville's past, to remain there, living in the family house inherited from her uncle. The house itself, a reminder of the Old South, underlines how instrumental the earlier Logans were in preventing changes in the town. Satisfied with their own wealth, they used their influence to preserve it as a specimen of the quaint, charming, old-fashioned Southern town, causing resentment in the local business establishment. "It was a Logan, for instance, who kept the railroad from coming through the town; it was another Logan who prevented the cotton mill and the snuff factory from locating here" (*CS,* 507).

The conflict of "Miss Leonora When Last Seen" centers on the decision of the town to condemn and tear down Miss Leonora's house, Logana, in order to make room for a new school. Their motivations for this project are, as we shall see, far from noble. Miss Leonora's loss of her home is particularly cruel because she has served Thomasville for twenty-five years as a teacher and devoted her life to the general goal of educating and elevating the town's citizens. Her displacement suggests the narrow insularity that characterized Southern life well into the twentieth century, and depicts the cost that such insularity extracts from those who fail to conform to their community's vision and values.

Miss Leonora, strong-willed and self-reliant, is thus a martyr to small-town values, even though the struggle of her life has been to educate Thomasville more broadly. The story's narrator, one of her former students, remembers the absolute way in which she assumed the role of teacher to the community, both in the school and outside it: "While you sat drinking coffee with her, she was still your English teacher or your history teacher or your Latin teacher, whichever she happened to be at the time, and you were supposed to make conversation with her about *Silas Marner* or Tom Paine or Cicero." Miss Leonora's ultimate goal has been "to populate the town with the sort of people she thought it ought to have" (509), a determination that shows her strong conviction about the social power of education. Although we might expect such a high-minded and nurturing attitude to have earned her a deep affection in her community, she becomes instead an irritating presence, resented by Thomasville as the representative of values that it rejects.

Her final displacement is really one in a series that has marked her life. As the last of the Logans to remain in Thomasville, she has lived under the protection of her family name, relying on her family past and on the protection that conformist communities sometimes grant to eccentrics who are deemed harmless. The narrator calls her "a natural-born reader, [who] enjoys reading the way other people enjoy eating or sleeping," a habit that made her the scourge of Thomasville's professional classes. "It used to be that she would bedevil all the preachers trying to talk theology with them, and worry the life out of all the lawyers with talk about Hamilton and Jefferson and her theories about men like Henry Clay and John Marshall." But she dropped the public role of intellectual when she retired from teaching and now reads privately, "the light in her office burn[ing] almost all night" (510).

This image of Miss Leonora reading alone in her office late into the night serves as one of the most vivid visual depictions of her place in Thomasville. It represents the isolation in which she lives, even while nominally a part of the community. But her isolation has its history, one that is an important part of the communal memory of Thomasville. Before teaching at the public high school Miss Leonora taught at the Thomasville

Female Institute, a boarding school that held a prominent place in the town for some time. Then in 1922 a fire completely destroyed the Institute in a spectacular blaze that lit up the sky "like Judgment Day" (523).

It is less the town's indifference than its callow ineptitude that disturbed Miss Lenora most. "She would not believe it when the firemen told her that the water pressure could not be increased. She threw a bucket of water in one man's face when he refused to take that bucket and climb up a second-story porch with it" (524). Once having accepted the school's inevitable destruction, however, Miss Leonora sat with a kind of morbid curiosity watching the course of the fire. "Poor Miss Leonora! The school was her life," the others in the crowd whisper, and the narrator notes that "she looked dead herself, but at the same time very much alive to what was going on around her" (525). Miss Leonora did witness something like her own death as the school burned, an erasure of the social identity and social role that had sustained her in Thomasville. After the fire, as she continued her career in the public schools, she carried this sense of personal loss and displacement with her, a form of tragedy that, once overcome, made her a stronger and more uncompromising witness for her values—and thus a sharper thorn in Thomasville's side.

The tension between Miss Leonora and her community is not entirely the result of the town's resentment of her aristocratic past or intellectual standards. There is also her violation of the town's segregationist code at her family home. The narrator mentions "the Negro families who live in the outbuildings up at her place," indicating arrangements rooted in the plantation culture of the slaveholding South. But Miss Leonora has transformed her own racial relationships in a way that makes Thomasville uncomfortable: "People say that some of them live right in the house with her, but when I used to go up there as a boy she kept them all out of sight. There was not even a sound of them on the place. She didn't even let her cook bring in the coffee things, and it gave you the queer feeling that either she was protecting you from them or them from you." (513). Miss Leonora of course understands the power of the taboo that she is violating, and her discretion is definitely—if ineffectively—self-protective. It is this violation, not the long-standing tension between her and the town over educational matters, that leads to her final ostracism.

Taylor's treatment of the issues of education and racial segregation, part of the historical context of the story, is complex. He commented in a 1987 interview with Barbara Thompson that he wrote the story "in simple protest" against the consolidation of public schools that he felt was destructive of community and family relations. Taylor worried that sending "your children off to those vast public schools, miles away" would result in an alienation from the family, that the children would return "with a certain contempt for their family, for their customs and manners" (*Conversations*, 171). Such consolidations, of course, often resulted in the racial integration of the schools. But whatever his concern for the integrity of local schools and their connections with family and community, he also wrote in clear opposition to the segregationist practices that persisted in the South. As Taylor structured the story, the town powers of Thomasville are attempting to eliminate racial integration by condemning Logana in order to build a new school there. They do so not "because they think Logana is such an ideal location" but "because it is the only way of getting rid of the little colony of Negroes who have always lived up there and who would make a serious problem for us if it became a question of zoning the town, in some way, as a last barrier against integration" (514-15).

Presumably, the town powers believe that the dispersal of the African Americans living at Logana will allow them to postpone school integration and, as a side benefit, exact revenge for the Logan family's long control of the town and Miss Leonora's dissent from its prevailing values. Even if the plan should fail to head off integration, "the truth of the matter is," the narrator tells us, "that there are people here who dislike the memory of the Logans even more than they do the prospect of integration. They are willing to risk integration in order to see that last Logan dispossessed of his last piece of real estate in Thomasville" (515).[5]

The plot has the effect of transforming Miss Leonora from an eccentric dissenter to a figure of resistance, and critical appraisal of the story (it has drawn some of the most interesting critical readings of all Taylor's work) divides over the question of how effective her resistance is. The story begins after Miss Leonora's apparent escape from Thomasville. "She has been missing for two weeks, and though a half dozen postcards have been received from her, stating that she is in good health and that no anxiety should be felt for her safety, still the whole town can talk of nothing else" (502). Her absence has temporarily forestalled the condemnation proceedings on Logana, and it gradually becomes clear to the reader that the talk about Miss Leonora among Thomasville's citizens is not entirely an expression of concern for her well-being.

Taylor retraces the causes of her disappearance in the narrator's attempt to explain his own and the town's complicated relationship with her. He is among her most promising former students, one of her "favorites among the male citizenry" (504) but one who never quite escaped Thomasville and its values as she hoped he would. It is because of his status as a favorite that the difficult task of informing Miss Leonora about the condemnation of Logana falls to him. His attempt to do so and her subsequent disappearance provide a climax that is both significant and highly ambiguous.

The climactic scene of the story emphasizes the narrator's combination of sympathy for Miss Leonora and his sense that she represents a threat to the values of Thomasville, about which he himself is ambivalent. He does not, ironically, recognize the significance of her progressive views on race but reveals this aspect of the story with an innocent openness that serves to underline the closed-mindedness of the rest of the community. But he does venerate Miss Leonora for other qualities, particularly for her courage and her dedicated and persistent attempt to be a teacher to the youths of the town. "She was eternally instructing us," he says, remembering her single-minded refusal to be distracted or to compromise in her work (521). She has impressed him as someone working against the pervasive complacency of Thomasville, and though he does not seem to have profited fully from her example, the end of the story suggests that her work has not been wholly fruitless in his case.

Taylor builds the story toward the narrator's awkward attempt to inform her of the condemnation, the final act of Thomasville's rejection of her. Miss Leonora, who has seen the inevitable, is already well prepared for the news and magnanimous in her refusal to blame the messenger. "I've felt so bad about your having to come here like this," she tells him. "I knew they would put it off on you. Even you must have dreaded coming, and you must hate me for putting you in such a position" (531). Her speech, both conciliatory and genuinely affectionate, confirms her partiality toward the narrator and emphasizes his own inner conflict over where his loyalties lie—with his old teacher, whom he respects and even reveres, or with the town's power structure, of which he is a doubting member.

It is this conflict of values, we must remember, that has generated his narrative; he tells it after his final meeting with Miss Leonora, and it is laden with a sense of guilt that results in elevating her to the status of heroic resister. His uneasiness about informing her of the town's decision is thus an important signal of a conferral of power: in the final scene the narrator, perhaps unwittingly, becomes the bearer of the values that Miss Leonora has represented by becoming her biographer. His telling of her story itself becomes an act of resistance to the corrupt course of Thomasville politics and culture.

The central critical question is the extent to which Miss Leonora has been defeated by Thomasville, making her a tragic and martyred figure and giving the story an essentially tragic tone. Taylor himself was not reticent in labeling Miss Leonora as "defeated"; she is, he commented in an interview with Hubert H. McAlexander, "defeated by [her] culture," and he described her also as "denied," "rejected," and "displaced," linking her with Major Basil Manley of "In the Miro District" and Aunt Munsie of "What You Hear from 'Em" (*Conversations*, 126). Clearly, Taylor was attempting to make a statement about Southern culture, using Thomasville as an example of a Southern city divided by conflicting attitudes toward economic and social change. He described his story to Stephen Goodwin as a "complete allegory," one of several that he constructed "just the way you'd work out a theorem" (*Conversations*, 12).

Still, his comments do not entirely solve the interpretive problems raised by the character of Miss Leonora. If Thomasville signifies the less appealing aspects of mid-twentieth-century Southern culture, Miss Leonora must be taken to represent some alternative to it. But is she a real and viable alternative, or a sign that a battle has been lost? Cleanth Brooks reads "Miss Leonora When Last Seen" as an allegory of the defeat of culture—in the sense of education, refinement, and moral commitment to the community—by the forces of false commercial progress.[6] Such progress is not only an enemy of culture but a corroder of the texture of community as well. Miss Leonora is in Brooks's reading a conservative sort of resister, an upholder of certain traditional values associated with education and the community. But this resistance is a radical act in the South, because these values, even if the culture officially endorses them, can threaten the established commercial and political order.

Miss Leonora's identification as a bearer of tradition through her role as a teacher, and therefore a builder of community, thus makes her a crucial figure of resistance to what Brooks calls the "shallow modernity" (212) of the powers-that-be in Thomasville. Those powers represent what we might call the "new South," although we must use that term with a full sense of irony. The "new South" originally denoted the forces of progressive change that were rising to replace the repressive, racist, and elitist qualities of the defeated "old South." Brooks finds that the story details the ways in which the progressive quality of change in the South was derailed by commercialism, conformity, and a settled resistance to intellectual culture. The South was becoming, at last, and alas, part of America.

But if Miss Leonora is defeated, she has not yet surrendered, and her remarkable act of holding on raises some doubts about the finality of her defeat. Two elements of the story's ending are significant. The first is the change that has seemingly overcome her, signified by the "bluinged hair" that the narrator last sees as she drives out of town. He fears that this is a sign of a newly adopted conventionality on her part, a departure from the eccentric and dissenting style of dress and habit of mind that she has displayed in the past. Miss Leonora, who has been known to leave Thomasville often for excursions through the countryside, has been seen during those excursions wearing one of two outfits: "outmoded finery," which included "the fox fur piece, and the diamond earrings, and the high-crowned velvet hat, and the kind of lace choker that even old ladies don't generally go in for any more," or, alternatively, dungarees and a "homeknit, knee-length cardigan sweater" (527-28). These outfits, different though they are, represent Miss Leonora's rejection of conventional ways of dressing. One exhibits her aristocratic disdain for the town and its standards, and the other her populist resistance to it. These are clothes that she is known to wear only outside the town on the excursions that mark her as a restless eccentric, unwilling to accept the drift of the town toward a bland modern commercial future. These trips seem to be a search for an acceptable alternative to Thomasville, a reaching back for a South that is quickly disappearing.

But when the narrator arrives at her house bearing his bad news, he is stunned to find that her aspect has changed yet again. "I saw at a glance that this wasn't the Miss Leonora I had known, and wasn't the one I had known about from her tourist-home friends, either." She has cut her hair and "set it in little waves close to her head, and, worse still, she must have washed it in a solution of indigo bluing" (530). It dawns on him that now Miss Leonora has conformed herself to a type: "one of those old women who come out here from Memphis looking for antiques and country hams and who tell you how delighted they are to find a Southern town that is truly unchanged" (531). Miss Leonora, it seems, may have gone over to the enemy, her commitment to culture reduced to a form of recreational consumerism.

One part of their conversation adds some fuel to this interpretation of her change. "When I think of the old days, the days when I used to have you up here," she says, "you and the others, too—I realize I was too hard on you. I asked too much of my pupils. I know that now." The narrator is certainly puzzled by this confession, and he explains his reaction in very significant terms: "It was nothing like the things the real Miss Leonora used to say. It was something anybody might have said" (532). He realizes that Miss Leonora is not just "everybody," or at least she has not been. Although her apparent alteration in both appearance and attitude poses an interesting critical problem in the story, it is the narrator's recognition of the change that is the most significant element of the ending. It suggests that Miss Leonora's teaching has not been entirely in vain and that her defeat—or at least the defeat of her values—has not been complete.

If the narrator is right and Miss Leonora's change is real—if, as the narrator fears, she has become just like everyone else—then her disappearance does indeed represent her defeat and the victory of Thomasville's shallow values. This seems to be the interpretive twist that Taylor has given the story in his interview with McAlexander, and it is the reading presented persuasively by Albert J. Griffith: "The terrible shock of the story is that Miss Leonora 'when last seen' is no longer the eccentric individualist she has always been before" (98). Griffith argues that her diminution is the community's loss; in this respect, the story stands as a tragic and prophetic warning about the change of values in the South.[7]

But has Miss Leonora really changed? Taylor leaves room for doubt on this important question. She *looks* different, but the reader instinctively wonders, with the narrator, whether there may be more to her final appearance—and uncharacteristic comments—than meets the eye. It is worth noting that she loses no time in leaving her house after she receives the news from the narrator, and this escape is significant because it delays the town's legal maneuvers to confiscate and destroy her property. If Thomasville is not defeated, its plans have at least been slowed, and the longer she stays away, the more difficult the town's legal and moral position becomes. For Brooks, her final departure from Thomasville is part of her continuing battle to resist its narrowness. "Miss Leonora's present trip is, then, more than the foible of a lonesome old maid," he argues. "It looks like a deliberate act of defiance"— no "hauling down of the flag" but instead "a gesture of defiance to the new order" (200, 203).

The resolution of these conflicting interpretations, though, is less important than the broader argument that either reading carries. Defeated or defiant, Miss Leonora is a character whose struggle reveals the narrowness and corruption of Southern cultural values at midcentury. She is a character through whom Taylor can represent a society at war with its better self. The sympathy he builds for her, communicated haltingly but nevertheless persuasively by the narrator, has ethical and political significance. The narrator, then, speaks for us all at the end: "And, anyway, I like to think that in her traveling bag she had the lace-choker outfit that she could change into along the way, and the dungarees, too; and that she is stopping at her usual kind of place today and is talking to the proprietors about Thomasville" (534-35).

❖ 6 ❖
The Racial Divide

Taylor's depictions of the patterns of family life in the South include, in some of his most perceptive stories, an analysis of the complicated relations of genteel families with their African American servants, relations rooted in the slaveholding culture of the old South and perpetuated by the economic hierarchies that persisted in our century. Taylor recognized that these inter-actions were a crucial aspect of the cultural constitution of the South, sub-ject to rapid change in the same way as other familial and interpersonal relationships. Several of Taylor's strongest stories from the late 1940s and 1950s center on African American servants whose complex relationships with their white employers, pursued within the framework of a rigid social hierarchy, had enormous power to mold psychologically the persons in-volved, white and black. These include "Cookie," "A Wife of Nashville," and "Bad Dreams."[1] Taylor is interested in both the cultural forms that govern these relationships and their resulting potential to reveal deeper elements of character.

His most dramatic and moving treatment of the tragic complexities of the master-servant relationship is his portrait of Aunt Munsie in "What You Hear from 'Em," a story that is also, as noted in the earlier discussion, a memorable depiction of a powerful individual's response to threatening social change. Munsie's experience of dispossession after the Tolliver boys abandon her in Thornton reminds us that the loss of freedom and denial of identity that were the results of slavery persisted for generations in the South. Munsie has shown her remarkable strength of character by entering into the role of servant so deeply that in some sense she transcends it to become, at least for a time, matriarch of the Tolliver family. Yet although she demonstrates that the role of servant can to some degree be trans-formed, she also shows that the hierarchy of power within the culture in-evitably extracts a cost from its victims. Independent and self-willed as she is, Munsie must unlearn the emotional dependence derived from her role as surrogate mother to the Tolliver boys.

One of Taylor's most direct treatments of the debilitating consequences of the dependency inherent in the Southern racial hierarchy is "A Friend and Protector" (1959), in which the narrator recounts his uncle Andrew Nelson's role as the white "friend and protector" of Jesse Munroe, an African American who becomes deeply dependent on Andrew's paternal watchfulness. The story's title is, we discover, ironic, for the protection and friendship that Andrew offers Jesse are, in many ways, destructive.[2] The ties between the two men originate in the small town of Braxton when Andrew, an attorney, extricates Jesse from the legal entanglements resulting from a murder case in which he is accused of being an accessory. "It was assumed in Braxton that there had been some sensible understanding arrived at between Andrew Nelson and the presiding judge. Jesse was to have a suspended sentence; Uncle Andrew was to get him out of Braxton and keep him out" (*OF,* 144). So Andrew takes Jesse with him to Memphis, where he and his wife Margaret establish a quasi-parental bond with him, rescuing him from repeated calamities. Jesse's occasional weekend binges and more troubling "escapades and scrapes" lasting up to a week usually result in the Nelsons' having to bail him out of jail or locate him at the hospital.

Although the pattern of the relationship seems to indicate an admirable devotion on the part of the Nelsons and Jesse's fierce loyalty in return, the story in fact suggests that this relationship is destructive to all three, especially to Jesse. The Nelsons serve as the audience for his debauchery, condemning it superficially but subconsciously relishing the glimpse it gives them into corners of life that are forbidden to them.[3] Jesse responds to their concern for him by exploiting his one sure hold over them, a capacity to allow them to rescue him. But even though his debaucheries seem to arise from his fundamental insecurity and answer a complicated need, they are ultimately self-destructive.

The story's narrator, more objectively reliable than the usual Taylor narrator, explains the dynamic of the relationship perceptively and is particularly astute in recognizing the Nelsons' culpability. Their interest in Jesse, mixing indulgence with censure, "most certainly forced Jesse's destruction upon him." Nor was this a simple lack of judgment on their part: "They did it because they had to, because they were so dissatisfied with the pale *un*ruin of their own lives. They did it because something would not let them ruin their own lives as they wanted and felt a need to do—as I have often felt a need to do, myself. As who does not sometimes feel a need to do?" (160).

The Nelsons' vicarious participation in Jesse's decadence thus reflects their own entrapment in a suffocating conventionality; their indirect contribution to his eventual demise signifies the actual lack of value that they place on him, despite their ostensible care for him. After a final horrifying mental breakdown, Jesse is committed to the state insane asylum, where he lives on as a trusty, his relationship with the Nelsons now ended. They can no longer rescue and rebuke him, and he can no longer test their devotion through his binges. Taylor's story, clearly emphasizing the destructiveness of such paternalistic relationships, can be read as an almost allegorical commentary on the superficiality of "constructive" or "positive" racial relations that are not based on genuine equality and empowerment.

Although Taylor's narrative stance is not usually that of the political or moral crusader, his portrayal of African American characters in the modernizing South demonstrates a deep sympathy for their situation. In a later interview he attributed that sympathetic stance to the attempt at deeper understanding that the creation of fiction requires. "I didn't know what I thought about blacks, for example, until I started writing about them—and saw that they got the short end of it," he told Robert Brickhouse in 1983 (*Conversations*, 50). Taylor might prefer to have us consider his fictional portrayal of political or moral positions entirely as the byproduct of his concentration on character and setting, yet his persistent attempt to illuminate the difficult situations of race relations in the South at midcentury forces readers to confront those political and moral difficulties. To approach "A Friend and Protector" exclusively as a story that delineates the psychological oddity of the bond between Jesse and the Nelsons is to miss Taylor's political meaning. He exposes the duplicity and self-delusion that account for the Nelsons' actions and shows that this self-delusion is necessarily connected with Southern racism. The role of master, Taylor reminds us, is inevitably corrupting.

In the 1946 story "A Long Fourth" (discussed in Chapter 5) the same moral blindness operates in Harriet's relationship with her maid. When Harriet rejects Mattie's plea for sympathy, she reveals not only the rigidity of the barriers separating whites and blacks but her own corrosive self-absorption. For Harriet, Mattie is a disturbing self-image, sharing as a woman Harriet's powerlessness and dependency but experiencing them much more sharply because of the South's racist social structure. The "special language common to both of them" (*OF*, 235) that emerges at the height of Mattie's crisis is understood only briefly, not to be recovered.

That failure is both social and personal, reflecting not only the cultural barriers against any meaningful, nonhierarchical relationship between blacks and whites but also Harriet's lack of capacity to overcome those barriers. "A Long Fourth" is primarily Harriet's story, but it can be told completely only with Mattie's presence.

Taylor pursues these interconnected themes of women's limited role in conventional marriage and the destructiveness of the Southern racial divide in "Cookie" (1948), a story that portrays the mistreatment of an African American maid but also reveals the hollow marriage of her white employers. This narrative depicts the powerlessness of both the maid and the wife, using the husband's callousness toward the maid as an indication of his hostility toward his wife. His wife's reduction to utter dependency on an absolutely empty relationship is one of Taylor's earliest analyses of the stifling effects of conventional patterns of marriage on women.

The story takes place during a tension-filled family meal in which a middle-aged couple, whose children are grown, play out a hollow charade of family life. The husband, a doctor who is frequently out on calls, has come to live an almost separate life, maintaining only the thinnest facade of connection with his wife. "Two nights a week, he *had* to be home for supper, and some weeks, when his conscience was especially uneasy, he turned up three or four times" (*CS*, 281). Taylor captures the subtle aggression lurking beneath ordinary civility as the husband registers his approval of the dinner.

> He served himself from the dish of beans and selected a piece of the side meat. He bent his head over and got one whiff of the steaming dish. "You're too good to me," he said evenly. He pushed the dish across the table to within her reach.
> "Nothing's too good for one's husband."
> "You're much too good to me," he said, now lowering his eyes to his plate. (282)

Whatever words are exchanged here, the eye contact and tone of voice belie any warmth or honesty. The wife's remark, which specifies "one's husband" rather than "you," is particularly suggestive of the way her marriage has deteriorated into an empty form.

As the dinner continues, the husband's inquiries about the children take on an aggressively judgmental tone when he learns of their failure to write home. His attitude brings his wife near tears. Taylor's strategy is to build the tension of the encounter slowly, gradually revealing the husband's callous insensitivity. The story thus moves from disclosure of the shallowness of the marriage to a deeper indictment of the husband's character. His meanness becomes clear in an interchange with Cookie, whom he sees as an appendage of his wife and a symbol of the domestic life that he holds in mild contempt. But Cookie is less inclined to take his subtle abuse passively. When he quizzes his wife about their children's failure to write, Cookie enters the conversation in her defense. "*He* hear from 'em?" she asks the wife, clearly conscious that it is a provoking question. "No, I have *not!*" he replies with a frown, threateningly turning his attention to Cookie (285).

This minor skirmish is prelude to the husband's initiation of a series of mocking questions designed to ridicule Cookie and assert his domination through her humiliation.

"Cookie, I've been wantin' to ask you how your 'corporosity' is."
   "M'whut, Boss-Man?"
   "And, furthermore, I understand from what various people are saying around that you have ancestors." He winked at his wife. She dropped her eyes to her plate.
   "What's he mean, Mizz?" Cookie asked, standing with the two dinner plates in hand. (287)

While the exchange deepens our revulsion at the husband's callousness, it also establishes the important point that racial oppression is part of the social milieu in which this family tragedy is played out. Cookie becomes the object of a hostility that the husband will not openly express toward his wife; as a black servant, she is not shielded by the unspoken social codes that give his wife at least some measure of protection.

Although Cookie is unable to defend herself directly from her master's initial assertion of dominance, she understands her own resources; she can be embarrassed by his mocking of her limited vocabulary, but the embarrassment does not cow her or make her passive. She retaliates by reporting servants' gossip about another doctor who seems to be playing host to wild parties where men of the town have been seen consorting with women. The husband has pushed Cookie for this information partly to shock his wife and partly to discover the extent of Cookie's knowledge of the goings-on at Doc Palmer's. As we soon discover, he has reason to be concerned.

Continuing his inquisition, he asks in a challenging way who has been seen at Doc Palmer's. "The cook turn[s] to him and look[s] at him blankly. 'You, Boss-Man'" (289). The story's tension builds to this revelation, which carries a strong dramatic impact, confirming our suspicion of the husband's disregard for his wife and underlining Cookie's defiance. Cookie's refusal to dissemble about her boss's dishonesty and hypocrisy makes her the primary means whereby Taylor exposes the evasions that preserve the shell of this marriage. When she is forced to play the role of revealer, she gains both our sympathy and admiration for her honesty and her courage.

But Cookie's revelation uncovers more than the husband's unfaithfulness. In an irony that underlines the tragedy of the marriage, the wife reacts not to her husband's infidelity but to Cookie's disclosure of it: "His wife stood up at her place, her napkin in her hand. Her eyes filled with tears. 'After all these years!' she said. 'Cookie, you've forgotten your place for the first time, after all these years'" (289). This is not, of course, the reaction we have been led to expect by the growing tension between wife and husband, but the unexpected turn broadens the theme significantly. Because of her reaction it is no longer possible to regard the story only as a commentary on a particular marriage. It is instead a commentary on the oppressive possibilities of marriage in the midcentury American South and on the persistence of a racial hierarchy rooted in slavery. The wife reacts as she does out of fear that any confrontation with her husband will further weaken or completely destroy her precarious position as wife; she is dependent financially, socially, and emotionally on the role in which she has invested so much.

Cookie's role as a dependent servant is thus an important corollary of the story's exploration of marriage, for her powerlessness mirrors and clarifies that of the wife. When the wife says that Cookie has "forgotten [her] place" she confirms for us that she has painfully remembered her own. In the conversation that follows we see the couple closing ranks against Cookie, whose breach of the family order seems to have been perceived as more serious even than the husband's infidelity.

> In a moment, his wife looked up at him and said, "I'm sorry. I'd not thought she was capable of a thing like that."
> "Why, it's all right–for what she said. Doctors will get talked about. Even Cookie knows the girl's a liar."
> His wife seemed, he thought, not to have heard him. She was saying, "A servant of mine talking to my husband like that!"
> "It's only old-nigger uppitiness," he reassured her. (289)

The husband has used Cookie's accusation to shield himself, knowing that his wife will refuse to accord credibility to such a charge if possible. That the accusation has come from an African American servant gives her the necessary excuse to turn away from the truth and thereby preserve the outer form of her marriage—something that, when she considers the alternatives open to her, she wishes to do. Taylor titled the story "Middle Age" when it first appeared in *New Yorker*, and that title underlines the precariousness of the wife's position. She is, like Harriet Wilson in "A Long Fourth," facing the stark limits of her role as wife and mother as she ages, and the surprising vehemence of her reaction against Cookie is a sign of her acute sense of vulnerability.

Both "Cookie" and "A Long Fourth" explore the experience of women through the implied analogy of the servitude of African Americans in the South. Taylor develops the analogy between wives and servants with greatest specificity in "A Wife of Nashville" (1949), a story that recounts the life of a middle-class white woman, Helen Ruth Lovell, through her relations with the series of African American maids whom she has employed during her marriage. Taylor uses the basic narrative of the comings and goings of the four maids——Jane Blakemore, Carrie, Sarah Wilkins, and Jess McGehee—to frame the difficult process through which Helen Ruth becomes resigned to her role as wife and mother.[4] His vivid portraits of the maids themselves, each a richly memorable character, add important dimensions to his characterization of Helen Ruth, augmenting his portrayal of women's experience and emphasizing the intersection of gender and race in the changing culture of the South.

Helen Ruth's relationship with each of her maids is to some degree antagonistic, since what they share as women cannot overcome the barriers of class and race that separate them. And, as in "A Long Fourth," Taylor shows that Helen Ruth's own dissatisfactions impinge on these relationships, adding tension to the already strained association of employer and employee. Carrie, for example, has a comically annoying tendency not to complete her tasks to Helen Ruth's satisfaction, a failing that is compounded by her inclination to offer advice on questions that Helen Ruth would prefer not to discuss. She proposes that Helen Ruth have her second child at home with Carrie herself serving as midwife; later she speaks to Helen Ruth about having her third child circumcised. Such advice, however well intended, seems to Helen Ruth to violate her privacy and to overstep the boundary between employer and employee, white and black. Yet despite these frustrations, she feels angry and betrayed when Carrie leaves her employ.

Sarah Wilkins, although both illiterate and unable to do heavy work because of her age, readily learns the family's favorite recipes and takes a warm interest in the Lovell boys. But a tension develops when Helen Ruth learns from Sarah that her ex-husband, Morse, killed her baby: "He rolled over on it in his drunk sleep and smothered it in the bed" (*CS*, 268). Helen Ruth is moved partly by pity but also by revulsion at the story, and it affects her ability to trust Sarah. She begins to worry about the men who pick the maid up after work every day, because she knows that Sarah is "living with first one and then another of them" (268-69). Morse returns one day in a drunken rage to take Sarah away, but at Helen Ruth's urging she refuses to go. In persuading Sarah not to go with Morse, Helen Ruth is in part concerned about her morals and well-being, but she is also in a struggle to control Sarah and command her allegiance. Her triumph is brief, however; a few months later Sarah leaves for Chicago.

Jess McGehee is the maid who forms the strongest bond with the Lovells, and her somewhat surprising departure occasions an important act of reflection on Helen Ruth's part, signifying her achievement of a deeper self-knowledge. Taylor's inclusion of the lives of these maids in the larger narrative of Helen Ruth's experience enriches the story's texture and underlines the barriers of class and race prejudice that contribute to her self-delusion. Her limited achievement of self-understanding is linked, as Taylor presents it, to a fuller understanding of the experience of the women she has employed.

Helen Ruth's husband, John R., kiddingly refers to his wife's succession of maids as her "affairs," suggesting when she hires Jess that "the honeymoon is over, but this is the real thing this time" (253-54). His teasing has the ring of truth. Each relationship that Helen Ruth works out with a maid is analogous to a courtship or marriage, with its mutual dependencies, conflicts, and attendant emotional ups and downs. Given its starkly hierarchical quality, with the power of her role as an employer magnified by the racial oppression of Southern culture, it is also analogous to the gendered hierarchy of conventional marriage. Though largely powerless in her own marriage, Helen Ruth has a measure of control over her servants, a control that she both desires and wields guiltily. Her maids enter the family structure as a part of it but also not a part of it, recognizing always the limits of their position and the firm boundaries between white and black that they must not transgress.

The story's underlying analogy between the roles of wife and servant is central to Taylor's delineation of Helen Ruth's character. She has defined her life primarily through her struggle to reconcile herself to her emotionally unfulfilling marriage with John R., a man whose essential disengagement from family life, though not overtly oppressive, is nevertheless poisonous to any hope Helen Ruth has of achieving meaning through her marriage. She is able to accept the situation for several years, but after the birth of her second child she begins to feel "a restlessness that she could not explain in herself" (263). When she responds to her loneliness by seeking more social interaction with her women friends, one unintended result of these attempts to widen her social sphere is that she gains a clearer perspective on the poverty of her marriage. In a conversation with Mamie Lovell—a distant cousin of John R.—and two other friends, Nancy Tolliver and Lucy Parkes, she is forced to answer inquiries about her home life. "'John R. and I each live our own life, Cousin Mamie,'" Helen Ruth says, explaining that she has little to do with what Mamie calls "the hound and hunt set" with whom John R. associates (264).

But her own explanation of her marriage has less impact on her than the approval of it offered by Nancy: "'Helen Ruth is a woman with a mind of her own, Miss Mamie,' Nancy Tolliver said. 'It's too bad more marriages can't be like theirs, each living their own life. Everyone admires it as a real achievement'" (264-65). Although Nancy intends this description as a defense of Helen Ruth and couches it in proto-feminist language, its effect on Helen Ruth is quite different. "She had never discussed her marriage with anybody, and hearing it described so matter-of-factly by these two women made her understand for the first time what a special sort of marriage it was and how unhappy she was in it" (265). This new perspective, the product of seeing herself through the eyes of her friends, prompts her to a temporary separation from John R., the most serious crisis of her life. She takes the children to Thornton, their old hometown, writing her husband that she will return "when he decide[s] to devote his time to his wife and children instead of to his hounds and horses" (265).

Helen Ruth's action emphasizes the depth of her unhappiness and suggests how vulnerable she is to others' perceptions of her. She is, as Taylor reminds us in his title, a "wife" of Nashville, a person defined by that particular social role. Although her crisis may in part be a rebellion against that role, she understands it as a flight from what she has internalized as her failure in it. Leaving her husband is an attempt not to flee her marriage but to succeed in it more completely by changing the dynamics of her relationship with him.

But her efforts fall victim to John R.'s obtuseness and unwillingness to communicate meaningfully with his wife. He never mentions Helen Ruth's letter but continues to correspond with her as if nothing significant has happened. He writes "about his business, about his hounds and horses, about the weather, and he always urge[s] her to hurry home as soon as she ha[s] seen everybody and had a good visit" (265). His trivialization of her act of separation underlines the superficiality of their emotional relationship and allows Helen Ruth see that her power to change her marriage in any substantial way is limited. Unable to affect it by this separation, she eventually returns to Nashville.

When she retreats to Thornton with her children, Helen Ruth takes her maid Carrie, who is also from Thornton and has family ties there. The barely urbanized Southerners in Taylor's fiction, both white and black, maintain a network of connections originating in small country towns. The white families who move to Nashville hire, if they can, black servants from back home, thus preserving both a common frame of reference and a shared understanding of the hierarchy of the relationship. For Helen Ruth the separation from her husband is a return to both family support and the more secure network of traditional relationships that Thornton represents, and thus to a world whose stability has not yet been undermined by change.

But one afternoon during her stay her former maid Jane Blakemore pays a visit to Carrie, a development that causes Helen Ruth great apprehension. The source of her anxiety is her realization that she is subject to judgment by those over whom she exercises authority. She herself has failed to meet her maids on the grounds of openness and equality and has enacted a husband-like tyranny at times in her dealings with them. She also recognizes that they know the sorry state of her marriage, about which she is acutely embarrassed. Seeing them together is "the most terrible hour of her separation from John R.," and as she watches Carrie "walking with Jane to the gate, there [is] no longer any doubt in Helen Ruth's mind" that she will return to her husband, and "return without any complaints or stipulations" (259).

Her observation of the two servants' meeting makes her intensely aware that her return to Thornton is a public enactment of the failure of her marriage and of her role as wife. If the earlier conversation with Cousin Mamie Lovell showed her the poverty of her marriage, the conversation that she imagines between Carrie and Jane suggests to her that her ultimatum to John R. is a futile gesture, with its own quality of self-centered pouting. Although she returns to Nashville and to her marriage in part to accept a certain diminishment of her earlier overly romantic expectations about life, such decisions by Taylor's characters usually suggest the acquisition of a tragic but important wisdom; the acceptance of such proscriptions is often a mark of necessary maturity.

But her wisdom in accepting the shape of her life should not be overemphasized, for Taylor is not inclined to believe that people change their lives or attitudes suddenly. He makes it clear that Helen Ruth still indulges in self-pity and continues to hold a presumption of superiority over her servants. "Had she really misused these women, either the black one or the brown one?" she thinks. That she couches the question in explicitly racial terms is significant, for it provides the basis of her evasive and self-justifying answer. "It seemed to her then that she had so little in life that she was entitled to the satisfaction of keeping an orderly house and to the luxury of efficient help." That is, the disappointments of her marriage entitle her to the privilege of these women's subservience: "There was too much else she had not had—an 'else' nameless to her, yet sorely missed—for her to be denied these small satisfactions" (259-60). By using her disappointments with her marriage to legitimize her exploitive relationship with her servants, Helen Ruth reveals her self-absorption and her insensitivity to the costs of the racial and economic hierarchy of the South.

Still, if the moment of crisis in the story suggests Helen Ruth's limitations of perception, it also indicates her capacity for change. The decay of her marriage has been largely beyond her control, and she comes to recognize that her separation and her ultimatum to John R. cannot heal it. Curiously, however, her marriage does achieve some emotional depth later on, when external events force her husband to change. His business success had led him to drift away from his wife and children; the economic setbacks of the Depression bring him closer to them, resulting in "the happiest years of their married life" (272). These are also the years that she has Jess, the most loyal and congenial of her maids, whose sudden departure is the stimulus for the entire retrospective narrative of Helen Ruth's life.

Jess's competence and devotion set the standard by which her predecessors are weighed and found wanting. She "not only cooked and cleaned, she planned the meals, did the marketing, and washed everything, from handkerchiefs and socks to heavy woolen blankets. . . . There was nothing she would not do for the boys or for John R. or for Helen Ruth." She even kept a scrapbook of family pictures and "begged from Helen Ruth an extra copy of the newspaper notice of their wedding" (272-73).

Her unusual devotion seems to make her a member of the family, and thus her decision to leave is the more surprising and hurtful to them. Unable to tell them of her decision directly, Jess resorts to subterfuge to make her escape, adding a humorously ironic twist to the story and also providing a gauge of Helen Ruth's growth in self-understanding since her earlier separation. The sequence of events begins one morning when Jess receives a telephone call and is soon "sobbing aloud" (276). She tells the family that her baby brother has died and, with Helen Ruth's encourage-ment, leaves to go to his family. But after Jess has gone, Helen Ruth realizes that there is "something that she knew she must tell the family," something that catches them by complete surprise: "Jess McGehee had no baby brother and had never had one"; her tale had been concocted to hide the fact that she was leaving for California to look for a job. "You knew that right along?" John R. asks with annoyance. "And you let Jess get away with all that crying stuff just now?" (277-78).

Helen Ruth's response indicates that she has developed a deeper com-passion for Jess and a more acute understanding of her own life as well. "What could she say to them, she kept asking herself. And each time she asked the question, she received for answer some different memory of seemingly unrelated things out of the past twenty years of her life." She rec-ognizes how little her family will understand her growing sense of connec-tion with Jess or grasp how her leaving has crystallized for Helen Ruth a tragic knowledge about her own life. "She felt that she would be willing to say anything at all, no matter how cruel or absurd it was, if it would make them understand that everything that happened in life only demonstrated in some way the lonesomeness that people felt" (279). She sees Jess's de-parture as an attempt to escape from the chains of loneliness and discon-nection that have bound her as well.

Helen Ruth understands that she cannot communicate her compassion for Jess, or her own loneliness, to her uncomprehending family, "that her husband and her sons [do] not recognize her loneliness or Jess McGehee's or their own" (280). Her recognition of the barrier, though painful, consti-tutes an important achievement in self-understanding and gives her the capacity to see Jess's subterfuge as an act of desperation originating in the impossibility of communicating openly with the Lovells. As wife and mother, Helen Ruth has faced a similar gap. Her frustration has, over time, yielded her the capacity to comprehend the frustration of another. We cannot call this form of broadened awareness a resolution of her problem. Resolutions of any finality are rare in Taylor's work, as, he argues by implication, they are rare in life. But we must accord Helen Ruth the value of a newly earned self-possession, and a self-understanding accompanied by a deeper and more sympathetic understanding of those around her.

"A Wife of Nashville" shares with both "A Friend and Protector" and "Cookie" the strategy of using African American servants to illuminate the characters of the whites who are finally the psychological focus of the stories. In "What You Hear From 'Em," Taylor uses the master-servant relationship to a somewhat different end by focusing the story on Munsie. Although both strategies of focus are effective, illuminating different aspects of the culture of the upper South and of the individuals who are a part of it, the characterization of Munsie is the most powerfully enduring of the character portraits from these stories. An element of that power, certainly, is Taylor's portrayal of the subtle process through which Munsie is victimized, however unintentionally, in the role of servant.

Taylor's analysis of such victimization is extended in "Bad Dreams" (1951), an astute and moving study of the marriage of Bert and Emmaline, former Thorntonites who are both in the service of the Tolliver family in St. Louis. Like "What You Hear from 'Em," "Bad Dreams" focuses on African American characters, leaving the white family that wields so much power over their lives in the background. But we understand the racial divide through the immense impact that the actions and attitudes of the whites have on the lives of the blacks.

The catalyst for the story is an ostensible act of kindness that James Tolliver performs for an "old Negro man [who] had come from somewhere in West Tennessee." Tolliver "had simply run across him in downtown St. Louis and had become obligated or attached to him somehow," first keeping him as a hand at his office but finally deciding, "without a word to his wife or to anybody else," to bring him home and install him "in an empty room above the garage" (*OF*, 116). Tolliver's act, though mysterious in some respects, suggests the codes of authority, dependence, and obligation that persisted to some extent between the races in the South well into the middle twentieth century. The old man's origins in West Tennessee establish the basis for a bond with Tolliver, who, even though he lives in St. Louis, has never entirely left Thornton. In taking care of the man, he is of course exercising a certain paternal authority and also, we surmise, using this particular act of kindness to exorcise some of the guilt attendant on his elevated place in the racially divided culture of the South.

Taylor is less interested in Tolliver's motive for the act than in its consequences for Bert and Emmaline, who also live in rooms above the Tollivers' garage. Moving the old man into the garage would "go almost unnoticed" by the Tolliver family—"They would hardly know he was on the place" (116)—but Bert and Emmaline, who must live in very close quarters with the man, most definitely would.

A full comprehension of the impact of the old man's presence requires some sense of the spatial configuration of the garage rooms that he comes to share with Bert and Emmaline and their four-month-old baby.[5] The description of the garage both establishes, with an air of mockery, the Tollivers' wealth and also emphasizes Bert and Emmaline's dependency. "When the Tollivers' two Lincolns were in their places at night, there was space enough for two more cars of the same wonderful length and breadth. And on the second floor, under the high mansard roof, the stairway opened onto an enormous room, or area, known as the loft room, in one end of which there was still a gaping hay chute, and from the opposite end of which opened three servant's rooms." Two of these rooms, and a bathroom are occupied by Bert and Emmaline, and with their new baby they have their hopes set on the third room, which has been "unoccupied for several years" (117). But that, of course, is where James Tolliver installs the old man. Such a move would under almost any circumstances have violated Bert and Emmaline's privacy, but that violation is compounded by another factor in the configuration of the garage rooms, which Emmaline realizes when Mr. Tolliver brings the man in: "He would have to pass through her very own bedroom to reach the bathroom" (121).

James Tolliver's apparently compassionate gesture to the old man thus comes to seem grossly insensitive from Bert and Emmaline's point of view, the perspective from which Taylor establishes the narrative. Emmaline instantly recognizes the inevitable obligation that Tolliver has, without considering it, placed upon her: "Here [the old man] had come—himself to be nursed and someday, no doubt, to die on her hands. She studied the room for a moment, mocking her earlier appraisals of it as a possible nursery"

(120-21). Emmaline's self-abusive despair is a sign of more than ordinary disappointment. The arrival of the old man has reminded Emmaline of the limits of her economic possibilities. She has internalized her culture's material desires, but because of its racism that culture also prevents her attainment of them. She and Bert are thus victimized by their ambitions.

This is not to suggest, however, that Bert and Emmaline are in some way unusually ambitious for material wealth. To the contrary, Bert holds Emmaline in high respect because her ambition seems pragmatically moderate. She has "no illusions about someday leaving domestic service" and has accepted her position with the Tollivers as preferable to life "in the leaking, lean-to-kind of shack she had been brought up in." Her fundamental desire is a modest one—to have "a family of her own" (128). This fuller sense of Emmaline and her ambitions allows us to understand more completely the depression into which the old man's arrival plunges her. When she is stripped of her dream of a nursery, she is also, in a sense, stripped of her conception of the possible dignity of her life and forced to see her situation without the veneer of hope: "She and Bert were still living, after all, in a barn. And yet she had named this room a nursery" (121).

As we have seen in stories such as "The Old Forest" and "Venus, Cupid, Folly and Time," the categories of social identity and psychological equilibrium are interdependent in Taylor's fiction. Social analysis often serves him as the mode of entry for psychological inquiry. "Bad Dreams" exemplifies this pattern as well; the arrival of the old man adds a new and unexpected element of stress to Bert and Emmaline's relationship, one that is already precarious. Taylor's strategy of exploring the psychological dynamics of their marriage is important for advancing his larger argument that social and economic oppression does have a high psychological cost. But his psychological analysis also allows us to see Bert and Emmaline as more than merely victims, and to find in their struggle for dignity and equilibrium a basis for sympathy.

Bert's reaction to Emmaline's seething anger at the appearance of the old man is our first indication of the nature of the strain in their marriage. "I *was* mad about it, Emmaline, but I'm not no more," he tells her, displaying an equanimity in the face of adversity that is characteristic of his personality. But his calmness irritates her: "'*Was* mad about it?' she said, taking a step toward him. The emphasis of his 'no more' was somehow irksome to her. 'I tell you I *am* mad about it,' she said. 'And I aim to stay mad about it,

Bert. I'm not going to have it'" (125). Emmaline has transferred part of her frustration with Mr. Tolliver to Bert, whose passivity she sees as part of her larger problem.

Bert is less passive about the situation than it seems. "We going to run him off" (129), he tells her. His plan of covert resistance signals an important difference between his personality and Emmaline's: when confronted with some difficulty, Bert is "always bound and compelled to get around at last to some happy, self-mollifying view of the matter" (126). His odd cheerfulness in the face of the invasion of his family's privacy is therefore less a gauge of his actual concern than an indication of the importance he places on self-control and the maintenance of at least a superficial measure of calm.

That emphasis is reflected in his attempt to calm Emmaline down as well: "No use my being mad about it and no use your getting that crazy-woman look in your eyes about it. . . . You been walking around like 'Stracted Mag" (125-26). Bert's reference to " 'Stracted Mag" is an appeal to a bond of humor that he and Emmaline share over "a poor demented old Negro woman wandering the streets of their hometown when Bert and Emmaline were children, jabbering to everyone, understood by no one, but credited by all with a fierce hatred of the white race" (126). He is attempting to humor Emmaline out of her anger, but his reference to 'Stracted Mag calls up the worst image of the old life of Thornton that they are trying to escape in St. Louis. Her "fierce hatred of the white race" makes it clear that an important source of their difficulty is the racial oppression under which they live. The old woman embodies the buried rage against racial oppression that they each keep under uneasy check in their lives in service with the Tollivers.

Emmaline lets her emotion surface more freely at first, but Bert's anger is buried very shallowly, and his superficial calm is more dangerous than Emmaline's open wrath. Bert cannot bear "protracted gloom" on any subject and has successfully found ways to maintain his cheerful temper—but he is irrationally ill-tempered when "awakened in the middle of the night" (126). Practiced in keeping his frustrations under check by force of will, he becomes a victim of his pent-up anger when sleep disables his willed vigilance. That weakness of course suggests the enormous strain under which Bert maintains his placid demeanor. His volcanic personality is the sign of the distortion that has resulted from his insistence on calm in the face of trouble.

The old man's arrival thus ignites smoldering emotions that Bert and Emmaline are barely able to contain. Bert's determined calmness helps to create a superficial peace at bedtime that night, but it is broken when they are awakened by "a terrible shrieking—a noise wild enough to be inhuman, and yet unmistakably human" (131): the cry of their baby. Emmaline, confusedly searching for the baby in the crib, screams out Bert's name, and Bert reacts in a rage, threatening both her and the baby even while he cradles the child in his arms. This scene of anguish and night terror effectively captures the emotional intensity generated by the conflicting drives that Bert and Emmaline try to manage day by day.

The piercing cry brings into open consciousness the bad dreams that Bert and Emmaline cannot keep entirely suppressed. Emmaline was dreaming of 'Stracted Mag approaching her on the town square in Thornton with "three or four cur dogs on a leash, . . . walking between two Thornton white ladies whom Emmaline recognized" (138-39). Emmaline feels the impulse to "run forward and throw her arms about old Mag and tell her how she admired her serene and calm manner," an impulse that suggests both her attraction to Mag as an embodiment of her own anger, and her desire to mask or control that anger by imagining Mag as a representation of serenity rather than anger. But then she realizes the threat that the woman embodies: "She saw old Mag unleash the dogs, and the dogs rushed upon her growling and turning back their lips to show their yellow, tobacco-stained teeth" (139).

Frozen at first in her attempt to scream, she manages to do so as she is awakened by her baby, her inner fear expressed through the cries of her child. Mag's vicious dogs are indications of the destructive forces, both internal and external, that threaten Emmaline. Mag's "walking between two Thornton white ladies" is also significant, for these white women represent the barriers to Emmaline's aspirations for her family and a life of dignity.

Bert's dream is equally revelatory of the fear and anxiety that he struggles to quell. "He had thought he was a little boy in school again, in the old one-room Negro grade school at Thornton." This is a dream that Bert has had many times before, its recurrence a sign that, like Emmaline, he has escaped Thornton only partially and remains haunted by a sense of oppression rooted in his childhood experience. Oppression has inscribed itself in him as a severe denial of impulse, a characteristic noted earlier in his suppression of rage and represented in his dream as the blocking of bodily needs: "He was seated in the back of the room, far away from the stove, and he was cold. It seemed he had forgotten to go to the privy before he left home, as he so often used to forget, but he could not bring himself to raise his hand and ask to go now." Bert's extreme passivity in the dream is indicative of his general stance of submissiveness before authority, exemplified in his refusal to confront James Tolliver to protest the living arrangements for the old man.

His submissiveness is reinforced by a deeper sense of insecurity, emphasized in the dream by Bert's fear of failure in the school: "The teacher was asking him to read, and he could not find the place on the page" (139). This sense of failure precedes a greater sense of dread that takes several forms in the dream: "Sometimes the teacher said, 'Why can't you learn, boy?' and commenced beating him. Sometimes he ran past the teacher (who sometimes was a white man) to the door and found the door locked. Sometimes he got away and ran down to the school privy, to find indescribable horrors awaiting him there" (139-40). These scenarios are all representations of imprisonment, made doubly significant by their association with the institution of the school, here shown as an instrument of oppression, and with the teacher ("sometimes . . . a white man") as a figure of repressive authority. The dream reflects Bert's sense of the social and economic imprisonment of life in the small-town, Western Tennessee environment of Thornton, imprisonment that has continued in a new form in his employment with the Tollivers in St. Louis. His method of escape from one intolerable situation has been to enter what seems now to be another.

Taylor's use of the dreams for detailed character revelation is one of his chief accomplishments in "Bad Dreams," but it does not exhaust the story. One of the most surprising elements is the intervention of the old man in the familial chaos brought on by the baby's cries. On his first appearance in the story we are told not only of Emmaline's despair over the loss of her hoped-for nursery but of her contempt for the old man as representative of a life she has tried to flee. When she sees him standing in "the ill-furnished bedroom,. . . dropping his bundle on the lumpy mattress," she is reminded of "all the poverty and nigger life she had known as a girl in Tennessee, before the Tollivers had sent back for her" (121-22). It is as if a reminder of a past that she has not escaped is shadowing her.

Although we may sympathize with her desire to transcend her past, her resulting attitude toward the old man is nevertheless harsh, for it denies him fully human status. He is, for her, "a dirty old ignoramus" (120), an "unwashed and ragged old man," or a "shiftless and lousy-looking creature" (122). She will grant him no identity other than as an object of revulsion, maintaining through her contempt for him her hope for a separate, higher status. Bert too is unable to see the old man as much more than a reminder of a past that he would like to forget and an object of frustration that he must somehow overcome.

In the ironic climax of the story the old man suddenly enters the bedroom to care for the baby. Neither Bert nor Emmaline, disoriented by their fear and anger, have been able to calm her, and their frustration builds into alarm and recrimination over her condition. The baby's distress grows along with that of the parents until Emmaline, near panic, feels "her baby being jerked away from her" and sees "the dirty old man holding the baby upside down by her feet, as he would have held a chicken" (134-35). The tactic works, and the baby's shrill cry becomes a softer one. Despite her extreme alarm, Emmaline is forced to recognize that the old man's voice is "fraught with kindliness" as he explains the baby's ailment: "Bad dreams," he says. "Bad dreams is all" (136).

The appearance of the old man allows Taylor to shift the focus from the psychological stress of Bert and Emmaline's marriage to a somewhat broader social commentary. But in making this shift, Taylor also reveals a tension in his own social perspective. He has, to this point, built considerable sympathy for the young couple, laying out persuasively their struggle for a domestic stability that is dependent on a certain level of economic attainment and security. Their dependence, and their somewhat callous treatment by the Tollivers, has been made clear, and the implicit message of the story has thus been the injustice of the Southern racial hierarchy. The old man James Tolliver has brought home has therefore functioned only as an extension of the Tollivers, a reminder of their final control over the nature and quality of Bert and Emmaline's life.

But Taylor insists, at the end, that we see this man more completely. His presence of mind in the moment of crisis, his experience with children, his sense of understanding for Bert and Emmaline all help to establish him as much more than an agent of James Tolliver. The old man is in many ways a reminder of the African American community of Thornton and other small Southern towns and the capacity of such communities to offer belonging and sustenance to their members.[6] In pursuing their dreams of a new life in St. Louis, Bert and Emmaline have consciously fled from that community and its poverty. But understandable as their desire to better themselves economically is, Taylor suggests that they must also maintain a positive bond with the past and with their own community.

The "bad dreams" that give the story its title are therefore not only the nightmares that Bert, Emmaline, and their baby suffer in the narrative. The bad dream is in a larger sense the "American Dream," which Bert and Emmaline have accepted in a somewhat constrictive and detrimental way. Although their material aspirations are presented as modestly reasonable ones, even those desires blind them to the necessity for compassion and respect for the old man and what he represents. Their unthinking exclusion of him is callous and shortsighted because they have been not only oppressed economically by the Tollivers and the system they represent but also robbed of a sustaining community and its values in their St. Louis lives. The old man represents Bert and Emmaline's ties to their heritage as African Americans, and their link to the crucial community of sustaining values inherent in that heritage.

Taylor's conflicting impulses are thus readily apparent at the end of the story. He is sympathetic with Bert and Emmaline, given the obvious barriers to their generally modest aspirations, but sympathetic as well to the old man, who is also a victim. His somewhat forced attempt to redirect the reader's sympathy from Bert and Emmaline to the old man places the young couple's aspirations in a larger critical framework and thus reaffirms the need for a rootedness of generational continuity and communal identity, even as the story has valorized Bert and Emmaline's efforts to establish themselves in the American middle class. Both these needs, Taylor argues by implication, are fundamental, even though they seem to collide. In struggling with very real economic difficulties, Bert and Emmaline run the further risk of losing connection with a cultural heritage that can be important to them. Whereas their bad dreams suggest the painful qualities of their connection with that heritage, the old man's appearance emphasizes the importance of retaining a constructive relationship with it. The story thus illustrates Taylor's repeated belief that any progress toward overcoming the past must be made not by complete rejection of it but through a positive engagement with it that will help to foster a more complete and balanced self-understanding and comprehension of the social world.

❖ 7 ❖
Dramas of Southern Identity

The principal characters of Taylor's fiction are almost all Southerners, most of whom have complicated and somewhat troubled identities *as* Southerners and deep but ambivalent attachments to the family heritage, social customs, and geographies that constitute their "Southernness." Taylor's portraits of them suggest his irreverent skepticism about the usual regional pieties and his recognition that a Southern identity is sometimes a barrier on the road to self-understanding. His engagement with his own Southern identity was complicated, he explained, by his family's residence in St. Louis during his late childhood and adolescence. As Senator Caswell remarks in *Tennessee Day in St. Louis*, "Sometimes the Southerners one meets out of the South seem more Southern than the South" (*TD*, 22), and it seems that the removal of Taylor's family from the South during important years of his development may have made the question of the nature of Southern identity important to him at a formative time in his life. In *A Woman of Means*, Quint Dudley's brief development of his identity as "the Southerner" while attending school in St. Louis probably reflects some aspects of Taylor's adolescent experience at the St. Louis Country Day School, which he attended from 1929 to 1932. Quint's adoption of that role and consequent ambivalence about playing it reflect Taylor's view of the false and destructive effect of assuming the burden of a Southern identity. At its extreme, this burden seems to inflict several of his fictional narrators with a form of paralytic nostalgia.[1]

Another contributing factor to Taylor's view of Southern culture was his educational experience under Allen Tate at Southwestern University in Memphis, John Crowe Ransom at Kenyon, and Robert Penn Warren at Louisiana State, and his developing friendship with Randall Jarrell, whom he met as a student at Kenyon.[2] As we observed in Chapter 5, Taylor's exposure to the Southern "Agrarian" school did not make him one of the Agrarians, and he viewed their ideas with increasing skepticism as he matured. Nevertheless, their attempt to identify some unique qualities of the

Southern cultural experience did hold a certain interest for him, for it represented a serious grappling with the problems of living out a "Southern" identity in a modern age.

As Louis D. Rubin has perceptively argued, the Agrarians did not write with a secure sense of possessing an established culture; rather, theirs was a sense of cultural loss and displacement: "A great deal of the impetus behind the writing of *I'll Take My Stand* [the central Agrarian manifesto], it seems to me, came out of this sense of community breakup, with its resulting loss of the individual role within the community."[3] The Agrarian project, therefore, in part a protest against modern commercial culture, implicitly recognized that the loss of community had already taken place. Taylor, writing a generation later, was even more sure of the loss of Southern community life but much less disposed to romanticize it. For him, the "South" and "Southernness" were deeply problematical terms.

The question of Southern identity usually haunts the characters of Taylor's fiction only indirectly. Although no one can miss the fact that they are, in most cases, Tennesseans, they are less Southerners than sons, daughters, lovers, husbands, wives, or parents. They are conscious of their traditions, customs, and regional values—sometimes in search of ways of living them out and sometimes in rebellion against them—but less obsessed with "the South" than with the difficulties of their own inner lives and personal relationships. In two key works for the stage, however, Taylor brings the theme of the Southern identity into the foreground, exploring characters who are representative of Southern culture or fundamentally concerned with it, and portraying situations intended to give form to the abstract concept of "the South." *Tennessee Day in St. Louis* (1955), and *A Stand in the Mountains* (1968) are ambitious works that speak authoritatively of Taylor's view of his Southern cultural heritage, depicting the struggle of modern Southerners to understand themselves during a period in which modern America is more completely subsuming its regions and thereby accelerating their movement away from their cultural roots.

In *Tennessee Day in St. Louis,* Lanny Tolliver, son of a Tennessee family displaced to St. Louis, demonstrates how an adolescent's hunger for Southern roots as a form of secure identity can result in a self-devouring and destructive compulsion.[4] A sensitive and intellectual boy who is deeply troubled about his place in the world, Lanny is captivated by the news that a distant cousin, Senator Cameron Caswell of Tennessee, will be visiting the Tolliver family on "Tennessee Day," an annual event when the tribe of transplanted Tennesseans in St. Louis gather to reaffirm their roots and maintain the network of connections that replaces their lost families and communities in Tennessee. The ninety-year-old Caswell is the type of the old Southern orator and politician, a man whose memory extends beyond the Civil War and who embodies in his nine decades the history of the South. Taylor paints him in broadly comic tones as a man with a large ego and a large appetite for good whiskey, good food, and bombastic oratory—a survivor of an earlier age, now almost a caricature of the old Southern patriarchy.

This antique quality in Senator Caswell appeals to Lanny, a soul who is unquiet in the modern world. Caswell's visit, Lanny confesses, "would be the answer to a million questions I have had about who I am and about our whole family" (*TD,* 35). Unable to find himself in the modern world, Lanny looks to his Tennessee heritage as a secure grounding for his identity.[5] But this hoped-for security is elusive because, as Taylor carefully shows, "the South" is in large part a shared fiction that can be destructively delusive.

Taylor represents Lanny's fascination with the old ways of the traditional South as a sign of dangerous intellectual imbalance that signals a deeper emotional turmoil. Caswell's fire-eating political oratory appeals to him the most, presenting an uncompromisingly defiant image of the South and thus the security of a vivid and well-defined social identity. At one point Lanny recounts Caswell's appearance in a dream, delivering an oration in which he proclaims "there is no new South; there is only the old South resurrected with the print of the nails in her hand" (37). Taylor later explained that this sentence was taken directly from one of the speeches of his grandfather, Robert Love Taylor, and that he had used it in the first paper he wrote for his freshman English class with Allen Tate (*Conversations,* 117). Here he uses this image of the defiant old South with a clear sense of how it might appeal to a troubled adolescent like Lanny, and how inevitably destructive that appeal might be. Insofar as the old South was endangered by modernity, it represented a way of resisting modernity. This is why Caswell is so crucially important to Lanny. "I am a traditionalist. *I* am a reactionary!" Lanny declares (38). But his traditionalism is based not on any desire to preserve important values but only on his fear of the emerging modern world.

Lanny's struggle to find and somehow live out his "Southernness" is thus a central theme of the play.[6] His identity crisis is also connected to another important strand of the play, the relationship between Lucy McDougal and her lover William, Lanny's uncle. Lucy and William are living together out of wedlock in conscious defiance of the norms of marriage and family. Their relationship constitutes a test of the continuing vitality of these norms and intersects with Lanny's rebellion against modernism in its questioning of "family," a quintessential locus of "Southern" values.

Lanny's tortured search for an identity and Lucy and William's attempt to forge a relationship outside of conventional marriage are therefore vehicles whereby Taylor can explore important aspects of the nature of the changing Southern culture. These strands of the play's narrative are linked through Lanny's close relationship with Lucy. Despite their age difference and fundamental disparity in outlook, Lanny and Lucy have the trust to be able to unburden themselves to each other. She sees him as a surrogate son, a painful reminder of all that she has foregone in her childless relationship with William.

Lanny resents William's treatment of Lucy, although he is still too innocent to realize that she and William are lovers until she reveals it to him in act 1, telling him also that William is breaking their relationship and leaving for the West Coast. Even though Lanny's perspective is marred by his jealousy of William and his emotional confusion, his sympathy for Lucy is genuine and, we come to see, well founded, for she is a woman who in some respects has been exploited by William's "modern" ideas about marriage and sexual freedom. Her own struggle with these ideas is profound, and her intellectual honesty and emotional openness make her one of Taylor's most interesting and appealing characters.

Lanny's effort to achieve self-understanding and Lucy's crisis in her relationship with William are brought together at the end of act 2, when it is revealed that Lanny has attempted suicide by taking an overdose of sleeping pills. The attempt suggests both his deep unhappiness and his flair for the dramatic gesture: it expresses his sense of lost alternatives but also seems designed to draw attention from both Lucy and Senator Caswell.

Lanny sees Lucy in some respects as a parental figure, but he is erotically attracted to her, as well, his desire adding to the emotional havoc in his turmoil-ridden state of mind. When Lucy confesses that she has been William's mistress for a number of years, he is shocked and angered; he first presses her to condemn William and then abruptly changes tone to declare,

"Lucy, I love you." When Lucy matter-of-factly responds, "Of course you do," he makes himself plainer: "No, I mean something worse than that." Lucy dismisses his declaration, with a certain perceptiveness, as the "play-acting" of a "child" (45), not realizing the lengths to which Lanny will go to dramatize his love and unhappiness. This exchange, from which Lanny takes a sense both of betrayal and of guilt, is a crucial backdrop to his suicide attempt.

The unexpected result, however, is to bring William closer to Lanny, and that closeness moves William to reconsider his insistent stance against marriage. It is William who discovers Lanny before the sleeping pills can do significant harm. "Without you, Lanny might not be alive now," Lucy tells him later (106), and even though he insists that Lanny was not in real danger, it is clear that the incident has had a powerful effect on him. "It doesn't seem likely to you that I could be 'touched' by anything that happened," he says to Lucy, but he explains to her that he *was* touched, quite literally, through his physical contact with Lanny: "That's when I was touched—dragging him into the bathroom, squeezing his middle, dragging him back to his room again. It was how he felt to me that touched me. Poor, skinny, helpless kid" (108).

William's contact with Lanny forces him to recognize his own mortality and his own age, a moment of self-confrontation that challenges profoundly his contempt for marriage, family, and the settled life. His relationship with Lucy has been part of a prolonged adolescent rebellion carried into middle age. But in saving Lanny he has understood something of the role of father which, in refusing to marry Lucy, he has rejected. A parent's physical contact with a child is always a subtle reminder of the fragility of the body and the preciousness and vulnerability of life. Such reminders have presumably been missing from William's bachelor life, but holding the helpless Lanny in this moment of urgent danger has been a powerful lesson. "Yes, I was watching you when you finally let go of him," Lucy says. "It was with a certain gentleness after all that roughness" (108). Although it happens offstage and is recounted to us at second hand in this dialogue, William's rescue of Lanny is the most important action in the play, working a transformation of both the savior and the saved.

William's change is revealed most explicitly when he explains to Lucy a dream that he had after saving Lanny. The dream makes it clear that at least subconsciously he has understood the significance of his act, and it is in the telling of it that he begins to draw out its implications for his course of life and his relationship with Lucy. "I dreamed we had a boy just Lanny's age," he tells her. "We *could* have had, Lucy! The kid in my dream *was* actually Lanny, except of course he wasn't." And, he adds, the boy "was threatening me somehow, and I was scared as hell of him. I called out to you" (111). William's account is, for Lucy, especially painful; as she angrily reminds him, his seeming change of heart is very ill timed, since she is "too old to have children" (112).

William's dream must thus be seen as compounded of both wish and regret, and his recollection of it brings to the surface some apparent doubt or hesitation about his decision to leave St. Louis and end his relationship with Lucy. The practical consequence is that he reopens the question of his leaving for the West, admitting to Lucy that although he has not been changed dramatically enough actually to want children, he has been brought to see his relationship with her in a different light and to consider staying with her. But Lucy knows William too well to accept this momentary tenderness as a sign of any permanent change. "It's a mirage you're seeing, William," she tells him. "Don't confuse your dreams with what's real. It's always been your peculiar strength that you didn't do that" (112). There is bitterness in Lucy's rebuff but also valuable wisdom won by hard experience. She recognizes the deep scars that William carries from his early family life, and she understands the extent to which he has formed his adult identity through the denial of family bonds. The momentary sense of loss that he feels in the aftermath of Lanny's suicide attempt will not permanently alter this identity.

Lucy's immediate dismissal of William's offer to resume the relationship is also a gesture of self-protection. She *cannot* allow herself to believe that his change is permanent for fear of deepening the hurt that she has already undergone. Having shared William's "modern" view of marriage and family at least to some extent, she has grown to see its tragic limitations and its increasingly dire consequences for her as she ages. Although William seems to be opening himself in a moment of rare vulnerability, Lucy is reluctant to take advantage of this momentary reversal. "It would have to have more thought from you than you have had time to give it," she tells him (112). She has come to accept the essential tragedy of their relationship, realizing that in running from the pain of marriage and family life, they have replicated it in a new form.

Lucy's outlook is elaborated more fully in act 3 through her dialogue with Miss Betty Pettigru, James Tolliver's cousin, a woman whose status as the spinster relative devoted to the family's welfare makes her an important analogue to Lucy. Taylor introduces her into the play to allow a fuller commentary on the inequity of gender roles in the Southern social structure. Through "Auntie Bet" he can illustrate the ruthless quality of the institution of the family, for she has, in her spinsterhood, been forced to the margins of the family and thus of the culture. Lucy, in the collapse of her relationship with William, has come to see her own condition as permanently unmarried, and thus she looks to Auntie Bet as a model of what such a life may hold for her.

Auntie Bet, who is accepted as part of the extended Tolliver family, suggests the importance of family life even to those excluded from its foundation in marriage. Their exchange is in some respects an icy one, for Lucy understands Bet's disapproval of the conditions of her relationship with William. Lucy returns her frank disapproval by bluntly asking her how she has been able to "make something out of a life that might have been a pretty sad and pointless affair"—a life, that is, as "an old maid in one of those country towns of ours" (116). This is the fate that Lucy thought she had escaped through her unconventional relationship with William. Her directness is not finally a hostile one but rather an attempt to find shared ground upon which she and Bet can establish some understanding. She approaches Bet as an independent woman who is aware of the difficult position of the unmarried woman in the Southern social structure, and she seeks her counsel on the possibility of reconciliation and marriage with William.

But Bet cannot respond as the independent woman that Lucy is seeking. Her answer is the conventional one: she encourages Lucy to settle for "nothing less" than marriage. When Lucy presses her for her reasons, she explains that a woman must "play [her] cards" in the most effective way in order to assure herself some place in the Southern family structure. "The legend of family pride in the South," she explains, has in large part been created and maintained by women who were in fact marginal to that structure, widows or maiden aunts who made themselves in some way or another a part of the family (120-21). Her advice implies that Lucy would play her strongest hand by marrying William and thus linking herself inextricably to the Tolliver family and to their children. To achieve some measure of family identification—even though she may not have her own children—would afford Lucy a sense of belonging in a world that otherwise ruthlessly excludes those outside its prescribed boundaries.

But such advice, making plain the extreme inequities of gender upon which the Southern social structure is based, horrifies Lucy. Bet tells her that she must make herself "indispensable," and the best way to do so is through marriage. But when Lucy presses her by asking, "To whom is it we are indispensable?" Bet answers frankly: "To the menfolks. To their sense of manliness, to their feeling of security and power and superiority." In revulsion, Lucy terms this a "very ugly picture." Bet can only agree but responds that it is nevertheless "a faithful one" (122-23).

The unintended effect of Bet's survival-oriented advice, however, is to make plain to Lucy that she cannot marry William, given the false position that she would be assuming were she to use the role or status of William's wife to solidify a bond with the Tollivers. Her orientation to the stability that the Tollivers represent would conflict with William's need for freedom—or, at least, his need to think of himself as "free." Lucy understands this aspect of his personality better than anyone else: "Does anyone understand, really, how much William hates all human ties that might be binding upon him in any way?" she asks Bet. "Have the rest of you realized that William's great satisfaction in living here has been the daily reminder that he *is* free of you all?" (118-19). Lucy is not one inclined to believe in the sudden transformation of character, and in this she represents Taylor's attitude with great accuracy. Bet's sermon on the necessity of her marriage to William only persuades her of its impossibility.

For William, however, the appeal of marriage seems to grow during the afternoon and evening following Lanny's suicide attempt. When he returns to the Tolliver house that evening, his parental attitude toward Lanny is even stronger. Encouraging the boy in a fatherly way to "be sensible" and to "begin using your head," he also offers him a promise about the future: "Lucy and I are going to get married, Lan. Right away" (160). Far from comforting Lanny, the announcement enrages him, revealing both his jealousy of William and his mistrust of the way his uncle treats Lucy.

Lanny's hostile reaction to his fatherly gesture is an important dose of realism for William. More potent still is his subsequent dialogue with Lucy, in which we see her enact a strategy to abort William's plans for the marriage. Rather than reject his offer, she wants to cause him to see for himself the superficial or fleeting nature of the family-oriented impulse that seized him after Lanny's attempted suicide. She therefore tells William that marriage is a "debt" that he owes her, and that his proposal offers her only what is hers "by rights" (161-62). The claim terrifies him, resurrecting his old fear of becoming captive to the institutions of marriage and family. He hastily exits, resuming his plan to leave St. Louis for the West.

Lanny witnesses this exchange and realizes that Lucy has consciously chosen to present William with a sense of obligation in order to force his rejection of marriage. "You *made* him go on without you," Lanny says to her. "You sent him off so he wouldn't be trapped here. . . . You felt that if he didn't get away tonight he might never get away" (163-64). But although Lanny understands the degree of calculation in Lucy's maneuver, he does not know that she has come to believe what she told William. While rehearsing her part of the dialogue, she admits, "I began to understand that the things I was going to say were truly what I felt" (165). She has recognized that her sense of having been wronged, her feeling that William owed her what he felt he was voluntarily giving, would shadow the relationship and make its flourishing impossible.

She knows moreover, that his impulse toward marriage, the act of formalizing the permanence of their relationship, has in fact been motivated less by the dynamics of the relationship itself than by the desire to reach out to Lanny and enact a parental role that might be helpful to him. "It was you that William and I were going to get hold of. William and I are nothing to each other any more, Lanny. But if we could have got hold of you, we would have had a common interest—that is, we could have begun deceiving ourselves, at your expense" (166). The delusion of extended childhood that she and William might have offered Lanny would have been based on a delusion of parenthood that they would have had to sustain between themselves. Lucy understands that just as Lanny must come to some acceptance of himself as he is, so must she. "The simple fact is it was too late for William and me to marry," she explains to Lanny. "The time had passed" (166). This is in one sense an admission of failure, but it is the kind of admission that signals a constructive acceptance of the past and the present moment, an acceptance upon which a future can be built.

As Lucy's difficult recognition that it is too late for her and William suggests, *Tennessee Day in St. Louis* moves its characters toward the destruction of their illusions. Although the action of the play takes place on a day given to tradition, ancestor worship, and the propagation of the myth that the old South is alive and well, that celebration ironically leads the central characters, Lucy and Lanny, to recognize that the "South" is really a name for escapism. Taylor underscores this argument by expressing it through Senator Caswell, the play's most unlikely vehicle for such thoughts. "I would have talked to you about old times back home as though it was all day before yesterday, as you no doubt believe it was," he tells Lanny. "But it isn't so!" (158). As an embodiment of the myth of the old South, and in many ways one of its chief propagators, Caswell nevertheless understands its power and its danger. Lanny must come to see that "by any sensible reckoning of history there are a thousand years between your generation and mine." Even what remains of a connection between present and past in the Tolliver family and the Tennessee Day ceremony that they help to sustain is doomed. "And in another decade or two," he tells Lanny, "even such a meeting as the one I addressed tonight—if anyone recalls it—will seem like something out of an age ancient and remote" (158). Caswell does not speak in bitterness, but his frank realism is clearly a warning to Lanny to put aside his dreams of the past and face the present.

Taylor's play does not take us beyond Tennessee Day, but by its end we have gained some confidence that both Lanny and Lucy have emerged from crises able to make decisions and adjustments that will serve them well in the future. Lucy's acceptance of her middle age and her seemingly permanent status as a spinster and Lanny's confrontation with the fact that he may not retreat into either a dependency on Lucy or a fantasy of the Southern past are the kinds of adjustments to the course of life that are Taylor's prime subjects. There is, in *Tennessee Day in St. Louis*, some indication that these adjustments have been negotiated positively, which is certainly not always the case in Taylor's work. The potential for tragedy still shadows the play—represented by Lucy's break with William, Lanny's near suicide, and Caswell's last speech, an old man's sobering farewell to the world he has known—but it offers at least a measure of hope in the unmasking of illusion as the first step toward emotional wholeness and moral integrity.

As *Tennessee Day in St. Louis* suggests, Taylor's ruminations about the South and the question of a Southern identity inevitably return to the problematics of family. The play's exploration of Southern identity entails an exploration of marriage and parenthood as the characters' connection to the Southern social system devolves into their place, or lack of place, as members of a family. The case of Lanny illustrates that one's cultural identification as a "Southerner" functions if anything as an illusory and possibly dangerous distraction.

The somewhat unusual directness and intensity with which *Tennessee Day in St. Louis* pursues the question of the South is amplified in *A Stand in the Mountains*, one of Taylor's most extensive explorations of the Southern social structure and its history. This play, with its lengthy prose introduction, presents formidable problems for stage production, but it provided Taylor with an opportunity to go beyond the realism that defined his fiction.[7] In so doing, he opened a Faulknerian world of psychic pain and violent conflict.

A Stand in the Mountains is set in the Cumberland Mountain resort of Owl Mountain Springs, the same setting Taylor used later in "The Witch of Owl Mountain Springs" and in a climactic late scene of *A Summons to Memphis*. Owl Mountain is a landscape of dreams for Taylor, in which inner drives and conflicts are vividly present and incapable of being repressed or fully controlled. Taylor's usual fictional strategy is to record the subtle patterns of interaction through which desire and memory are expressed obliquely or indirectly. In this work his keen sense of the nuances of Southern manners is his most important tool. But at Owl Mountain, for some reason, characters do not mask themselves, and their deeper motivations—often aggressive and violent—are much nearer the surface.

In speaking of Owl Mountain as a symbolic and psychological landscape, we must remember how deeply it is anchored in Taylor's personal experience. The mountain resort is based loosely on the resort at Monteagle, Tennessee. "My family has been going to Monteagle for hundreds of years, it seems, and people I've known for hundreds of years," Taylor explained in an interview with J. William Broadway. And in conversation with Hubert H. McAlexander he specified that "a cottage that we owned [in Monteagle] is the house I had in mind for my play *A Stand in the Mountains*" (*Conversations*, 105, 123). Taylor met and married his wife, Eleanor Ross Taylor, there, and summer stays at Monteagle provided his family a place of continuity with Tennessee friends and relatives, and with a family past, during years in which "we lived all over this country and in Europe" (*Conversations*, 105). For Taylor, Monteagle was a formative and sustaining part of his relation to the South, and it remained imaginatively for him a last vestige of the Southern past: "When everything else had changed, it was very much the same up there" (*Conversations*, 97).

Conscious of the potential uses of such a setting for a literature concerned with cultural change and social displacement, Taylor delineated the significance of Owl Mountain in a prefatory essay to *A Stand in the Mountains*, "a sort of history of the imaginary place and the imaginary people that I have here put together" (*Stand*, 9). If we remember Taylor's sense of Owl Mountain as a surviving island of the Southern world in the flood of modernism, the essay assumes a crucial relation not only to the play it prefaces but to his entire fictional creation.[8]

Taylor describes Owl Mountain through a fundamental class division between "summer people" and "mountain people," a distinction that becomes very important in the development of the play. "The summer people," who come to the mountain as a resort, come to it "in the most real sense—from another world" (10), with their economic power and their pretensions to aristocratic lineage. The "mountain people" are marginalized Southerners: a racially mixed group, excluded from the course of Southern development, whose history took a different course from that of the whites who established the Cotton Culture. "These are a race that the modern world, and the not-so-modern world of the Old South, had passed by, passed up, passed over" (10).

Although this division between summer people and mountain people is the fundamental class difference represented at Owl Mountain, it should also be recognized that the summer people cannot be regarded simply as plantation aristocrats. In the early years of the resort, Taylor explains, "all manner of people commingled on the hotel veranda and in the shade of the maples and oaks on the mall." More a refuge from the yellow fever at that time than a leisure resort, Owl Mountain came to be a microcosm of the white South: "Nearly all classes of Southerners of that period were represented there, and perhaps they tolerated each other because they knew that they were all refugees from the Fever" (14-15). This bond of adversity gave the resort something of an exotic identity to begin with, and as it continued into the twentieth century, its chief supporters and patrons were not the dying Southern aristocracy but "sons and daughters of the old regime" whose "energy" and "vitality" made them reject "shabby gentility" (17) and the limited economic sphere of rural and small-town Southern life. These new Southerners, familiar in the Nashville and Memphis settings in so many of Taylor's stories, returned to Owl Mountain in an attempt to retain something their new lives were incapable of producing: a connection with nature and continuity with family and social tradition. Modern urban life had effaced that continuity. Consciously or not, they also sought the moun-

recognition of the false basis of Harry's commitment, is "a drab creature, dispossessed of the girlish prettiness she once had and nowadays making no effort at attractiveness" (21). "I can't bear the sight of her," Harry declares late in the play, after which, realizing what he has said, he "gasps audibly" (60).

The complex layers of denial and self-delusion resulting from his decision to live among the mountain people have made Harry a powder keg of repressed conflict—which explodes in the play's melodramatic climax, his murder of Lucille and his children. Harry has kept his terrible energies in check by devoting himself to a scheme for the economic reformation of the Owl Mountain area. He wants to incorporate the village, including the grounds of the resort, and bring through a four-lane highway—projects that would violently wrench this preserve of the past into the present. He also hopes to run for mayor of the newly incorporated town. His grandiose plans for the community and his attempt to position himself as its leader, suggest that he shares the essential nature of his father, a wealthy and influential attorney who once ran for mayor of Louisville.

Transforming Owl Mountain would in large part be self-serving entrepreneurship in that it would establish Harry as the chief purveyor of the local crafts. While profiting financially from his adopted mountain culture, however (and thus changing its nature fundamentally), he would also accomplish a second task: the destruction of the Owl Mountain Resort, a key part of his mother's world. His Uncle Will, hopelessly devoted to his sister-in-law Louisa and dependent on Owl Mountain as a place of refuge from the changing world, is horrified when he hears of Harry's plan to incorporate the area. "Why do you want to ruin this place?" he asks in shock. He has assumed that Harry came to the mountains to escape the world of conventional business: "Our mountains are about the last place where that Chamber of Commerce image hasn't prevailed" (49-50). The motives that Will attributes to Harry describe his own sense of Owl Mountain as a refuge from the modern world.

Whereas Zack's rebellion results in a diffident non-involvement, Harry's entails a purposiveness that represents self-transformation to him. But it requires the making over the mountain and its people in his own image. Will accuses him of a "Chamber of Commerce" mentality in seeking economic development on the mountain, and Harry eventually confirms this in an oblique way. "I'm part of something real now. It took me a long time, but I've learned to want the things that most other people want. I'm like the other people on this mountain now" (52). In referring to "the other people," Harry pointedly means that he is no longer of the summer people—no longer, that is, his mother's son. The scheme for incorporating the mountain and bringing the highway through is thus crucial to the change of identity that Harry feels he has effected. When he discovers following the ballot for incorporation that this change is illusory, his tightly wound psyche comes violently apart.

Louisa is the play's unmoved mover, a figure whose personality is revealed more through reactions to her, which originate in the past, than by anything she says or does. Her sons' pent-up anger and Will's weak and hopeless love for her are indications of her forceful and charismatic personality, her will to control, her capacity for manipulation, and her self-absorption. But the figure that she presents on stage is far from that of an ogre; her personal magnetism explains in part the violent struggle that her sons have to engage in to try to free themselves from her. That magnetism makes her the play's catalyst, and all its action is a kind of competition for her approval or attention.

But Louisa herself is not the confident individual that she seems; she has transformed her identity in a rise to social prominence and must constantly reaffirm her self-construction. In moving from West Tennessee to Louisville after her marriage to Ned Weaver, she entered a world of status and comparative power which, in its forms and relations, gave her purpose. As she explains, "The chance to move in society in an old-fashioned American city is—or was—something no woman could reject with her whole heart." Even though she admits that it was in part "superficial and silly," it nevertheless provided "an energetic, imaginative, intelligent woman" with important "outlets for her especially womanly talents" (70). The Louisville world that had threatened to stifle Zack and Harry had given Louisa a context for self-expression, an arena in which her character could develop. Her conscious ambivalence about whether that world still exists, suggested by her hesitation over whether to choose "is" or "was" in describing it, is a telling sign of the insecurity that she now feels. Her passion has been to share her opportunity by selecting other young women, from backgrounds similar to hers, for introduction into Louisville society. It was just such an abortive attempt at initiation that came to epitomize her relation with Zack and Harry, the opportunity that she offered representing to them a form of imprisonment.

The focus of Louisa's attention now, the latest in her series of young protégées, is Mina, a distant Weaver cousin from Forkèd Deer, Tennessee, whom she hopes to present to Louisville society. Mina is in many respects a younger version of Louisa—strong-willed, magnetic, and sexually attractive. While visiting Louisa at Owl Mountain in preparation for her introduction to Louisville in the fall, she becomes something of a manifestation of the life force to the contentious and exhausted Weaver clan.

But unlike the women of Louisa's generation, Mina does not necessarily regard marriage into Louisville society as the only, or even the best, of her options for the future—and she definitely has her eye on the main chance. She is ambivalent about taking Louisa's help, in part because she instinctively feels the older woman's enormous power and recognizes its potential threat. As Louisa's surrogate daughter—and surrogate self—she has much to gain, but she admits to Harry that "in a way she frightens me" (63). At Owl Mountain Mina becomes increasingly aware of her own personal power when Harry and Zack fall in love with her, becoming Louisa's rivals for her attention and for her future. "You're nineteen," Zack tells her, "and no matter how hard you try to bury yourself here, or in Louisville, the world will come and find you. You're too good to miss" (111).

Louisa's ally in the struggle to control Mina is her brother-in-law Will, who has been part of her household since her husband's death, only recently becoming a year-round resident of Owl Mountain. Will's permanent move to the mountain is consonant with his detached antiquarianism; he is a Tennessee historian with a special interest in the mountain region and an intimate knowledge of the origins of the Owl Mountain Resort. Having immersed himself in the study of Southern history, he sees himself as an upholder of tradition and an opponent of the new South's direction of commercial development. An intellectual with both an antiquarian turn of mind and some of the early attitudes of the Agrarians, he has persisted in his resistance to modern America until he has become an irrelevant and crotchety conservative.

Will is in love with Louisa, and though he is unable to express it directly, he does so indirectly by assisting in her plans to introduce young women into Louisville society through the debutante system. As he explains to Zack, his relationship with her has been balked by a past incident in which he assumed financial responsibility for a child that was not, in fact, his own. Louisa "doesn't find me ridiculous," he insists to Zack. "She heard stories about me and Thelma, about Thelma's baby, and about how I paid certain expenses" (83). Will's confession here leaves the strong impression that Thelma has been his mistress, as the rumors in the Owl Mountain community have had it. But the rumor is, for Will, a convenient fiction. It is not until the end of the play that he admits to Zack, "You're looking at a man who has never slept with a woman!" (108).

Will's seeming victimization by the rumors is in the deepest sense self-created. Trying to unravel the mystery of his mother's relation with his uncle, Zack pushes Will for clarification late in the play, telling him that "if [Louisa] wouldn't marry you, she ought at least to have become your mistress." But his question forces Will into an admission of his destructive passivity: "How could she do either, when I never asked her?" Will recognizes that his passivity and seeming aloofness have masked his urgent love for Louisa. "I have loved her as a child would, wanted her as a child wants its mother, feared losing her like a child" (109). Will's childlike regard for Louisa is a confession of a profound weakness of character, his lack of the necessary courage to assume the commitment and responsibility that might create a meaningful bond. His childlike love is in reality a sign of his shirking of the role of lover, husband, and father. Although he remains emotionally dependent on Louisa, he withdraws from the responsibilities of personal attachment to her. He is instead content to remain in her presence, finding an odd fulfillment in supporting her attempts to nurture certain young women in the social graces and introduce them into Louisville society.

This is, for both Will and Louisa, a form of pantomime parenting, and it suggests his place in the family as a kind of shadow father, his presence a continuing reminder of his failure to assume that role in reality. Will's impotence is of the heart and the will, not of the body, and he represents a version of the sexual and familial failure that characterizes each of his nephews. He recognizes this failure, blaming himself for the anger and frustration that he sees in Zack and Harry. "If your father had lived," he says to Zack, "I suppose it would be him you would blame for your frustrations." Will understands that his distance has contributed to their failure to achieve a stable emotional maturity, and that their anger is connected in part to a lack that he helped create. "Maybe you're getting at me through her. No doubt if I had the cunning to make your mother marry me, you would have come at me directly. Don't you see I'm the one who failed you? I'm the one you must get" (55).

Despite his sympathy for Zack and Harry and his sense of guilt for their failures, Will is adamant about his loyalty to Louisa and his intention to protect the Owl Mountain Resort as he has known it, seeing it as a last refuge for his threatened values. The battle over the future of the land is thus central to the play, emerging as an allegory of the fate of the South. The value of the land is represented in a literal way by one of its commodities, a deposit of clay near Potter's Cove which is prized for its ceramic uses. When Zack inquires about the ownership of Potter's Cove, hoping to allow his lover, Georgia, to use its clay for her pottery, Will adamantly tells him that "Potter's Cove is *mine*" (56), an assertion of control that by implication extends to Will's desire to preserve the entire mountain from change.

Zack's plans to use the clay threaten to put him in competition with Harry, exacerbating a long sibling rivalry. Harry already has begun to exploit the clay deposit with a commercial pottery business aimed at weekend and summer visitors, which he hopes will be greatly expanded by his larger plans to bring through a highway. Will is appalled at the aesthetic quality of the pottery that Harry sells, but Harry remains resolutely concerned with the bottom line. "My ambition is to manufacture polka-dot toilet bowls. What I make sells, and I'm not afraid of new competition—especially of the artistic sort" (55). This naked and unapologetic commercialism is one more element of Harry's war against the pretensions to refinement of his upbringing, a calculated desecration of the Owl Mountain that has stood for the genteel life.

Harry has staked his identity on an initiative to incorporate the town and is confident that he has the support of the mountain people for his economic development scheme. But in a cruel joke on his ambition he is first informed that the measure has passed and then, after his initial exulting, learns that "almost to a man they voted against it—to a man, and to a woman." Harry labels this defeat "their brand of vengeance" (99), and that remark signals his recognition that he has been the target of their long-pent-up class resentment. No matter how hard he tries to embrace their ways and become one of them, he remains to them a Weaver, one of the rich summer people from Louisville. His plans to remake the mountain only reinforce their sense of having been exploited by the class he represents.

Harry's political rejection is a denial of the new identity that he has created for himself, and the blow dealt him unleashes a violent process in which he destroys all vestiges of that identity, including his family. His defeat and destruction are of course a hollow victory for Will, and we find later that he is unable to save Owl Mountain: it is decided that the highway will be put through despite the vote against incorporation. In Harry's battle with his past there are no victors. "We're Lee in the Mountains," Zack says to Will late in the play. "If they had let General Lee go to the mountains, he might have held out indefinitely" (107). But the allusion at this point is an indication of tragic and wrong-headed defeat more than of heroic defiance. The play closes with Will and Louisa's decision not to return to Louisville in the winter but to make the cottage at Owl Mountain a permanent home. Louisa's abandonment of her Louisville life is an important signal that Harry's defeat has been hers as well, and that even she has lost her sense that the world she has presided over still lives.

This quasi-allegorical rendering of the demise of the "South" is the intellectual framework upon which Taylor builds the play. The Owl Mountain Resort, indicative of the genteel life of the Southern upper class, is destroyed by the modern encroachment of the freeway. Louisa abandons her part in the debutante system of Louisville as a viable social role. Harry destroys himself and his family in an act of shocking violence, thus ending his quest for an alternative "Southern" identity among the "mountain people." It is as if all manifestations of Southern culture are systematically destroyed in the play. But in the experience of reading it, the Southern allegory is distinctly secondary to the psychosexual tension that is fundamental to the characters' perceptions and motivations.

The play's original title, *The Girl from Forkèd Deer*, emphasized the centrality of Mina, whose sexual magnetism is a catalyst. The play begins with an account of Zack's late arrival the night before and his mistakenly entering Mina's bed in the dark. The sexual suggestiveness of the encounter is augmented when Mina mistakes Zack for Harry; this initiates the gradual revelation of her affair with Harry and of a developing rivalry between the brothers for her affections. Their rivalry is complicated and intensified by the fact that they are also competing with Louisa, recognizing that they could upset her plans to introduce Mina to Louisville society. The sexual pursuit cannot be divorced from the mother-son struggle that has so powerfully formed both Zack's and Harry's personality.

A conversation in scene 3 offers the explicit confirmation that Harry and Mina's affair is inextricably linked with Harry's tortured relationship with Louisa. "I was never awed by the old battle-axes" at the Mississippi State College for Women, Mina tells him, "the way I am by your beautiful mother." Harry assents, calling Louisa "an awesome phenomenon" and "one of the most graceful and beautiful women the world has ever known." As he continues, his emotions seem to run even stronger: "She seems so utterly feminine, so appealingly feminine. And there is something masculine about her very attractiveness." Mina is not entirely prepared for this effusive praise of Louisa and finds something disturbing in the passion with which Harry declares his mother's attractiveness: "It's as though you wanted to make love to her, not me" (63-64).

We do not know how much Freud Mina read at the Mississippi State College for Women, but her comment is perceptive. Louisa holds her sons under a maternal control that derives its energy in part from her sexuality, and the force of their rejection of her is a measure of their attraction to her. Harry's initial attempt to establish his personal and sexual identity is to marry Lucille, a woman very different from his mother. This fleeing from the reality of his sexual nature rather than attempting to heal it has proved disastrous. Mina, on her way to being made over into a new Louisa, thus proves irresistibly attractive; through her he can simultaneously attain his mother and deny her control.

Taylor's strategy of placing sexual desire at the center of the play serves to emphasize the quality of dissolution that is the central message of *A Stand in the Mountains*. The sexual bond, which should serve as the basis of marriage, family, and a fruitful and ongoing community, has become a destructive agent, fueling the destabilizing energies that Harry's rage epitomizes. The world of Owl Mountain comes down, therefore, as the structure of the family comes apart. For Taylor, this is a significant conjunction of events. "The reason the South interests me primarily is that I think of it in terms of the family," he commented in a 1987 interview (James Curry Robison, 143). *A Stand in the Mountains* is his most ambitious attempt to work through this conjunction systematically.

But it would be reductive to conclude that Taylor has expressed a retrograde wish for a return to a simplistic world of "happy families," a term he used with a full sense of its Chekhovian irony in the title of one of his story collections. Taylor makes it plain that Ned Weaver's death, and Will's refusal of the role of husband and father, played a large role in the derailed lives of Harry and Zack. When Harry remarks on his mother's "masculine" quality—"there is something masculine about her very attractiveness" (64)—he is in part admitting that he has resisted her as a mother *and* as a father. But although the play is a fable of family fragmentation, it is not didactic in its aims. In other work, Taylor has demonstrated the inability of the stable patriarchal family to nurture whole and well-balanced individuals, and we should not be led to assume that, given a strong father, Harry's childhood might have been without problems. Taylor's allegory of the demise of the Weaver family cannot therefore be reduced to an endorsement or rejection of a particular family structure; it must instead be seen in the larger terms of the sense of tragedy that frames Taylor's entire imaginative work. Harry and Zack can be said to be victims of their fatherlessness and thus condemned by the absence of a force which, had it been present in their lives, might well not have saved them.

A Stand in the Mountains lacks the restraint and nuance of character revelation that gives Taylor's fiction much of its impact. Nor can the play's dialogue substitute for the engaging qualities of his prose narration. But the play helps us see more clearly that the restraint characteristic of the mannered world of his fiction covers psychic drives and instabilities that are dangerous and destructive. There is little compromise in Taylor's dark view of human experience, as it manifests itself both in his depictions of interpersonal relationships and in his representation of larger social structures and forces. In his account of the world a courageous stoicism is the most reliable stance, and it requires a measure of self-knowledge that is often elusive. Such affirmations as there are in his fiction consist of limited achievements in self-understanding, often embodied in the act of narration and self-presentation that constitutes the stories themselves. The primary work of the inner life for Taylor is the struggle toward such achievements, which always require a new refusal of self-delusion and a sympathetic understanding of the condition and experience of others.

Although *A Stand in the Mountains* is not the last, or the best, of Taylor's works, it is appropriate to end with it because it brings together so many of his essential concerns and demonstrates how his interest in larger social and regional themes always circles back to the nature of the family. The Weavers are one of Taylor's most tortured families, and they exemplify both the needs and the tensions between generations which simultaneously require the family and condemn it. In the play the family is the fundamental context of both social experience and psychological development, and Taylor's somewhat extreme delineation of the connection between generational conflict and psychic imbalance is an illuminating commentary on his entire fictional achievement. Harry Weaver's profoundly troubling anger is shared in one form or another by almost all Taylor's male narrators, who, like Harry, identify a parental figure as the source of their frustration. Will Weaver's indecisive passivity is also shared by many of Taylor's narrators, as Nat Ramsey and Nathan Longfort remind us. And Louisa Weaver's obsessive insecurity about her place in the social world is enacted by many of Taylor's important female characters in both the early and late stories.

What is fascinating about *A Stand in the Mountains* is its conviction that these conflicts are symptomatic of a culture doomed to destruction. The highway through Owl Mountain, representing the final destruction of the old South by its own modern self, also represents Taylor's deepest fear and his deepest desire. The lost world that he recreated so precisely in his stories is symbolically destroyed by it, and the survivors forced to live in the world in a new way.

Taylor understood the limits of the old way. His stories carefully document its repressive and destructive narrowness, its fundamental injustice, and its profound tendency to wholesale self-delusion. But he saw little promise of redemption in any new way of life arriving in the guise of the modern world. Taylor's world will not accommodate either nostalgia for the past or salvific visions of the future. Honest self-understanding and stoical courage are, in a world denuded of possibility, the only virtues that matter.

Notes

INTRODUCTION

1. For a thorough compilation of Taylor's record of publication, see Wright, *Peter Taylor: A Descriptive Bibliography, 1934-87.*

2. McAlexander, *Conversations with Peter Taylor* (hereafter cited simply as *Conversations*), 13.

3. Taylor's use of retrospective narration is beginning to emerge as an essential aspect of his achievement. Paine has termed Taylor's use of a "digressive retrospective monologue" an important element of his accomplishment ("Interview with Peter Taylor," 21); and Lynn has persuasively described the "narrative irony" that marks Taylor's later fiction, an irony produced in part by the shuffling and rearrangement of chronology in his retrospective stories ("Telling Irony," esp. 193).

4. Other works employing a similar technique include "Venus, Cupid, Folly and Time" (1958), "In the Miro District" (1977), *A Summons to Memphis* (1987), "The Oracle at Stoneleigh Court" (1993), and *In the Tennessee Country* (1994). For analyses of "The Old Forest," see Shear, "Peter Taylor's Fiction," 60-61; and Towers, "Master of the Miniature Novel." Taylor commented in several places on the biographical significance of the story; see in particular Thompson's interview in *Conversations,* 142. Taylor also helped prepare the script and did the voice-over narration for a film version of "The Old Forest." On the making of the film, see Taylor's comments in DuPree (*Conversations,* 54-59); and Ross's account in "'The Old Forest': Story Into Film."

5. For an astute and impassioned appreciation of this collection and of Taylor's achievement, see Yardley, "Peter Taylor: The Quiet Virtuoso." Taylor is, in Yardley's view, "the American writer who, more than any other, has achieved utter mastery in short fiction" (51).

6. For positive reviews of *A Summons to Memphis,* see Robinson, "The Family Game Was Revenge"; and Gray, "Civil War in the Upper South." For an important dissent, see Updike, "Summonses, Indictments, Extenuating Circumstances."

7. Taylor told Paine that the oral tradition in the South had a particular relevance in his case because "I lived in a family of great story-tellers. My mother and grandfather were great raconteurs and anecdotalists" (27).

1. FATHERS AND SONS

1. In a revealing reading that concentrates on Taylor's use of spatial relations as means of psychological revelation, Vauthier ("Peter Taylor's 'Porte Cochere': The

Geometry of Generation") notes that both the house and the remembered spaces of Ben's childhood constitute meaningful spatial contexts within Ben's psyche, as he revisits conflicts with his father by creating new conflicts with his own son. "While acting as a father," she observes, Ben "remembers his suffering as son, indeed remains son" (354).

2. Asked by McAlexander about the autobiographical elements of the story, Taylor said, "You write a story in which you are the protagonist, but you have to change him for the theme's sake. It is true that my father's business partner betrayed him, and that my grandfather was betrayed in a Senate race and 'died of a broken heart,' according to family story" (*Conversations,* 119).

3. As Richmond has noted, in "Peter Taylor and the Paternal Metaphor," this narrative, based on the experience of Taylor's father, plays an important role in both "Dean of Men" and *A Summons to Memphis.* She reads it in both works as "a prototype of the power of the paternal figure to determine the identities of his children and the role these children subsequently assume in the fabric of their society" (56).

4. The liberal arts college portrayed here is based on Kenyon College, from which Taylor graduated in 1940 and where he taught in the late 1950s. He demonstrates his familiarity with the more depressing side of university politics by having his narrator spin out a rather elaborate tale of faculty and administrative infighting and retaliation. To summarize briefly, the narrator had used his influence with a friend on the college board of trustees to help a group of young faculty members block the appointment of an unqualified on-campus candidate for the presidency. In retaliation, the narrator was denied an opportunity to improve his housing assignment at the college; he had expected his colleagues to support his promotion at a faculty meeting, thus qualifying him for the desired house, but for reasons of what they considered prudence they had failed to bring up the issue, a failure that the narrator took as a betrayal.

5. Although the symbolic resonance of the name is undeniable, it is also of interest that Taylor noted that "Basil Manley [Taylor] was the name of my [father's] grandfather" (*Conversations,* 22).

6. See Lynn, 97. Lynn offers a persuasive account of Taylor's manipulation of chronology in the story, and its connection with the narrator's search for the significance of the events he relates.

7. As Graham has noted, Manley has maintained his independence by refusing to conform to his children's conventional expectations of him, but that refusal of his family has "also shut his grandson out" (*Southern Accents,* 23). The narrator's behavior and expectations, though they seem self-destructive, are actually aimed at establishing himself as a son in his grandfather's eyes.

8. The description of Manley as having suffered a defeat is used both by the narrator (*MD,* 200) and by Taylor himself in commenting on the story (*Conversations,* 890).

9. Recognizing that Manley's change is in many ways a loss of self, Balthazor

characterizes his retreat as "metaphorically, a funeral" ("Digression and Meaning," 224), noting his black dress and sudden meek surrender to the ways of his children.

10. Metress offers a useful discussion of the division of critical opinion on Phillip's achievement of self-comprehension ("The Expenses of Silence in *A Summons to Memphis*," 202-3). This issue is complicated by Phillip's tendency to use the narrative as a form of self-justification. Lindsay has called attention to the rhetorical qualities of Phillip's lawyer-like narrative, terming it "one long polemic" ("Phillip Carver's Ethical Appeal in Peter Taylor's *A Summons to Memphis*," 168). See also Brinkmeyer's characterization of Phillip's narrative as a work of memory that bears "striking resemblance to Taylor's (and [Katherine Anne] Porter's) conception of artistic endeavor" ("Memory, Writing, and the Authoritarian Self in *A Summons to Memphis*," 112).

11. Brinkmeyer observes that Phillip connects George Carver's authoritarian paternalism to his professional insecurity, describing his "obsessive desire to wall the family off from the rest of the world in order to maintain the security he enjoys as a patriarch of the family" (113).

12. Commenting on their seeming failure to achieve full psychological maturity, Robinson notes that their style of dress—"like girls in corpulent middle age"— represents "a sort of taunting allusion to the time when the rituals that would have supported their passage through life were disrupted" (63).

13. For an effective statement of the case against Phillip's reliability, see Lindsay, 174-81.

14. As readers of his other works will recognize, the Owl Mountain Resort, Taylor's version of a resort at Monteagle, Tennessee, is associated in his mind with the fading Tennessee aristocracy and the problems of the Southern identity. He uses this setting in his play *A Stand in the Mountains* and in the late story "The Witch of Owl Mountain Springs" (see chapters 7 and 4).

15. Taylor's allusion here to his earlier story underlines the theme of emotional entrapment that the two stories pursue. It is important to note that at this moment it is the son, Phillip, who is engaged in the act of preventing the father's movements.

16. Lindsay (176-77) notes the contradictory and evasive quality of Phillip's attempt to explain his reasons for preventing his father's leaving.

17. Brinkmeyer regards these phone calls as evidence that Phillip is slowly moving toward "a meaningful reunion with his father" (119), one that is not, however, finally accomplished. He believes that although Phillip had, in reconstructing his past relationship with his father, the opportunity to break through to a deeper self-understanding, he was never quite able to move beyond his self-defeating resentment.

2. MOTHERS AND SONS

1. Smith's "Narration and Themes in Taylor's *A Woman of Means*" reminds us of the novel's overlooked achievement and argues for its accomplishment in both narration and thematic statement.

2. Smith (100) describes the award as a sacrifice of Quint's "true identity," calling attention to the fact that such external or superficial recognitions can go only partway toward resolving his inner conflict.

3. See Graham's commentary on the scene (109-10).

4. Anna's delusion of course reveals her desperate desire to achieve some unalterable relationship, a desire that explains her quick acceptance and ardent love of Quint.

5. *In the Tennessee Country* expands Taylor's earlier story "Cousin Aubrey" (1990), adding much depth and detail to the psychological portrait of the narrator.

6. Although the novel diverges significantly from autobiography, it is interesting to note, again, the parallels with Taylor's own experience: Nathan's father discourages him from taking up a career as a painter, while his mother insists on it; Taylor's father forbade him to be a writer, while his mother encouraged his ambition.

7. Frank Desprez's "Lasca," a declamation piece anthologized in Felleman's edition of *The Best Loved Poems of the American People*, 257-59, is a cowboy's recollection of the death of his lover, Lasca, in a cattle stampede "in Texas, down by the Rio Grande." The poem's focus on the loss of a lover may be indicative of Nathan's mother's sorrow over her earlier separation from Aubrey.

8. It is important to note that Taylor's use of the motif of the supernatural in several later stories seems to be an extension of his longstanding concern with the distortions of perception arising from psychological tensions and imbalances in his characters. On this basis, one could reasonably maintain that elements of the affair, or Linda Campbell's very existence, were either deliberate falsifications or examples of extreme self-delusion on Nathan's part.

9. It should be noted, however, that Nathan tells of these past events *after* having learned of the earlier affair between his mother and Aubrey. He must interpret the past through that knowledge.

10. We might even consider the possibility that Nathan is Aubrey's natural son, given the earlier romantic attachment between Aubrey and his mother.

3. FABLES OF MATURITY

1. For a discussion of the story in the context of Taylor's exploration of the erotic component of identity formation, see Williamson's "Identity and the Wider Eros."

2. This reading goes against the grain of the usual interpretation of the Dorsets as an incestuous couple. I read them instead as frozen in a condition in which their sexual natures have gone unacknowledged except through the indirect revelation of desire that is enacted at their parties. The issue is finally unresolvable, given the evidence we have.

3. See Beattie's insightful discussion of the differing reactions to the Old Forest among men and women. As she notes, Taylor, through Nat's narration, consistently connects women "with the natural order, the 'good' forest, whereas Nat as-

sumes that the world is interesting only in hierarchical, historical terms" ("Peter Taylor's 'The Old Forest,'" 108).

4. This is a good example, I believe, of the "narrative irony" that Lynn has identified as a defining aspect of Taylor's later work. Lynn recognizes that Taylor often defuses suspense about plot but, in so doing, augments tensions about motive. Taylor's narrators, and his readers, attempt "not to discover *what* happened—something we know largely (though not entirely) from the start—but *why* it happened and with what significance" (193).

5. Phillip Carver in *A Summons to Memphis* and Nathan Longfort in *In the Tennessee Country* share this characteristic.

6. Shear's analysis is astute: "Caroline, the one who in the situation seemed most vulnerable socially, . . . acts most effectively and gains the clearest sense of the only kind of power she believes she can ever have" (61).

4. MEN AND WOMEN

1. See Thompson's 1987 interview with Taylor in *Conversations*, 148-49.

2. For a reading of the implications of the story in terms of the differing psychological theories of Sigmund Freud and Alfred Adler, see Sodowsky and Sodowsky's "Determined Failure, Self-Styled Success." They argue that from a Freudian perspective Betsy is "trapped by the forces of parent-child relationships and sexual fears," but from an Adlerian perspective she is "choosing and controlling the unsocial direction of her life" (148). Taylor was far from a dogmatic Freudian, but he made use of the popular Freudianism of the early and middle twentieth century to enhance the psychological depth and emotional conflicts of his characters. "A Spinster's Tale" is a good example.

3. As Andrews has noted in "A Psychoanalytic Appreciation of Peter Taylor's 'A Spinster's Tale,'" Elizabeth's fear of Speed is a displaced version of her fear of her own developing sexuality. Her failure to accept her physical maturity eventually results in her becoming "a spinster whose sleep is still haunted by images of the drunken old man" (157).

4. Griffith, *Peter Taylor*, 20. Griffith adds that Elizabeth "associates Mr. Speed subconsciously with the cause of her mother's death: with the male principle to which her mother submitted in pregnancy" (21).

5. Both Sodowsky and Sodowsky (149) and Andrews (158) observe that Elizabeth's house functions in Freudian terms as a symbol of the body. If we accept this symbolic association, then Speed's entry into the house is the symbolic equivalent of a sexual assault.

6. Graham writes that Josie's personality is marked by a lack of "self-esteem and self-control," the result of being "controlled and degraded through her relationships with men" (64).

7. The actual events of the evening, given mainly from the perspective of Josie,

who has been drinking heavily, are not entirely clear. But it seems that her suspicions have some basis.

8. Among these later works I would include the two novels *A Summons to Memphis* and *In the Tennessee Country,* and many of the stories in his last collection, *The Oracle at Stoneleigh Court.*

9. Harry Weaver rejects his lineage, in an act of rebellion against his mother, by marrying beneath his class and taking on the life of the "mountain people." See Taylor's discussion of the Tennessee class structure in his preface to *A Stand in the Mountains,* (9-19) and my discussion of that play in Chapter 7. "The Witch of Owl Mountain Springs" has clear thematic affinities with *A Stand in the Mountains,* and in both cases the Owl Mountain setting is symbolic ground, a landscape of dreams that allows Taylor to bring forward the psychic extremes of his characters' inner lives.

10. As I noted earlier, there is room for disagreement about how much Nat finally learns, although I believe he does indeed make some progress toward maturity. The story's revelation of Caroline's growth and understanding seems to me to be clear.

11. See Taylor's comments on the "mystery" of the story in his 1993 interview with Metress ("An Oracle of Mystery"), 148-52.

12. Other versions of this character are Nathan Longfort's grandfather in *In the Tennessee Country* and Senator Caswell in *Tennessee Day in St. Louis.* The autobiographical model for the character is Taylor's maternal grandfather, Robert Love Taylor.

13. Ruthie Ann is the cousin of Alex Mercer, the close friend of Phillip Carver in *A Summons to Memphis.* Taylor's allusion to his novel here serves to connect his narrator, in both class experience and personality, with Phillip.

5. LOSING PLACE

1. In considering the influence of Ransom, Tate, and Robert Penn Warren on Taylor, Griffith persuasively argues that they "undoubtedly had more influence on Taylor as literary critics and theorists than they had as Agrarians" (7). I believe that Griffith is right to caution against seeing Taylor as an "Agrarian." What Taylor shared with that movement was a concern with the problem of cultural displacement and alienating social change.

2. Bell, "The Mastery of Peter Taylor," 259. Bell's thoughtful consideration of Taylor's accomplishment stresses the accuracy of detail in his representation of a particular time and place.

3. In "A View of Peter Taylor's Stories," Casey notes Taylor's shift, with *In the Miro District* (1977), from a focus on women to a focus on men. She argues that Taylor used the female perspective in his early fiction "as a screen through which he observed disorder," associating men with "trampling the social restraints enforced or represented by women" (125-26).

4. Graham's reading of the story emphasizes its exposure of Southern racism. She argues that here "Taylor confronts the central issue of the oppression of African-American women" (53). She notes that Taylor "portrays the African-American servant without sentimentality" (55) and that he "avoids stereotypes and political symbols in his representations of African-American women because he focuses on the peculiarities and familiarities of their struggles as human beings" (55-56).

5. Taylor's comments to Barbara Thompson about writing the story to protest school consolidation are a misleading guide to interpreting the story, it seems to me. He makes the town powers favor consolidation in order to prevent school integration, thus reversing the usual racial politics of the school zoning question. Whatever his original intentions, the story evolved into a character study of Miss Leonora, and a commentary on the difficult role of the educator and intellectual in the small-town South.

6. Brooks argues that Taylor offers a familiar character type in American fiction, "a genteel and high-minded spinster somewhat warped by her isolation," but gives it a "characteristically Southern" treatment by revealing how closely her love of culture is bound up with a commitment to community (*A Shaping Joy*, 202). Brooks emphasizes the hold of community on its individual members as a quintessentially Southern theme, and he casts Miss Leonora as the exemplar of these values. Brooks's work (along with Warren's introduction to *A Long Fourth and Other Stories*) has been influential in focusing critical attention on Taylor as a "Southern" or "regional" writer.

7. For Taylor's comment on the story in the interview with McAlexander, see *Conversations*, p. 126. See also Robison's view that Miss Leonora "has surrendered all personality" (*Peter Taylor*, 61) and Graham's view that Taylor depicts Miss Leonora as one who "conforms and becomes only another faceless, modern sight-seer" (133).

6. THE RACIAL DIVIDE

1. Taylor published these three stories, as well as "What You Hear from 'Em," in his 1954 collection, *The Widows of Thornton*. See Griffith, 46-64, for extended and illuminating commentary on this volume.

2. See the discussion of the story, based on an interview with Taylor, in Dean, "Peter Taylor: A Private World of Southern Writing," 34; see also Griffith's commentary, 82-83. Taylor's original title for the story, "Who Was Jesse's Friend and Protector?" emphasizes the irony.

3. This theme of the voyeuristic surrogate of debauchery is also prominent in "The Gift of the Prodigal" (discussed in Chapter 1).

4. Bell argues that the story illustrates Taylor's mastery of his fictional craft, and he comments perceptively that "the black women are the mirror in which [Helen Ruth] sees herself and as she learns to accommodate herself to them she becomes a wiser and better person in all the departments of her life" (256).

5. Taylor's precisely rendered stories often depend not only on the nuances of individual psyches but on the details of physical surroundings. Indeed, Taylor's work presents us with a series of memorable houses and interiors, some of which carry enormous significance for the interpretation of the stories. The Dorsets' house in "Venus, Cupid, Folly and Time" and Old Ben's house in "Porte Cochere" are important examples of richly significant living spaces that both shape and reflect the identities of their occupants. Taylor himself was, by the way, interested in the restoration of old houses and renovated a number of them. See the interview with Broadway in *Conversations,* 102-4.

6. Critics of the story tend to agree that the old man's actions help to establish something of a bond among the black characters. Griffith observes that the old man's actions bring about "an uncertain reconciliation of the two generations effected" (63), and Robison argues that at the story's end "the young couple and their child are united with the old man as fellow sufferers" (38).

7. DRAMAS OF SOUTHERN IDENTITY

1. One might include the narrator of "Venus, Cupid, Folly and Time," Nat Ramsey from "The Old Forest," the narrator of "The Oracle at Stoneleigh Court," and, perhaps quintessentially, Phillip Carver from *A Summons to Memphis.*

2. For biographical information on Taylor's education and widening circle of literary friendships, see Griffith, 5-9, and his many comments on these friendships in interviews collected by McAlexander in *Conversations.*

3. Rubin, *The Writer in the South,* 92-93. See also Rubin, *The Wary Fugitives,* 187-250.

4. See Griffith's discussion of the relation of the Tolliver family represented here with that in Taylor's stories "Two Ladies in Retirement" and "Bad Dreams," both of which appeared in his collection *The Widows of Thornton* and again in *The Old Forest and Other Stories.* As Griffith notes, the setting of St. Louis is "one of those Midwestern metropolises in which so many of Taylor's old-time Southerners find themselves transplanted but not yet fully acculturated" (66-68).

5. In Lanny, Taylor is undoubtedly offering commentary on the Agrarians, whose attempt to rehabilitate the South intellectually in the 1930s (the play is set in 1939) promised a renewed sense of the Southern identity. Alienated from the direction of modern culture, they sought imaginative alternatives to it and hoped to find in the Agrarian South models that would inform their social and artistic goals. If one found it intolerable to write and live as an American, given the shape of American culture, one might write and live as a Southerner, finding in the different identity and sense of orientation a new energy and hope for fulfillment. The Agrarian position combined elements of utopian social criticism and reactionary nostalgia into an imaginatively potent vision. Lanny illustrates the pull of Agrarian ideas that Taylor himself had once felt: "Those were the ideas that dominated my young manhood, my thought, when I was beginning to write." But as Taylor came to understand,

Agrarian theories lacked the substance from which actual life might be drawn, and as his skepticism about Agrarianism deepened, he came to realize that "it is a *truly* lost cause because of what's happened in the world" (*Conversations,* 94).

6. Griffith has noted that "all the external action of the play is related to the maturation process that takes place in Lanny" (69), which links this play with other Taylor stories that explore the same process.

7. Though Taylor's great artistic achievement was in fiction, he wrote plays with a belief in both the artistic possibilities of stage performance and the value of the dramatic form as a text for readers. "I wanted to write plays before I wrote stories," Taylor told Paine (22), describing his enthusiasm for the work required to see a play through to production. At one point he even declared that he was through with the short story entirely and in the late 1970s, as Griffith explains, entered a period of deep commitment to dramatic writing and to experimentation with a "broken-line free-verse format" (118). Taylor's experimental mood also seems to have affected other aspects of his work. Several of the one-act plays collected in *Presences: Seven Dramatic Pieces* (1973) employ ghosts or supernatural presences as devices to amplify character revelation and dramatic conflict.

8. McAlexander argues that the preface "contains some of Peter Taylor's most insightful social commentary" ("History, Gender, and Family in *A Stand in the Mountains,*" 95) and believes that it is a key text in understanding Taylor's historical and social perspective.

9. Griffith comments that the play "has no paucity of dramatic ideas or provocative themes" but lacks unity and economy: "Too many of the characters and subplot complications seem superfluous, dragged awkwardly in to illustrate tangential motifs that Taylor could not bring himself to discard, however distracting they might be to dramatic cohesiveness" (109).

10. See McAlexander, "History, Gender, and Family," 96. See also Sullivan's reading of the play as representative of Taylor's regional focus and themes ("The Last Agrarian").

Works Cited

Andrews, Maureen. "A Psychoanalytic Appreciation of Peter Taylor's 'A Spinster's Tale.'" *Journal of Evolutionary Psychology* 9 (Aug. 1988): 309-16. Rpt. in McAlexander, *Critical Essays on Peter Taylor*, pp. 154-61.

Balthazor, Ron. "Digression and Meaning: A Reading of 'In the Miro District.'" In McAlexander *Critical Essays on Peter Taylor*, pp. 216-26.

Beattie, Ann. "Peter Taylor's 'The Old Forest.'" In Stephens and Salamon, eds. *The Craft of Peter Taylor*, pp. 105-10.

Bell, Madison Smartt. "The Mastery of Peter Taylor." In McAlexander, *Critical Essays on Peter Taylor*, pp. 254-61.

Brickhouse, Robert. "Peter Taylor: Writing, Teaching, Making Discoveries." In McAlexander, *Conversations with Peter Taylor*, pp. 48-53.

Brinkmeyer, Robert H., Jr. "Memory, Rewriting, and the Authoritarian Self in *A Summons to Memphis*." In Stephens and Salamon, *The Craft of Peter Taylor*, pp. 111-21.

Broadway, J. William. "A Conversation with Peter Taylor." In McAlexander, *Conversations with Peter Taylor*, pp. 67-114.

Brooks, Cleanth. *A Shaping Joy: Studies in the Writer's Craft*. New York: Harcourt Brace Jovanovich, 1971.

Brown, Ashley. "The Early Fiction of Peter Taylor." *Sewanee Review* 70 (Fall 1962): 588-603. Rpt. in McAlexander, *Critical Essays on Peter Taylor*, pp. 77-86.

Casey, Jane Barnes. "A View of Peter Taylor's Stories." *Virginia Quarterly Review* 54 (Spring 1978): 213-30. Rpt. in McAlexander, *Critical Essays on Peter Taylor*, pp. 124-35.

Dean, Ruth. "Peter Taylor: A Private World of Southern Writing." In McAlexander, *Conversations with Peter Taylor*, pp. 28-34.

Desprez, Frank. "Lasca." In *The Best Loved Poems of the American People*, ed. Hazel Felleman, pp. 257-59. New York: Doubleday, 1936.

DuPree, Don Keck. "An Interview with Peter Taylor." In McAlexander, *Conversations with Peter Taylor*, pp. 54-59.

Goodwin, Stephen. "An Interview with Peter Taylor." In McAlexander, *Conversations with Peter Taylor*, pp. 6-21.

Graham, Catherine Clark. *Southern Accents: The Fiction of Peter Taylor*. New York: Peter Lang, 1994.

Gray, Paul. "Civil War in the Upper South." *Time*, Sept. 29, 1986, p. 71.

Griffith, Albert J. *Peter Taylor*. Rev. ed. Boston: Twayne, 1990.

Lindsay, Creighton. "Phillip Carver's Ethical Appeal in Peter Taylor's *A Summons to Memphis*." *Mississippi Quarterly* 44 (Spring 1991): 167-81.

Lynn, David H. "Telling Irony: Peter Taylor's Later Stories." *Virginia Quarterly Review* 67 (Summer 1991): 510-20. Rpt. in McAlexander, *Critical Essays on Peter Taylor*, pp. 193-200.

McAlexander, Hubert H., ed. *Conversations with Peter Taylor*. Jackson and London: Univ. Press of Mississippi, 1987. (interviews included in this volume are also listed separately here.)

———, ed. *Critical Essays on Peter Taylor*. Boston: G.K. Hall, 1993. (Essays collected in this volume, also listed separately here, are cited by page number from this volume.)

———. "History, Gender, and the Family in *A Stand in the Mountains*." In Stephens and Salamon, *The Craft of Peter Taylor*, pp. 96-104.

Metress, Christopher. "The Expenses of Silence in *A Summons to Memphis*." In McAlexander, *Critical Essays on Peter Taylor*, pp. 201-15.

———. "An Oracle of Mystery: An Interview with Peter Taylor." In Stephens and Salamon, *The Craft of Peter Taylor*, pp. 143-56.

Paine, J.H.E. "Interview with Peter Taylor." *Journal of the Short Story in English* 3 (1987): 14-35.

Richmond, Linda. "Peter Taylor and the Paternal Metaphor." In Stephens and Salamon, *The Craft of Peter Taylor*, pp. 56-64.

Robinson, Marilynne. "The Family Game Was Revenge." *New York Times Book Review*, Oct. 19, 1986, pp. 1, 52-53. Rpt. in McAlexander, *Critical Essays on Peter Taylor*, pp. 61-65.

Robison, James Curry. *Peter Taylor: A Study of the Short Fiction*. Boston: Twayne, 1988.

Ross, Steven John. "'The Old Forest': Story into Film." *Sacred Heart University Review* 5 (Fall/Spring 1984-85): 3-18.

Rubin, Louis D. *The Wary Fugitives: Four Poets and the South*. Baton Rouge: Louisiana State Univ. Press, 1978.

———. *The Writer in the South: Studies in a Literary Community*. Athens: Univ. of Georgia Press, 1972.

Shear, Walter. "Peter Taylor's Fiction: The Encounter with the Other." *Southern Literary Journal* 22 (Spring 1989): 50-63.

Sides, W. Hampton, "Interview: Peter Taylor." In McAlexander, *Conversations with Peter Taylor*, pp. 129-36.

Smith, James Penney. "Narration and Theme in Taylor's *A Woman of Means*." *Critique* 9 (1967): 19-30. Rpt. in McAlexander, *Critical Essays on Peter Taylor*, pp. 98-107.

Sodowsky, Roland, and Gargi Roysircar Sodowsky. "Determined Failure, Self-Styled Success: Two Views of Betsy in Peter Taylor's 'A Spinster's Tale.'" *Studies in Short Fiction* 25 (Winter 1988): 49-54. Rpt. in McAlexander, *Critical Essays on Peter Taylor*, pp. 148-53.

Stephens, C. Ralph, and Lynda B. Salamon, eds. *The Craft of Peter Taylor*. Tuscaloosa: Univ. of Alabama Press, 1995. (Essays collected in this volume are also listed separately here.)

Sullivan, Walter. "The Last Agrarian: Peter Taylor Early and Late." *Sewanee Review* 95 (Spring 1987): 308-17.

Taylor, Peter. *The Collected Stories of Peter Taylor*. New York: Farrar, Straus & Giroux, 1969.

———. *In the Miro District*. New York: Carroll & Graf, 1983.

———. *In the Tennessee Country*. New York: Knopf, 1994.

———. *The Old Forest and Other Stories*. Garden City, N.Y.: Dial Press, 1985.

———. *The Oracle at Stoneleigh Court*. New York: Alfred A. Knopf, 1993.

———. *A Stand in the Mountains*. New York: Frederic C. Beil, 1985.

———. *A Summons to Memphis*. New York: Knopf, 1986.

———. *Tennessee Day in St. Louis: A Comedy*. New York: Random House, 1957.

———. *A Woman of Means*. New York: Harcourt, Brace, 1950; New York: Avon, 1986.

———. *The Widows of Thornton*. New York: Harcourt, Brace, 1954.

Thompson, Barbara. "Interview with Peter Taylor." In McAlexander, *Conversations with Peter Taylor*, pp. 137-73.

Towers, Robert. "A Master of the Miniature Novel." *New York Times Book Review*, Feb. 17, 1985, pp. 1, 26.

Updike, John. "Summonses, Indictments, Extenuating Circumstances." *New Yorker*, Nov. 3, 1986, pp. 158-65.

Vauthier, Simone. "Peter Taylor's 'Porte Cochere': The Geometry of Generation." *Southern Literature and Literary Theory*, ed. Jefferson Humphries. Athens: Uiversity of Georgia Press, 1980, pp. 318-38. In McAlexander, *Critical Essays on Peter Taylor*, pp. 162-79.

Warren, Robert Penn. Introduction to Peter Taylor, *A Long Fourth and Other Stories*. New York: Harcourt, Brace, 1948.

Welty, Eudora. "Place in Fiction." In *The Eye of the Story: Selected Essays and Reviews*. New York: Random House, 1977.

Williamson, Alan. "Identity and the Wider Eros: A Reading of Peter Taylor's Stories." *Shenandoah* 30 (1978): 71-84. Rpt. in McAlexander, *Critical Essays on Peter Taylor*, pp. 136-47.

Wright, Stuart. *Peter Taylor: A Descriptive Bibliography, 1934-87*. Charlottesville: Univ. Press of Virginia, 1988.

Yardley, Jonathan. "Peter Taylor: The Quiet Virtuoso." *Washington Post Book World*, Jan. 27, 1985, p. 3. Rpt. in McAlexander, *Critical Essays on Peter Taylor*, pp. 51-54.

Index